When Our Mothers Went to War

Members of the Army Nurse Corps and Civilian Women who were in Malinta Tunnel when Corregidor fell

Edith Shacklette
Helen Hennessey
A Williams
Frances Nash
Oz Putman
Eunice Young
Adele Foreman
Phyllis J. Arnold
Letha McHale
Magdalena Eckmann
Minnie L Breese
Hattie R Brantley
Adolpha Meyer
Blanche Kimball
Gwen Henshaw
Mina Aasen
Myra V. Burris
Edith M Corns
Madeline M Ullom
Doris A. Kehoe
Eula Fails
Alice M Zwicker
Clara L Mueller

Maude C Davison
Ann Mealer
Sallie P Durrett
Kathryn L Dollason
Earlyn M. Black
Beulah Greenwalt
Dorcas E. Easterling
Edith M. Wimberly
Mildred J. Dalton
Mary Reppak
Dorothy Scholl
Helen M. Cassiani
Eleanor O. Lee
Winifred P. Madden
Ruth M Stoltz
Dorothy Ludlow
Verna V Henson
Mary B. Brown
Marcia Gates
Ethel Thor

Josephine M Nesbit
Rose Rieper
Frankie Lewey
Inez V. McDonald
Mary Jo Oberst
Anne B Wurts

CIVILIANS

Denny Williams
Ruby Motley
Brunetta A Kuchlethau
Vivian Weissblott
Fontaine Porter
Betty Bradfield
Catharine L Nau
ANNA WINGATE
MARIE ATKINSON
Marie Wolf
Rita E. Johnson
Marie Gould

Mildred Roth

A J. Hahn
Jean Kennedy
Bertha Dworsky
Clara Mae Bickford

Eleanor R

Betty Brian
Helen MacChalten

When Our Mothers Went to War

AN ILLUSTRATED HISTORY OF WOMEN IN WORLD WAR II

Margaret Regis

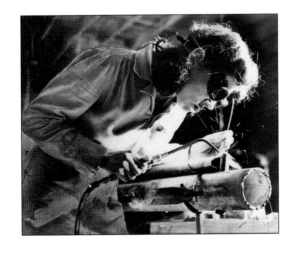

NAVPUBLISHING ▪ SEATTLE, WASHINGTON

NavPublishing, LLC
P.O. Box 5624
Bellingham, WA 98227 USA

www.navpublishing.com

Printed and bound in Canada.

Library of Congress Cataloging-in-Publication Data

Regis, Margaret, 1957–
    When our mothers went to war : an illustrated history of women in World War II/Margaret Regis.
        p. cm.
Includes bibliographical references and index.
ISBN 978-1-879932-05-0 (pbk. : alk. paper)
1. World War, 1939–1945—Women—United States. 2. World War, 1939–1945—Women—United States—Pictorial works. I. Title.
D810.W7R44 2008
940.53082'0973—dc22
                        2008002833

To Sally

Books by Margaret Regis and Larry Kimmett

THE ATTACK ON PEARL HARBOR: AN ILLUSTRATED HISTORY
U.S. SUBMARINES IN WORLD WAR II: AN ILLUSTRATED HISTORY

On the front cover: (foreground) Army flight nurses, whose plane crashed in occupied Albania, show off their worn boots after trekking 800 miles through the mountains to safety. Left to right: Lois Watson, Lillian Tacina, Pauline Kanable, Elna Schwant, Ann Kopsco and Frances Nelson; (above them) A C-47 transport plane, the plane most commonly used to carry flight nurses and other women in the war zones; (background) Battleship Row burns at Pearl Harbor, December 7, 1941.

Half title page: A cloth signed by army nurses and civilian women in Malinta Tunnel on Corregidor when the U.S. forces surrendered the Philippines to the Japanese on May 6, 1942. Fearing they might not survive, the women signed their names to leave a record of their presence.

Title page: (left) Shirley Schwake, a 17-year-old welder at the Laister-Kauffman glider factory in St. Louis, Missouri, brazes a part for the cockpit of a training glider; (right) The Andrews Sisters hug a GI during their 1945 USO trip to Italy.

Back cover: (top) "We Can Do It" poster by J. Howard Miller; (bottom) Singer Frances Langford and Tony Romano entertain soldiers in New Guinea during their USO tour of the South Pacific with the Bob Hope Show in August 1944.

Contents

Acknowledgments

Many books have recorded the history of World War II, highlighting the dangers and heroism of soldiers in battle. Women experienced a different war, equally compelling and fraught with risks and victories. This books tells *their* story. Because of its vast scope, I have concentrated my view on the actions of American women, as well as women who came to the United States at the end of the war. I have presented experiences that are representative of the widely varied roles of women during the war. There are many more notable women and events, but with limited space and such an ample subject, I regret I could not include them all.

I am grateful to the people who generously contributed to this work, in particular to the women and their families who brought back sometimes happy, sometimes painful memories of their experiences. My sincere gratitude goes to Ethel Thor Nelson (Army Nurse Corps) and her daughter, Carla Kingsbury; Betty Willett Mowery and Oscar Rea Mowery; Muriel Daggett Olsen (SPAR); June Sargent Schmidt and Ervin Schmidt; and Ada Ulmer (Pearl Harbor survivor). Thanks also to Anne Fadiman, daughter of Annalee Jacoby Fadiman, who provided insight into her mother's activities as a war correspondent. In addition, I would like to thank the National Park Service for the presentation of "The Women of Pearl Harbor: A Feminine Perspective" at the Pearl Harbor 60th Anniversary Conference in Honolulu, December 3, 2001, which included eyewitness accounts from navy nurse Lenore Terrell Rickert and other female survivors.

Further, I express my appreciation to the Bainbridge Island Historical Society for their January 25, 2004 presentation, "Rosie the Riveter, More Than a Legend," which featured a number of women, including Joan Wilt, who told their stories of work on the home front, and to Evelyn Whitfield, author of *Three Year Picnic,* who in an appearance at the Eagle Harbor Book Company, Bainbridge Island, Washington, shared her experiences as a prisoner of the Japanese.

My thanks also goes out to photo researchers, friends and others who assisted me in myriad ways, from finding World War II memorabilia and resources to recommending contacts or working with the photographs. These included Eileen France of Sweets & Savories, James Frusetta, Carol Gibbens, Dennis Gobets, Lynn Gordon, Ben Kimmett, Lauren Lester, Ruth and George Maupin, Tim Mickleburgh, Franklin Noll, and Sally Van Natta.

Gathering the photos for this book was a monumental enterprise which could not have been accomplished without help from numerous libraries and archives. Individual archivists, historians, curators and librarians also provided information and resources that broadened and enlivened this history. I would like to thank Jacalyn Blume, Diana Carey, and Marie-Hélène Gold of the Schlesinger Library, Radcliffe Institute; Federico Baldassarre; Susan Barker at the Sophia Smith Collection, Smith College; Columbia University, Rare Book and Manuscript Collection; Carolyn Davis at Syracuse University Library, Special Collections; Michelle Franklin at Time & Life, Getty Images; William Galvani at the Naval Undersea Museum; Denise Gose at the Center for Creative Photography; Britta Granrud at the Women in Military Service for America Memorial Foundation; Harvard University Archives; the John Fitzgerald Kennedy Library; Paul Johnson at The National

Archives Image Library, United Kingdom; Dianne Keller at the Montana Historical Society Library & Archives; the Library of Congress; Jessica Kratz at the National Archives, Center for Legislative Archives; Kristine Krueger at the Margaret Herrick Library, Center for Motion Picture Study; The Museum of History & Industry, Seattle; the National Archives and Records Administration; The Netherlands Institute for War Documentation; the New York Public Library, Schomburg Center for Research in Black Culture; Maj. Jennifer L. Petersen, Army Nurse Corps Historian; Mark Renovitch at the Franklin D. Roosevelt Presidential Library and Museum; John Sforza, author of *Swing It! The Andrews Sisters Story;* Dawn Stitzel at the U.S. Naval Institute; Richard Suico and the staff of the Sno-Isle Library, Edmonds; Susan Thorsteinson and the staff of the Kitsap Regional Library, Kingston; the United States Holocaust Memorial Museum; and the Wisconsin Historical Society.

A special thanks goes to Larry Kimmett, whose insight, advice, and encyclopedic knowledge of World War II was invaluable throughout the writing of this book.

And most of all, I thank the women of the World War II generation who met the challenges of wartime with practicality, courage, and love.

"A woman's will is the strongest thing in the world."

—*Eleanor Roosevelt*

Introduction

No women were on the deck of the battleship USS *Missouri* on September 2, 1945 to witness the Japanese surrender at Tokyo Bay, but they should have been. Women built the battleship *Missouri,* as they built much of the structure of the Allied victory. In shipyards, factories, offices and farms across America, the work of women during the war was the vital element that sustained community and country. Women did this work while rearing their children, growing victory gardens, selling war bonds, donating blood, and holding together households without their husbands. Donning the uniforms of military and service organizations, many women also supported Allied forces as Army WACs, Navy WAVES, Marines, Coast Guard SPARs, Women Airforce Service Pilots, and Red Cross volunteers.

Overseas, from camps and bomb-ravaged cities, female correspondents reported firsthand news of the battles. In hospital ships, air evacuation planes, field hospitals, and internment camps while they themselves were prisoners of war, army and navy nurses treated the ill and the wounded. USO performers went "on with the show" in spite of frostbite and plane crashes, to entertain GIs in the war zones, while Red Cross clubmobile women traversed muddy, rutted roads to bring food to fighting men.

This is the story of many women—of housewives who saved tin cans and bacon grease, and of mothers with small children who trekked through the Philippine jungles, one step ahead of the Japanese. It is the tale of flight nurses shot down behind enemy lines, and of women gathered in family parlors to assemble care packages for their boyfriends, husbands, and sisters overseas. The Allies could not have triumphed in World War II without the participation of women. Guided by hope, patriotism, a sense of adventure, or the stark need for survival, women set their will to a common goal: a swift end to the world's most devastating war.

First Lady Eleanor Roosevelt (opposite) at Pearl Harbor in 1943 at the start of her tour of the South Pacific. She wore a Red Cross uniform during her travels to the war zone.

War Breaks Out

World War II officially broke out September 3, 1939, two days after German tanks and planes roared into Poland, but it began long before then. From the early 1930s when Adolf Hitler and the fascist Nazi Party gained power in Germany, the specter of repression and anti-Semitism grew across Europe. Beginning in 1936, Hitler defied the World War I Versailles Peace Treaty and armed the demilitarized Rhineland. Two years later, allied with Italy's fascist dictator, Benito Mussolini, he took over Austria and part of Czechoslovakia. By 1939, Germany was poised to invade most of the continent and ultimately to implement a plan of efficient, systematic genocide against Jews and other "racial enemies."

In Asia, fueled by a militarist drive to expand its empire and seize needed raw materials, Japan invaded Manchuria in 1931, China in 1937, and Indochina in July 1941. In response to the occupation of Indochina, the United States froze Japanese assets in the U.S., and on December 7, 1941, Japan launched a surprise attack on the U.S. Pacific Fleet at Pearl Harbor. By March 1942, the Japanese controlled nearly all of Southeast Asia and held 130,000 Allied civilians prisoner. In the United States, the country's isolationism changed to patriotic shock, and the rapid Japanese victories in the Pacific stoked prejudice and war hysteria. The U.S. government ordered 110,000 west coast Japanese Americans into desolate internment camps.

War had come. World war. And with its destruction, fear and injustice, came purpose, organization and a will to fight.

USS Shaw (*opposite*) *explodes at Pearl Harbor, Hawaii during the second wave of the Japanese attack. Japan's surprise raid on Pearl Harbor killed 2,389 Americans, including 49 civilians.*

Caught Abroad

As the 1930s drew to a close, thousands of American women in Europe and the Pacific anxiously watched the signs of impending war. They were the wives of engineers, businessmen, government workers and military men who had long-established homes abroad. Some were missionaries, university students or wives of foreign nationals. Others were single women with careers as teachers, nurses, or journalists.

Expatriates in Europe watched with alarm as Hitler's army seized Austria, Czechoslovakia, and then Poland, igniting full-scale war in September 1939. The United States remained neutral, and up until December 1941 when the U.S. entered the war, Americans in Europe felt somewhat secure. Some moved to safer areas like England or unoccupied Vichy France, competing with throngs of refugees for passage out on a diminishing number of transports. Ships traveling the Atlantic ran the risk of German submarine attack. In unoccupied France, Americans became "targets of suspicion." After December 1941, the Vichy government deemed them enemy aliens, and in late 1942 interned U.S. women at Vittel Spa in eastern France.

The threat of war also grew in the Far East. In 1937, Japan invaded China and chilled the world with its brutal assault on Nanking. The U.S. State Department urged American civilians throughout Asia to take refuge in the Philippines. With strong U.S. defenses at Manila Bay, it considered the Philippines unassailable. The U.S. military, however, was still building its forces and did not expect to have full defenses in place until the spring of 1942. In May 1941, the U.S. Army ordered 700 army wives and dependents sent home. The Navy soon followed suit.

Still, the State Department did not issue an official evacuation order for civilians. In the absence of clear directives, many Americans misread the severity of the situation. Families wanted to stay together; many had long-established homes, important work or lacked the resources to leave. Also, a prevailing racism against the Japanese—the belief that if they attacked, the U.S. would defeat them in a matter of weeks—weighed in favor of remaining. Margaret Sherk, a mining wife, decided to stay after the high commissioner's office assured her Manila was the "safest place in the Orient." Gwen Dew, an American journalist in Hong Kong, booked passage to leave on December 8th—too late.

With war upon them, American women abroad faced change and danger. Thousands, like Margaret Sherk, spent the war in internment camps. A small number, including Gwen Dew, were repatriated. Others went into hiding and eventually escaped. And a few formed resistance networks and provided essential aid to Allied soldiers.

A family (below) *passes through U.S. Customs. At the outbreak of the war, thousands of Americans traveled home by whatever means they could.*

U.S. CUSTOMS

The Correspondents' Wives: Fleeing Europe

Among Americans scrambling for the safety of the United States were Tess Shirer and Lois Sevareid, wives of two pioneering CBS Radio correspondents from Edwin R. Murrow's famous team, "the Murrow Boys." When the Germans invaded Austria on March 12, 1938, Tess Shirer lay in a Vienna hospital bed critically ill with phlebitis. She had given birth two weeks before in an emergency Cesarean section, to a baby daughter, Eileen Inga. With a chance to provide an uncensored eyewitness report of the fall of Austria, her husband, William L. Shirer, flew to London and in a landmark broadcast became the first CBS newsman ever to go on the air and report events firsthand. While he was gone, Tess lived through a week of terror: bombers roared overhead, Nazi thugs rampaged through the hospital, and Tess' doctor (a Jew) fled in fear. After a new surgery to remove surgical instruments left inside her, Tess slowly recovered. On June 10, 1938, the last day her visa to Switzerland was valid, the Shirers left Austria for Geneva. Gestapo women guards at the airport strip-searched Tess and tore off her bandages. Tess and Eileen Inga stayed in Geneva until October 1940. Deciding finally to leave Europe, they traveled across Vichy France to Lisbon, where they got passage on a ship to New York. Bill Shirer returned home in December 1940.

Meanwhile, in Paris, Lois Sevareid, wife of correspondent Eric Sevareid, struggled with her own difficult pregnancy. In the spring of 1940, with the Germans massed across the French border, she risked losing her two babies if she didn't lie flat on her back for three months. When labor began on April 25th Lois was in grave danger, but in the end she gave birth to two healthy sons. Eric left on assignment while she was still in the hospital, unable to walk. The next morning, May 10th, the Germans invaded Holland, Luxembourg and Belgium and launched air attacks on France. The nurses and patients at the clinic fled, leaving Lois and the twins alone. With sirens and distant bombs exploding, Lois feared that she wouldn't be able to protect her newborns. At midnight, in the blackout, Eric found her, and took her and the babies home. Just weeks later, with the Germans advancing on Paris, Lois, not yet fully recovered, loaded the boys and their diapers into two wicker baskets and left by train for Italy, where she boarded SS *Manhattan* for the dangerous crossing of the Atlantic. Eric returned to the U.S. in the fall of 1940.

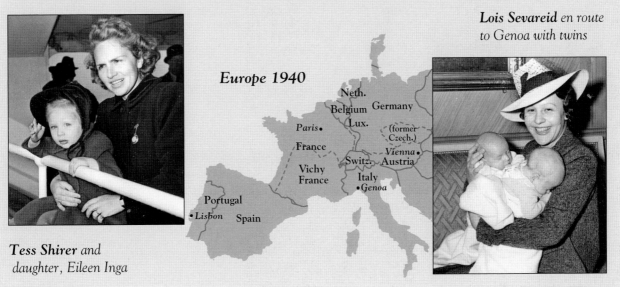

Lois Sevareid en route to Genoa with twins

Europe 1940

Neth.
Belgium Germany
Lux.
Paris•
France (former Czech.)
Vienna•
Switz. Austria
Vichy
France Italy
•Genoa
Portugal
•Lisbon Spain

Tess Shirer and daughter, Eileen Inga

Pearl Harbor

PACIFIC

Pearl Harbor U.S.
/ Oahu
Hawaii

Battleship USS
Arizona *(right)*
burns in the late
morning of De-
cember 7th.

Aerial view of
Pearl Harbor,
Hawaii (below).
On the left is Ford
Island lined by
"Battleship Row."
Across, to the right,
are Hickam Field
and John Rodgers
Civilian Airport.
Honolulu lies in the
distance.

In the United States, the clamor for isolationism ended abruptly Sunday December 7, 1941 when Japanese carriers launched 350 fighters and bombers in a surprise raid on the U.S. Pacific Fleet at Pearl Harbor and its surrounding airfields. Thousands of American women came under attack that morning.

The first bombers struck just before 8 a.m. Military personnel raced to their battle stations. As planes thundered overhead, families living at the bases huddled in their houses or rushed to shelters. On Ford Island in the center of the harbor, shrapnel from the *Arizona*, exploding just offshore, rained down on Mary Ann Ramsay and her mother as they ran across the lawns to the air raid shelter. At the housing near Hickam Field, army wife Virginia Huggins and her daughters took cover under a steel dining room table. In Honolulu, forty explosions from poorly-fused U.S. antiaircraft shells fell back to earth, scattering residents and starting fires throughout the city. Forty-nine civilians died and 35 were wounded.

In the aftermath, women volunteered to help in any way necessary. Civilian nurses joined army and navy nurses already at their posts. Others helped in food service, hospital laundries, shelters, and with Red Cross, Civilian Defense and Salvation Army relief efforts. On Monday December 8th, President Roosevelt declared war on Japan. Pearl Harbor lay in ruins—the U.S. Pacific Fleet broken and 2,389 Americans dead. Life in the islands had changed, irrevocably.

Under Fire: Cornelia Fort

When the Japanese attacked, flight instructor Cornelia Fort was in the air above nearby John Rodgers Airport in an Interstate Cadet monoplane, practicing takeoffs and landings with a student pilot. At age twenty-two, Fort was one of the country's most experienced pilots.

Just before 8 a.m., as her student, Mr. Suomala, headed in for a landing, Fort noticed a military aircraft coming directly toward them. She jerked the controls away from her student and pulled up over the oncoming plane. Red Rising Suns shone up from the wings. She looked toward Pearl Harbor and saw billows of black smoke. Then she saw formations of silver bombers.

"If danger comes as suddenly as this did, you don't have time to be frightened. I'm not brave, but I knew the air was not the place for our baby airplane," she said. Fort dropped the Cadet down quickly. Machine-gun fire burst around the plane. They touched down and Suomala, not yet understanding, asked plaintively, "When am I going to solo?" Seconds later a plane strafed the runway, and she and Suomala ran for cover. In the hangar, no one believed the Japanese were attacking until a mechanic ran in and said, "That strafing plane that just flew over killed Bob Tyce" (the airport manager). The Japanese shot down two student planes that morning.

Fort left Hawaii in late February. Seven months later she became one of the original 25 women pilots recruited for the Women's Auxiliary Ferrying Squadron.

Ships burn and antiaircraft fire explodes at Pearl Harbor (above) during the second attack wave. The Japanese sank or damaged 19 U.S. ships and destroyed more than 165 U.S. planes in the attack. Over 3,500 Americans were killed or wounded, including 84 civilians. The Japanese lost only 29 planes, five midget submarines, and 185 men in the raid.

Pilot Cornelia Fort's (left) quick reactions saved her plane during the Japanese attack.

Awakened by the Attack

PEARL HARBOR
Ford Island
Housing — Naval Hospital
Hickam Field

Evelyn Bell and Ada *"Jonnie" Ulmer (seated) in the bomb shelter Jonnie's husband dug for them. After the attack at Pearl Harbor, the Red Cross distributed gas masks to civilians on the island. Fearful of invasion, Evelyn kept a revolver and Jonnie slept with a butcher knife under her pillow. "All I could think about was staying alive . . . not getting caught by the Japanese," Jonnie said.*

Jack and Jonnie Ulmer (opposite) in November 1941.

Ada "Jonnie" Ulmer, a young navy wife, spent the evening before the attack with her neighbors, Evelyn and Reg Bell, at a picnic at their housing unit near Hickam Field, Pearl Harbor. Her husband Jack, a navy bosun's mate, was en route to Wake Island on a tugboat.

About 8 a.m. December 7th, Jonnie awoke to the sound of planes and gunfire. "I went out to see what was going on, and there was Reg Bell climbing the telephone pole. He said, 'It's the . . . Japs and they caught us with our pants down.'" Jonnie looked up and saw Red Rising Sun insignias on the planes. "There was firing going everywhere and planes coming down in flames." Bullets ripped into walls; people crawled under their houses for protection.

Reg ran into the house, got his revolver and gave it to Evelyn and said, "You keep this and you take care of Jonnie. We don't know where Jack is." Then he left for his battle station aboard the *Helena*. That morning, a torpedo hit blew him onto the dock and broke his back.

In the neighborhood it was bedlam after the attack. "The radios went crazy. They reported there were a hundred ships coming and the Rape of Nanking would be nothing when the Japanese got through with us," Jonnie said. She and Evelyn, both nurses (Jonnie, a former navy nurse, had to leave the service when she got married), volunteered to help and were sent to Tripler General, the army hospital. In the blackout, they worked around the clock, caring for shrapnel victims with head injuries, many of them delirious. "I don't know how we took care of them," she said. "We just did."

"There was no such thing as getting off. We would pile in a corner somewhere—men and women. You just laid there until somebody took you by the hand and said, 'Come on, I need you.'"

After two weeks, the registry sent Jonnie and Evelyn to the Naval Hospital where they cared for some of the worst burn victims—men pulled out of the flaming oil in the harbor. "Some men were so burned you knew they'd die. You hoped they'd die, because their fingers were down to nothing, there were no lips left. . . . It was just awful. You looked at them all and wanted to cry." The nurses salved the men with the new drug, sulfa, and on those who survived, the skin healed pink, not withered as burns had up until that time.

Meanwhile, the Navy listed Jack Ulmer's ship as sunk. Jonnie's brother-in-law told her, "Jack is gone. Make up your mind he's gone." But Jonnie thought she would feel it. She said, "I think he's somewhere hoping I'm safe." On December 21st Jack returned. His ship had maintained radio silence for two weeks during its treacherous return from Wake Island.

The military ordered all dependents back to the mainland. Each person could take one suitcase. For Jonnie this was the hardest. "You just had to walk off and leave everything." Evelyn Bell returned to the mainland first. Jonnie followed in May 1942. Reg Bell had three surgeries and was back at work doing salvage as soon as he could walk. Jack Ulmer served in the South Pacific, "lost his ship," and returned home at the end of the war.

December 7, 1941

The word went out: Pearl Harbor attacked! Later, people recalled how they first heard the news and how it changed their lives. After watching the fighting build in Europe and Asia, the United States was at war.

Nancy Potter was in high school at the time. "I was standing on the stairs when the Pearl Harbor announcement was made, and the declaration of war followed very suddenly. I can remember looking down at the carpet and thinking life would never be the same again."

Betty Willett was in the car with her family. "My mother, father, sister and I were going up to visit my uncle. We got halfway there, were listening to the radio and they announced Pearl Harbor. My father had recently gotten out of the navy. He just turned right around because he knew he'd be back in the navy immediately. We were very shocked—especially that my father was leaving."

Actress Eve Arden didn't quite believe the radio report. "I was running the vacuum over our sublet carpet and could catch only an occasional phrase from the radio. . . . 'Attacking in waves,' I heard. 'Battleships already sunk,' and the words 'Pearl Harbor' and 'Japanese planes.' Well, I thought, Orson's done it again."

Yoshiko Uchida, a Japanese American student, heard the news with her family. Believing it was only an "aberrant act" and it didn't mean war, she went to the library to study. "When I got home, the house was filled with an uneasy quiet. A strange man sat in our living room and my father was gone. The FBI had come to pick him up, as they had dozens of other Japanese men."

First Lady Eleanor Roosevelt was hosting a luncheon when the news came. It was not until she went upstairs afterwards, that she knew something had happened: "All the secretaries were there, two telephones were in use, the senior military aides were on their way with messages. I said nothing; the words I heard over the telephone were quite sufficient to tell me that, finally, the blow had fallen and we had been attacked." That night, in her weekly radio broadcast, Eleanor said, "There is no more uncertainty. We know what we have to face and we know we are ready to face it. . . . Whatever is asked of us, I am sure we can accomplish it; we are the free and unconquerable people of the U.S.A."

Civilians Interned

Internees at Santo Tomás Internment Camp in Manila built shanties (above) to have a place to meet one's spouse, prepare extra food, or eat in privacy. Later when over-crowding became severe, more than 1,000 lived in these structures.

Women internees (opposite) wash their hair at a communal tub at Santo Tomás.

PACIFIC

Philippines

"There was never a time when we were not hungry."
—*Evelyn Whitfield, Santo Tomás, Camp Holmes and Bilibid Prison*

When the U.S. entered the war, Americans living in occupied countries faced internment. In Europe, the Axis held a few thousand U.S. civilians, but repatriated most of them in 1942. The Japanese interned more than 130,000 Allied men, women and children—7,500 to 14,000 of them Americans—for the duration, with only a fraction repatriated.

On December 8, 1941 in the Far East, the same day as the Pearl Harbor attack in Hawaii, Japan struck the Philippines and began a major assault on Southeast Asia. U.S. forces in the Philippines withdrew to Bataan, and on December 26th declared Manila an open city, leaving civilians defenseless. The islands soon fell. By March 1942 Japan controlled all of Southeast Asia. Stunned by the swiftness of the invasion, some 6,000 Americans in the Philippines fled with little more than a hastily packed suitcase. Margaret Sherk, a mining wife from Suyoc, whose husband

volunteered to fight with the army, found herself alone in Manila with her young son when the Japanese entered the city: "What was to happen to us now? . . . I had such vivid imaginative pictures of what could be done to us," she said

Contrary to their fears, the invaders did not rape American women. The Japanese ordered Allied civilians in Manila to pack food and clothing for three days, and bussed them to Santo Tomás University, the largest internment camp in the Philippines. There, approximately 4,000 remained imprisoned for the next three-and-a-half years. Other camps eventually transferred their populations so that by February 1945, Santo Tomás, Bilibid Prison in Manila, and Los Baños, south of Manila, held all the Philippines' internees.

Conditions in the camps violated the Geneva Conventions and grew worse as the war turned against the Japanese. The conquerors required prisoners to bow, slapped or beat internees for minor infractions, and executed several men who went over the wall. At Santo Tomás, the Japanese did not provide *any* food for the first six months, and then supplied such inferior rations that by 1945 internees subsisted on less than 1,000 calories a day. Dysentery and tropical diseases flourished in the absence of good food and medical supplies.

The Japanese housed men and women separately, and prohibited sexual relations. Sleeping quarters crammed 50 internees in a room. In the main building at Santo Tomás, Elizabeth Vaughan had a space seven feet by 26 inches. Bathrooms lacked adequate plumbing, with a few stools for several hundreds. Privacy was unknown. "Harder to bear than hunger," Evelyn Whitfield recalled, "was the incessant chatter, the curiosity about each others' personal life, the gossip and anger."

Organized by a Central Committee comprised mostly of men, internees worked to improve sanitation, food distribution, and perform essential camp jobs. A small town economy sprang up. In addition to assigned camp details, internees earned money for services such as knitting, teaching, and barbering. At Santo Tomás, those with money could buy from the outside until 1944. There were few other resources. The rare packages that got through, and the Red Cross comfort kits delivered in 1943 and 1944, made the difference between life and death for many.

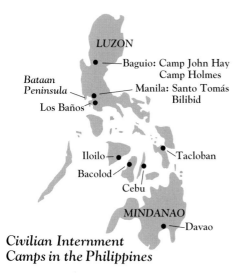

Civilian Internment Camps in the Philippines

LUZON
Baguio: Camp John Hay
Camp Holmes
Bataan Peninsula
Manila: Santo Tomás
Bilibid
Los Baños
Iloilo
Tacloban
Bacolod
Cebu
MINDANAO
Davao

Daily Life: Margaret Sherk

A typical day at Santo Tomás began at 6 a.m. for Margaret Sherk and her 4-year-old son, David. Because David awoke early, Margaret spent the first hour at the outdoor wash trough, doing laundry away from the room she shared with about thirty other mothers and children. Around 7 a.m., she and David took their tin plates and spoons and got into line for a breakfast of cracked wheat with pink worms floating upside down. This was the first of many lines in any given day: lines for meals, lines to get soap, to use the bathrooms, to take showers. . . .

After breakfast they aired their bedding and checked for bed bugs. Then David went off to a kindergarten run by a woman internee, and Margaret worked at the camp library, mending books. Margaret earned about 12 cents per book at her library job, enough to pay for David's schooling and to buy extra food. Without a reserve of money she also became adept at bartering.

Mothers and children were entitled to a midday meal, so at noon she and David waited in line for the lunch—usually a soup made from the evening's leftovers. During the afternoon heat they showered and had a siesta. While David slept, Margaret worked on clothes or picked worms out of rice. By the time David awoke it was almost time to stand in line for the evening meal. A typical dinner was boiled rice with a watery stew, often containing talinum, a spinach-like vegetable, and fish heads or shreds of carabao (native oxen). After the meal they took another shower (to cope with the heat) and David went to bed. Margaret spent the evening at her camp details: "toilet duty" and vegetable cleaning, and occasionally listened to music. The day ended with roll call and lights out at 11 p.m.

Bowing to the Emperor

Celebes: Darlene Diebler

In January 1940, Darlene Diebler, a young bride from Boone, Iowa, ventured into the wild interior of Dutch New Guinea with her husband, Russell, to establish a Christian mission for the Kapauku natives. The threat of war forced them to evacuate in 1941 to the Celebes. Less than a year later, the Japanese invaded the Celebes, put Darlene and her fellow women missionaries under house arrest, and imprisoned the men at Parepare. Darlene never saw Russell again.

In May 1943, the Japanese sent the women to Kampili Internment Camp. There, along with some 1,670 women and children, Darlene lived in grass-roofed barracks with dirt floors. The women coped daily with flies carrying dysentery, free-roaming rabid dogs, and inadequate food. Women maintained the camp and performed forced labor for their captors; they knitted socks for the army, cleared land, unloaded trucks, and raised pigs for Japanese consumption. "The pigs . . . had better accommodations than the women prisoners," Darlene recalled. One of only three Americans in the camp, Darlene was nevertheless named a barracks leader, perhaps because she spoke English, Dutch and Indonesian. The women feared the commander,

Mr. Yamaji, who was known for his brutality. Easily enraged, he beat women with his cane for minor infractions. When Darlene made a suggestion about drinking water, he struck her a blow to the neck, saying, "You talk too much."

In late 1943 Darlene found out Russell had died of illness at Parepare. "My whole world fell apart," she said. Mr. Yamaji called her into his office and said, "What you have heard today, women in Japan have heard." In response she told him about her religious beliefs and how she held love in her heart, even for her enemies. Mr. Yamaji was deeply moved, and from that day on she felt he trusted her.

On May 12, 1944, the Japanese secret police, the Kempeitai, arrested Darlene, falsely accused her of spying, and imprisoned her in solitary at the Kempeitai prison in Makassar. Through the walls she heard the cries of others being tortured, among them Philoma Seely and Margaret Kemp, the two other American women missionaries. The Kempeitai interrogated Darlene repeatedly and beat her with karate chops to the neck and jabs between the eyes. Weak from malnutrition, dysentery, malaria and beriberi, Darlene sustained herself by walking around her cell. She concentrated

on the positive: how grateful she was to have a tile floor rather than dirt; how fortunate she had on her dress with the full-circle skirt. In early July, Mr. Yamaji came to see her and gave her a bundle of 92 bananas—food that undoubtedly saved her life. After four months of interrogation, the Kempeitai released Darlene and the two other Americans to the camp at Kampili.

Allied bombing raids increased over Kampili as Japanese soldiers made a last stand in the Celebes. On July 17, 1945, Allied bombs destroyed most of the camp while the women and children huddled in nearby trenches. The internees moved to a rudimentary camp in the jungle where they lived under the most basic conditions until the Australians liberated them in September 1945. Darlene left the Celebes on September 19, 1945 in fragile health. "I was going home alone in borrowed clothes. Widowed at 26, with not a thing in the world I could call my own. . . ." She returned to her family and spent the next two years recovering. In 1948, she married Gerald Rose, a missionary, and together they returned to work among the natives in New Guinea.

Borneo: Agnes Newton Keith

In 1939, when World War II broke out in Europe, American writer Agnes Newton Keith and her English husband, Harry, were on leave in Canada from their home in Sandakan, North Borneo. With England at war, Harry was ordered to return to his post as Director of Agriculture. Pregnant and determined to stay with Harry even if war spread to the Pacific, Agnes sailed with him to Borneo, and in April 1940, gave birth to a son, George.

In January 1942, the Japanese invaded Sandakan. In spite of Agnes' desire to "face it together" with Harry, the Japanese interned women and children in a separate camp from the men. Agnes and 2-year-old George, accustomed to comfortable colonial life, coped with the shock of living crowded with 40 women and children in leaking, rotted, unlighted quarters. The women dug holes, cleared the land, and ate the poorest grade of rice sweepings, while struggling to provide for their children. Agnes learned to take risks, buying food on the black market and smuggling money into camp. Against all reason except her intense need, she made dangerous nighttime crawls under the fence to meet Harry.

In January 1943, the Japanese moved the women and children to Kuching. They said goodbye to their husbands from across the ditch, uncertain they would ever see them again. During the 10-day boat trip, squatting in the rain on the open deck, Agnes and the mothers felt the weight of their children: "Each one now, like myself, knew she must go it alone. . . . Our children were all that was left to us of our men. We were the preservers of our children now."

Women internees *in Southeast Asia (above) learned to bow to their Japanese captors or face severe punishment.*

At Batu Lintang near Kuching, with over 240 Dutch and British women and children, Agnes suffered semi-starvation, tropical diseases, face-slapping and other punishments while performing forced labor for the Japanese. It was "prison camp," she noted, not "internment" because at Kuching, camps with civilians ran under prisoner-of-war rules. After she fought off a guard who tried to molest her, the Japanese command dealt with Agnes' complaint by breaking her ribs.

As starvation in the camps reached its peak in 1945, Allied planes bombed Kuching. On September 11, 1945, the 9th Australian Division marched in. Everyone cheered, cried, and clasped hands. Agnes and George were reunited with Harry, who had been in a nearby camp. Soon afterwards, they sailed for the United States.

I am an American

Restricted Areas

The attack on Pearl Harbor and the rapid Japanese victories in the Pacific completely changed the political climate in the United States. Japanese Americans on the West Coast, long the targets of racial prejudice and economic envy, suddenly became focal points for fear and war hysteria.

The prejudice had deep roots. In 1924, the Exclusion Act outlawed Japanese immigration to the U.S. and prohibited those already in the country—the *Issei* generation—from owning land or becoming citizens. As their children born in the United States—the *Nisei* generation—came of age, Japanese American land and business holdings grew, and powers like the Hearst press fueled hate with campaigns against "the Yellow Peril."

When war came, the press and economic powers played on widespread fears of sabotage to whip up public fervor against Japanese Americans. A few voices dissented. On a visit to the West Coast just after Pearl Harbor, First Lady Eleanor Roosevelt called for tolerance towards Japanese, Italian and German Americans. "The biggest obligation we have today is to prove that in time of stress we can still live up to our beliefs and maintain the civil liberties we have established as the rights of human beings everywhere," she said.

Her words held no sway with the president, who believed the threat of internal subversion was real, even though investigations found no hard evidence of Japanese American sabotage. Under pressure to take action, President Franklin Roosevelt signed Executive Order 9066 on February 19, 1942, authorizing the establishment of "military areas" on the West Coast from which "any or all persons may be excluded." The practical effect of this order—which Roosevelt may not have fully foreseen—was to forcibly remove all people of Japanese descent from the West Coast, arguably the worst violation of civil rights of American citizens in 20th century U.S. history.

Within three months, the U.S. Army evacuated 110,000 Japanese Americans (out of a total of 127,000 in the continental

Evacuees of Japanese ancestry in Los Angeles (left) board the train for Manzanar War Relocation Authority Center, 250 miles away in the California desert. Following army directives, they brought only what they could carry, leaving behind their homes and possessions.

U.S.) from the West Coast. Two-thirds were U.S. citizens. Ironically, in Hawaii, where martial law was in effect, the government removed fewer than 2,000 of the 158,000 people of Japanese ancestry. Their evacuation would have spelled economic disaster for the islands. The U.S. also interned or relocated more than 22,000 people of German or Italian descent deemed potentially dangerous.

The army instructed evacuees to bring no more than they could carry. Families had only days to liquidate their businesses, homes and possessions. In their haste, many suffered great financial loss. Some left possessions with trusted friends, but most lost everything—the earnings of generations.

The biggest shock to many, however, was that it happened at all. Mabel Ota, a *Nisei* from Los Angeles said, "It was really sort of unbelievable. . . . I kept saying all along, we're American citizens and the government couldn't possibly put us into camps. I really didn't believe it would happen until it did."

Aleutian Evacuation

Japanese invade Attu and Kiska June 7, 1942

Alaska

Aleutians

Camps

In June 1942, the Japanese military bombed Dutch Harbor, invaded Attu and Kiska islands in the Aleutians, and imprisoned 42 American civilian Aleuts in Japan. This was the only ground attack on U.S. soil in World War II. In response, the U.S. military evacuated 881 Aleuts to southeastern Alaska. There, evacuees lived in dilapidated camps with inadequate food, water, and electricity. Some found work in canneries and on fishing boats. "If we had waited for the government to take care of our medical, food, and housing needs, we would not have survived," said Alice Snigaroff Petrivelli. Evacuees, including Lukenia Prokopeuff and her daughter (above), returned at the end of the war to find their villages ravaged.

Manzanar to Heart Mountain

Manzanar (above) stands out bleakly in the California desert in this July 3, 1943 photo by Dorothea Lange. Hired by the War Relocation Authority to document the evacuation of Japanese Americans, Lange's images juxtaposing courage with the indignities of incarceration led the government to censor many of her photos.

Chiyeko Juliet Fukuoka (top opposite) a Nisei released from Topaz to attend school in New York City.

● **Internment Camps**

Japanese American Internment in the United States

The army ordered West Coast Japanese Americans to report to civil control stations for registration and numbering. From there, they bussed evacuees to assembly centers to live while awaiting completion of permanent camps further inland. Crews rushed to make unused fairgrounds, racetracks and stockyards into assembly centers, even as internees arrived.

At Tanforan near San Francisco, families lived in 10 by 20-foot horse stalls. Yoshiko Uchida, a Berkeley student whose father was taken to Montana in the initial Federal Bureau of Investigation roundup, arrived with her mother and sister. "Dust, dirt and wood shavings covered linoleum that had been laid over manure-covered boards; the smell of horses hung in the air."

As soon as construction allowed, the army transferred internees to permanent camps in remote desert or swampland areas. In all, the government set up 16 assembly centers, most of them in California, and 10 internment camps scattered in California, Arizona, Utah, Idaho, Wyoming, Colorado and Arkansas.

Miné Okubo, whose art fellowship was disrupted by the war, arrived at Topaz in Utah after a restless 36 hour trip in a blacked-out train. "It was a desolate scene," she said. "Hundreds of low black barracks covered with tarred paper were lined up row after row. A few telephone poles stood like sentinels, and soldiers could be seen patrolling the grounds."

Conditions in the camps, although crowded and uncomfortable, complied with the Geneva Conventions and did not approach the brutal internment civilians suffered under the Japanese in Southeast Asia or in the Nazi death camps.

Families lived in barrack "apartments" with up to seven people to a 20 by 25-foot room. "There were no chairs, nothing to use for partitions nor closets. Dust from windstorms covered us, coming in through the knotholes," Elaine Yoneda recalled of Manzanar. Camps consisted of blocks of 12 or 14 barracks, each with a central mess hall, laundry, and public bathrooms. The lack of privacy in the showers and latrines was especially embarrassing to older women, who brought in cloths or newspapers to cover themselves, until the army agreed to install partitions.

Mess halls served 250 to 300 people. Food was rationed, as it was across the country. The diet included two meatless days a week and emphasized starches. At times meals consisted of bread, potatoes and spaghetti only. Yet, there was no shortage. "No matter how bad the food might be," Jeanne Wakatsuki recalled, "you could always eat till you were full."

Cooperative organizations developed in each camp, with internees volunteering (they were not required to work) for jobs as nurses, teachers, journalists, cooks, garbage collectors, block wardens and even camouflage net makers for the war effort for a salary of no more than $19 a month (about 10% of wages outside).

As time passed, confinement took its toll. Families broke up and morale suffered. In January 1943, the War Department allowed American-born *Nisei* who signed a loyalty oath to enlist in a special army combat unit. Some 33,000 *Nisei* served in the military during the war.

After a visit to Gila River in April 1943, Eleanor Roosevelt urged the President to relax the exclusion order. With military necessity no longer a viable reason for internment, the government issued exit permits for *Nisei* to work or attend school on the outside. Most of the *Issei* generation remained in the camps until 1945.

In early 1943, facing the high costs of maintaining the camps, and seeing public fears about Japanese Americans subside, the War Relocation Authority (WRA) issued loyalty questionnaires to all internees over age 17. Ostensibly for use in expediting release, the loyalty oath instead became a divisive rod that split many Japanese American families.

The problem stemmed from the carelessly-worded Question 28, which asked if an internee swore allegiance to the United States and foreswore allegiance to Japan. For the *Issei,* a "yes" answer would renounce Japanese citizenship and make them stateless persons. Some *Nisei* saw the question as a trap intended to make them admit a previous allegiance to Japan.

The WRA segregated the "disloyals" and their children in a high-security camp at Tule Lake. *Nisei* "loyals" received leave clearance to go east. Women signed on for defense jobs and government work, or attended school, often with assistance from the Quakers or other religious groups.

It took considerable courage for internees to venture into the prejudiced world that had so recently pushed for their incarceration. Miné Okubo left Topaz to take a job with *Fortune* magazine. She looked back as she departed. "Only the very old or very young were left. Here I was alone, with no family responsibilities, and yet fear chained me to the camp."

On the outside, most assimilated without much problem. In Boston, Lillian Ota noted, "People stare at me, but not so much as to make me feel uncomfortable." In spite of the hostilities some encountered, release was infinitely preferable to life behind barbed wire. By the end of 1943, one-third of all evacuees had left camp for work, school or to join the military.

War Correspondents

War brought change to women journalists long confined to covering the "feminine beat." As the U.S. military drafted the men, newsrooms emptied out and one-time copy girls and secretaries moved up to positions as hard news reporters. About 150 determined women fought for assignments overseas. During the 1930s, women journalists had covered the Japanese invasion of China and the build-up to war in Europe. After the U.S. entered the war in 1941, more than 100 women became accredited war correspondents attached to military units in North Africa, Europe and the Pacific. In an era when most people got their news from print, these women worked for influential newspapers, magazines and wire services. A few reported for radio.

Their work exposed them to the dangers of war, and many learned firsthand what it was to survive bombing, strafing and torpedo attacks. They roughed it in tents and marched long distances in uniform, carrying their portable typewriters. Fighting hostility from men and restrictive policies that hampered their access to the action, women found ways, with courage and resourcefulness, to report the news. No women correspondents were killed in World War II; that distinction would come later when veteran reporter, Dickey Chapelle, died covering the Vietnam War. Women journalists proved their excellence and daring in World War II. Although many were pressured to give up their jobs at war's end, their endurance and demands for equality during the war permanently raised the level of opportunity for women in journalism.

Associated Press correspondent Ruth Cowan (opposite) in uniform in 1942. Accredited correspondents wore uniforms with helmets, and carried a canteen, a gas mask, and two bags in addition to their portable typewriters. The "C" armband signified "correspondent."

War Correspondents

War Correspondents in London, 1942. (Left to right): Mary Welsh, Time *magazine; Dixie Tighe, International News Service; Kathleen Harriman, International News Service; Helen Kirkpatrick,* Chicago Daily News; *Lee Miller,* Vogue; *and Tania Long Daniell,* New York Times.

Women had long faced discrimination and challenges in journalism "I never minded hard work or long hours, but to waste time on articles that must have been as boring to the readers as to me was infuriating," wrote newspaperwoman Sarah McClendon of her work in Texas in the 1930s. In those days, editors relegated female reporters to the society page. In World War I, the U.S. Army refused to accredit women correspondents to cover the war front. In fact, up until the Second World War, publishers largely kept women out of hard news reporting.

World War II brought new opportunities to female journalists. As men joined the military or accepted assignments on the war front, positions opened up and women took on increasing responsibilities in the newsroom. By 1943, women made up 50 percent of the staffs of many newspapers. In addition, female journalists pleaded for, cajoled and demanded overseas assignments in Europe, North Africa and the Pacific. Despite obstacles to allowing women on the battle front (no

general wanted a female correspondent killed on his watch), by war's end 127 of the 1,700 accredited war correspondents with American forces overseas were women. Representing magazines, newspapers, wire services, and in a few instances, radio broadcasters, their small numbers belied the impact of their work.

Some of the more seasoned women reporters gained their experience in the 1930s when First Lady Eleanor Roosevelt began to hold press conferences for women only. (Female journalists had long met opposition in trying to attend presidential press conferences, and this was Mrs. Roosevelt's response.) The move forced editors to hire female reporters. Most women, however, got their start from wartime newsroom vacancies.

Helen Thomas, who moved up from copy girl to cub reporter at the *Washington Daily News,* had the difficult task of reporting war casualties that came in on the wire: "They seemed endless at times, and it was painful just to watch as the copy paper filled up with name after name. We had to look for those casualties who were from the Washington area and contact the families. How I dreaded that."

Sarah McClendon, expelled from the Women's Army Corps (WAC) because she was pregnant, found herself in early June of 1944 in Washington, D.C., abandoned by her husband, alone, and giving birth to a baby girl. By the end of June she stood in the Oval Office, a reporter for the *Philadelphia Daily News*, the newest member of the White House press corps, and one of the first women to attend presidential press conferences.

Two women gained prominence as political columnists: Pulitzer prize winner Anne O'Hare McCormick of the *New York Times*, and Dorothy Thompson. Famous as the first correspondent Hitler expelled from Germany, Thompson used her syndicated "On the Record" column to attack the German leader and campaign for the rescue of Jews fleeing Germany. With lecture appearances, radio news broadcasts, and a column that appeared in 200 newspapers, she was a major influence.

Women correspondents were on the scene in Europe and the Far East well before the United States entered the war. After Pearl Harbor, the War Department accredited correspondents to report from combat areas. Bucking arguments that a war zone was no place for a lady, female reporters, with pressure and persuasion, won their accreditations. Once the War Department ordered the Women's Auxiliary Army Corps (WAAC) overseas, objections to women correspondents lost force. Ruth Cowan and Inez Robb arrived in North Africa with the WAAC in January 1943, the first accredited women correspondents assigned to a military unit overseas. Women who covered the Pacific had to wait until the fall of 1944 for navy accreditation.

Accredited correspondents wore uniforms and held the assimilated rank of captain (a military precaution in case of capture). Unlike male reporters who traveled with the fighting troops, women could go no farther than WAC contingents or field hospitals without permission from the commanding officer. Press camps, where most briefings took place, were off-limits to female reporters until late in the war, as were on-site censors; women in Normandy had to send their stories to London by messenger to clear the censors.

Although threatened with court-martial, some women found the regulations overly restrictive and interpreted them in new ways or flouted them altogether. In France, Virginia Irwin successfully dodged all-points bulletins seeking her return, meanwhile filing front page stories from the battle zone. Martha Gellhorn joined up with Polish and Canadian forces fighting in Italy in order to be at the front.

Through rain and mud, blistered feet and tent dwelling, in danger from snipers and bombs, women followed the action and filed eyewitness accounts that captured not only the events, but also the human face of the war. Looking back, Martha Gellhorn wrote, "War was always worse than I knew how to say—always. And probably from an instinct of self-preservation, one tried to write most often what was brave and decent."

Virginia Irwin of the Saint Louis Post-Dispatch, *Marjorie Avery of the* Detroit Free Press, *and British reporter, Judy Barden (left to right) crossed the English Channel to Normandy with the first WAC contingent in July 1944 and lived in tents while reporting on the Allied advance into France. On warm days they wrote their dispatches from a folding table in an apple orchard.*

Standing up to Hitler: the Early Days

Two women in Berlin, Dorothy Thompson and Sigrid Schultz, witnessed Adolf Hitler's rise to power. In 1933, the ailing President Hindenburg appointed Hitler—head of the extremist Nazi Party since 1925—chancellor of Germany. By August 1934, with military backing, Hitler seized the power of president and chancellor to become *führer* (supreme leader). In a country worn down by defeat in World War I and the Great Depression, Hitler's drive to rebuild German infrastructure and secretly rearm brought employment and won him support among the common workers. At the same time, he crushed all political opposition and revoked civil liberties. Militarism arose, and a virulent racial and religious intolerance took hold.

Dorothy Thompson, bureau chief for the *Philadelphia Public Ledger* and the *New York Post* in Berlin, may not have realized her criticism of Hitler would later become the rallying cry of her career. In 1931 when she first interviewed him, she misjudged his power: "When finally I walked in . . . I was convinced I was meeting the future dictator of Germany. In something less than fifty seconds I was quite sure I was not. It took just about that time to measure the startling insignificance of this man who has set the whole world agog. . . . He is the very prototype of the Little Man." After the Reichstag fire in 1933 and the ensuing Nazi rampage, Thompson vocally condemned Hitler and wrote warnings of the violence he planned against Jews. In response, Hitler expelled her from Germany—the first of many correspondents he would order to leave.

Unlike Thompson, who openly criticized Hitler, Sigrid Schultz, Berlin bureau chief for the *Chicago Tribune*, knew how far she could go. Her experience covering central Europe since 1916 made her an expert on German affairs. Although critical, she reported only facts, and thereby managed to remain in Germany in spite of Nazi entrapment attempts. One of the few women reporters, Schultz learned to drink with the men at the Hotel Adlon, a political watering hole, and cultivated contacts like number two Nazi, Hermann Goering, who introduced her to Hitler. In one interview, Hitler told her, "You cannot understand the Nazi movement because you think with your head and not with your heart." At another he shouted, "My will shall be done!"

In 1937, Schultz began to write secretly under the byline John Dixon to report the real story of Nazi intimidation. In August 1939, "John Dixon" was the first to break the news of the Soviet-German nonaggression pact. When war broke out in September 1939, Schultz remained in Berlin and reported by radio even after shrapnel from a British bomb pierced her leg. Feeling increasing personal danger from the Nazis, she left in early 1941.

EUROPE
August 1939

Great Britain
London •

GERMANY
Berlin •
Poland
Rhine-land
Sudetenland
Alsace-Lorraine
Czecho-slovakia
France
Austria
Hungary
Italy
Portugal
Spain
Yugoslavia
Albania

■ German-controlled

Dorothy Thompson (top) appeals for aid to Britain at a major rally in Chicago in 1940. In 1936, two years after her expulsion from Germany, she began the political column, "On the Record" for the New York Herald Tribune. *She used it to attack Hitler and U.S. isolationists, to alert the nation to the plight of refugees, and as early as 1938, to reveal the existence of Nazi concentration camps. With numerous lecture appearances, her widely syndicated column, and her own radio news broadcasts, Thompson was a huge force in shaping public opinion.*

Sigrid Schultz in Berlin in 1932 with U.S. ambassador William Dodd (on left) and Nazi propaganda chief, Joseph Goebbels. Schultz used her many contacts to report the rise of Nazism in Germany. After she complained of intimidation, Hitler's number two man, Hermann Goering labelled her the "dragon lady from Chicago." Journalist Quentin Reynolds called her *"Hitler's Greatest Enemy." Her 1941 book, Germany Will Try it Again, influenced U.S. President Roosevelt to insist on "total surrender" from the Germans in World War II.*

German dictator Adolf Hitler (bottom) at the Nazi Party Congress in 1935. On his orders, the Nazis systematically annihilated 6 million European Jews.

Women reporters were on the scene in Europe throughout the late 1930s. In March 1936, in violation of the World War I peace treaty, Hitler invaded the demilitarized Rhineland. Two years later, Germany annexed Austria and set its eye on Czechoslovakia's Sudetenland. Fearful of war, Britain and France signed the Munich Pact with Hitler in September 1938, ceding the Sudetenland to Germany. In the London *Sunday Times*, Helen Kirkpatrick reported on British prime minister Neville Chamberlain's triumphant return from Munich and his declaration of "peace for our time." Dorothy Thompson cut through the British rhetoric: "What happened on Friday is called 'Peace.' Actually it is an international Fascist *coup d'état.*"

On November 9, 1938, *Kristallnacht* (the night of broken glass), Nazis smashed, looted, and burned Jewish property and forced 26,000 German Jews into concentration camps. Sigrid Schultz, in Berlin, reported, "Eyewitnesses saw how systematically the 'spontaneous demonstrations' had been organized." Hitler seized the rest of Czechoslovakia in March 1939. Finally awake, Britain and France vowed to defend Poland from German attack.

In Berlin on August 31, 1939 for the London *Sunday Times*, Virginia Cowles saw *Luftwaffe* fighter planes massed for the invasion of Poland. The next day the German tanks roared across the border. Roving correspondent Sonia Tomara survived the intense bombings in Poland and remained long enough to report on the defeat of the demoralized and ill-equipped Polish army. Britain and France declared war on Germany on September 3rd. World War II had begun.

Dateline: Europe and North Africa

Moscow under
attack (above),
July 1941. The
only foreign corres-
pondent in the
Soviet Union when
Germany attacked,
Life magazine
photographer
Margaret Bourke-
White, captured the
night bombing of
the Kremlin from
her hotel balcony.
Refusing to take
shelter, she stayed
in her room and
risked shrapnel and
explosions to record
this scene. She
developed her film
in the hotel bathtub.
Bourke-White was
one of only a
handful of Western
journalists allowed
on the Russian
front during the
entire war.

In the early months of the war, two women correspondents, Mary Marvin Breckinridge and Betty Wason, reported from northern Europe for CBS radio's pioneering evening news roundup. Breckinridge broadcast reactions to Hitler's aggression from Holland, Norway, Belgium and Germany. When the Germans invaded Norway, Betty Wason sneaked in from Sweden, hitched a ride through the mountains, dodged bombs, assessed the British defenses, and rushed back to Stockholm to broadcast the news that the Allies were faltering.

Britain's failure in Norway led Parliament to oust Neville Chamberlain. Winston Churchill became the new prime minister of Great Britain. On May 10, 1940, Hitler launched *Blitzkrieg* air assaults and invaded neutral Belgium, Holland and Luxembourg. French and British forces mobilized in northern France, but the Germans encircled their armies. With their backs against the English Channel at Dunkirk, the British called in warships, merchantmen, ferries and even pleasure boats for a massive evacuation of 338,226 Allied troops. Virginia Cowles watched the exhausted men disembark at Dover. "Hundreds of them filed through the docks, dirty and tired," she wrote.

With the surrender of Holland and Belgium, the Germans advanced toward Paris. Sonia Tomara, fresh from her flight out of Poland, joined the throngs fleeing south. She was in a cafe in Bordeaux when Marshal Philippe Pétain came on the radio and told the French to lay down their arms. "'It is armistice,' a woman said near me. 'It is defeat,' a man replied in a strange voice. There were no gestures, no words of rebellion," Tomara wrote. Under the armistice, the Germans occupied northern and western France, and Pétain's collaborationist regime governed southern France.

No sooner had the French signed the armistice than Hitler launched intensive air attacks on Britain to open the way for invasion. From the streets and air raid shelters, correspondents Mary Welsh, Tania Long, Virginia Cowles, Helen Kirkpatrick and Martha Gellhorn lived

Photo by Louise Dahl-Wolfe

through and reported on the Blitz. *Time/Life* reporter Mary Welsh later wrote: "For the succeeding 56 nights, without surcease, London shuddered and burned."

Stymied by England's resistance, Hitler turned his sights on the Soviet Union. By chance, Margaret Bourke-White, the celebrated *Life* magazine photographer, was in Moscow in June 1941 when Germany broke its nonaggression pact with Josef Stalin and invaded. From her hotel balcony which faced the Kremlin, Bourke-White photographed German bombs exploding. On one spectacular night she watched parachute flares light up the city "like mammoth blazing parasols." Risking personal safety, she hid from the blackout wardens and worked through the air raids, positioning her cameras, and then developing the film in the hotel bathroom. In September, she traveled to the front. "We drove through plains scattered with helmets of the dead, and battlefields that looked like the end of the world." It was the start of the protracted Russian war which demanded great sacrifices from both sides, and which the Germans ultimately lost.

In the spring of 1942, shortly after the U.S. entered the war, Margaret Bourke-White became the first woman correspondent accredited to the U.S. Army Air Force. Assigned to cover the Allied offensive in North Africa in January 1943, she traveled in a ship convoy because the army deemed it unsafe for her to fly there with the male correspondents. While the men arrived safely in Algiers, a German U-boat torpedoed her ship in the Mediterranean. Taking only two cameras and her five most precious lenses, she spent the night bailing her life boat and waiting for rescue.

In the same convoy, but not torpedoed, Associated Press reporter Ruth Cowan and Inez Robb of the International News Service arrived only to face hostility from male correspondents and army brass. Determined to do her job, Cowan cabled First Lady Eleanor Roosevelt: "Don't encourage more women to come to Africa. The men don't want us here." Her cable never made it past the censor, but shortly afterward, doors opened and she and Robb were allowed to visit the front.

Meanwhile in Algiers, Margaret Bourke-White finally received permission to go on a bombing mission—an opportunity routinely denied to women correspondents. ("Well, you've been torpedoed," General Doolittle told her, "you might as well go through everything.") Working in the 40-below-zero temperatures of an unpressurized, vibrating B-17 bomber, Bourke-White photographed the fiery flashes of Allied bombs as they exploded below on the German El Aouina airfield at Tunis. The raid was a major success. In May 1943 the Allies captured 240,000 German and Italian troops, ending the North Africa campaign.

Margaret Bourke-White (left) in 1942. Her career in World War II was storied. In 1941, she photographed Soviet dictator, Josef Stalin, capturing a momentary smile from the "most ruthless personality" she had ever met. In North Africa, she made headlines as the first woman to fly on a bombing raid. And in Italy, she recorded the war from a Piper Cub above "Purple Heart Valley."

- ■ Axis-controlled
- ▨ Allied Territory
- □ Neutral

Norway Sweden Finland
Stockholm
Moscow
Great Britain Dunkirk
London Neth. Berlin
Belg. Germany Poland USSR
Paris Lux.
France Czechoslovakia
Switz. Austria Hungary
Portugal Italy
Spain Albania
Greece
Mediterranean Sea
Morocco Algiers Tunis

Eyewitness D-Day

Martha Gellhorn (above) in 1941. One of the great war correspondents of the century, Gellhorn's bravery and commitment to journalism spanned over 50 years from the Spanish Civil War to the U.S. invasion of Panama in 1989. In World War II, she covered Czechoslovakia, the Blitz, Finland, Italy, Holland and Germany. She trekked across China, flew on a fighter mission in the Battle of the Bulge and was at the liberation of Dachau.

Troops land at Normandy (above right) on D-Day.

With victory in North Africa, the Allies turned their sights on fascist Italy. Italy had begun aggressive expansion in 1935 with an attack on Ethiopia. Four years later, in April 1939, Italy invaded Albania and United Press reporter Eleanor Packard watched Italian troops roll into the capital city, Tirana. CBS radio correspondent, Betty Wason, continued the coverage in October 1940 when Italy attacked Greece, and when Germany finished the conquest the following year.

The Allies landed in southern Italy on September 3, 1943 and within a week secured the Italian surrender. The Germans, however, fought on in Italy. As the Allies slowly advanced up the Italian peninsula, correspondents Martha Gellhorn, Helen Kirkpatrick, Virginia Cowles and Sonia Tomara reported the battles. Margaret Bourke-White joined her colleagues in the campaign in October 1943. Cramped inside an unarmed Piper Cub that flew low to scout enemy artillery positions near Cassino, Bourke-White photographed a terrain so hard-fought and pocked with shell holes the soldiers called it "Purple Heart Valley." "The earth seemed to be covered with glistening polka dots. . . . I could hardly believe so many shells could have fallen in a single valley," she wrote. "It was cruelly contradictory that with all this evidence of bloodshed and destruction, the valley seemed to clothe itself in a sequin-dotted gown." Moments later, German fighters attacked the Piper Cub. Her pilot went into the "steepest dive" she had ever experienced and they escaped back to base.

While the war ground on in Italy, the Soviet Union mounted a massive offensive in its three-year-old struggle against the Germans, and the Allies launched the long-awaited invasion of France: D-Day.

At dawn on June 6, 1944, British, American and Canadian forces landed on the Normandy coast in the face of intense German fire. The War Department refused to let women accompany the forces, so war-hardened reporters like Ruth Cowan and Helen Kirkpatrick covered the invasion from England. Women correspondents chafed at the restrictions and sought ways around them. On D-Day, International News Service reporter Lee Carson managed to get up in a plane for an exclusive aerial view of the invasion. *Boston Globe* correspondent Iris Carpenter flew in on an ambulance plane to a tiny strip of Omaha Beach on D-Day plus four. Martha Gellhorn, however, got the biggest scoop.

On D-Day plus one, breaking all rules, Gellhorn stowed away on the first British hospital ship sent to Normandy. Arriving off the coast of France, she was amazed by the size of the invasion force: "a floating city of huge vessels." Planes buzzed overhead and water ambulances brought wounded to the ship. Gellhorn rode in on a motor ambulance and waded to the beach in waist-deep water. "Everyone was violently busy on that crowded, dangerous shore.... We walked with the utmost care between the narrowly placed white tape lines that marked the mine-cleared path."

Her eyewitness account ran front-page in *Collier's*. It also won her the wrath of the army press officials back in England, who restricted her to a nurses' training camp and delayed her orders to go to France. After a day of confinement, Gellhorn climbed the fence and hitched a flight to Naples. Without her passport or press credentials, she attached herself to Polish and Canadian forces fighting in Italy and continued to report for *Collier's* out of the reach of the Army Press Office.

Ten days after D-Day, Hitler unleashed a terrifying and unpredictable weapon on England: the V1 rocket, or buzz bomb. *Chicago Daily News* reporter Helen Kirkpatrick, veteran of the Blitz, North Africa and Italy campaigns, once again saw London streets covered with bricks and broken glass. In an interview with General Dwight D. Eisenhower, the supreme Allied commander, Kirkpatrick remarked on the buzz bombing: "It's too damned dangerous here. I want to go to France." Eisenhower laughed and issued orders the next day.

In July 1944 the army finally allowed women reporters to cross the Channel. Restricted to WAC units and field hospitals, the women wrote about the wounded and the camps. At the 44th Evac Hospital, *Vogue* photographer Lee Miller dispelled the image of the clean-shaven, valiant hero: "The wounded were not 'knights in shining armor' but dirty, disheveled stricken figures—uncomprehending."

Ostensibly for their safety, the army denied women correspondents access to the jeeps, press camps, teletypes, and on-site censors the male reporters used. When *New York Times'* Tania Long Daniell asked why she couldn't stay at a press camp, she was told it had no women's latrines, and there were no plans to dig any.

These arbitrary rules did not keep women out of danger. Often, field hospitals were farther forward than male reporters' units and came under fire. Without jeeps, women hitchhiked to the front. At a crossroads near Saint-Lô, Iris Carpenter and Ruth Cowan had to hit the dirt when German bombs suddenly fell. Carpenter's ear drum shattered. An Allied command car drew up and the outraged officers asked, where was their jeep and driver? Cowan replied: "We're *women* correspondents," as if that explained everything.

War correspondents in Normandy (below) from left: *Ruth Cowan, Associated Press; Sonia Tomara,* New York Herald Tribune; *Rosette Hargrove, Newspaper Enterprise Association; Betty Knox, London Evening Standard; Iris Carpenter,* Boston Globe; *and Erika Mann,* Liberty *magazine.*

D-DAY INVASION
England
Normandy ●Paris
France

With the Army in Europe

Helen Kirkpatrick, Chicago Daily News *correspondent, (below) in Europe, February 1944. Covering the story at headquarters and the action at the front, she reported on the London Blitz, the North Africa campaign, the Italian surrender at Malta, the liberation of Paris, the Allied advance into Germany, and the war crimes trials at Nuremberg.*

In August 1944, with most of the women correspondents in Normandy confined to WAC units and field hospitals, *Vogue* photographer Lee Miller found herself by chance in the "prohibited" combat zone. Sent to do a public relations piece, she arrived to find St. Malo, France still in the midst of battle. "I was the only photographer for miles and I owned a private war," she said. Over the next few days she photographed Allied air attacks on the German holdouts in Old St. Malo Fort, at times putting aside her camera to aid the wounded. Her photographs of a mushroom cloud explosion, later confiscated by censors, documented one of the first uses of napalm.

This secret weapon, along with conventional ground tactics, helped the Allies advance on Paris. Helen Kirkpatrick, traveling with the Free French Forces, was one of the first reporters to enter the city on August 25th. Wild with joy, Parisians lined the city streets and cheered their liberators. "The Germans are still holding out, but Paris is free," wrote Kirkpatrick. "Its freedom is heady and intoxicating." But as the Allies settled in, the dark side of the German occupation came into the light. Helen Kirkpatrick

and Martha Gellhorn were among reporters who toured the shocking Gestapo prisons and torture rooms where thousands of French citizens suffered.

It was not the first Martha Gellhorn had heard of atrocities. As early as 1938 in *Collier's,* she reported on the Nazi terror campaigns in occupied Czechoslovakia. In 1943, after interviews with escaped refugees, she revealed the horrors in Poland: of the Nazis' systematic roundup and deportation of Jews to concentration camps, jammed into cattle cars; of mass showers that were actually gas chambers. Now, following U.S. forces into Holland, Gellhorn reported on the disappearance of Jews from that country.

The farther the Allies moved into German-held territories, the more dangerous reporting became, with constant threats of shelling and snipers. For their safety, the army eased limitations on women correspondents. Women no longer slept in tents, but instead stayed in hotels or press camps and traveled with male reporters in jeeps. Although still officially barred from combat areas, access to the front depended mainly on a woman's boldness and the discretion of her commanding officer.

Among the few women actually accredited to fighting units in World War II were Iris Carpenter and Lee Carson, who traveled with the U.S. First Army in Belgium and across the border into Germany. Entering the newly-taken city of Aachen, they met sullen crowds—the citizens of a defeated country. Germany was falling, but not yet ready to surrender.

In early December 1944, in the snowy Ardennes highlands, German forces broke through and carved a "bulge" in the Allied line. "Retreat in the face of Germany's smashing counteroffensive on the Luxembourg-Belgium frontier today is a

"The Germans are still holding out, but Paris is free. Its freedom is heady and intoxicating."
—Helen Kirkpatrick, liberation of Paris

> *"The mountainside was a mess of craters. Hitler's own house was still standing . . . the fire which the SS troopers set as a final salute was lashing out the windows."*—Lee Miller, Berchtesgaden

new experience to the battle-tested doughboys of the American First Army," Lee Carson reported. The Americans halted the offensive on Christmas Day at Bastogne, Belgium in a bloody battle. Arriving in the bomb-blasted village, Martha Gellhorn observed that is was "a German job of death and destruction and it was beautifully thorough." She wrote: "You can say the words 'death and destruction' and they don't mean anything. But they are awful words when you are looking at what they mean." The Battle of the Bulge cost the U.S. 81,000 and the Germans 80,000 to 100,000 casualties.

With the Allied line secure, the U.S. Army pushed on into Germany. In early March 1945, Virginia Irwin, with Patton's Fourth Armored Division, reached the Rhine River, the last barrier to the German heartland. Iris Carpenter and Lee Carson reported on the Ninth Armored Division's incredible victory at Remagen, where the Germans were about the blow up the last standing bridge on the Rhine. Racing to disengage the charges in the face of German fire, army engineers and infantry saved the structure and secured a path over the river for Allied troops. At the bridge two days later, Carpenter and Carson were nearly hit by strafing German ME-109s. A London *Daily Telegraph* correspondent was killed. "One minute he was there, alive, talking to us," Carpenter said. "I realized it could happen to any of us."

Throughout April the Allies surged across northern Germany, capturing key cities in the race to the Elbe River where the Soviets moved in from the east. Refugees clogged the roads. "We all wondered when the war would end," Margaret Bourke-White wrote. "Logically it should have been over; there was no real reason

for the Germans to go on fighting. Prisoners were being taken by the tens of thousands."

The doors to the German death camps, with all their horrors, were also flung open. At Buchenwald on April 11, 1945, Sigrid Schultz, Helen Kirkpatrick and Marguerite Higgins saw the living dead: 20,000 people starved to emaciated skeletons. Lee Miller, at Dachau, photographed dead bodies in cord wood stacks, and bodies spilling out of box cars. "I implore you to believe this is true," she cabled her editor. The Nazi genocide numbed comprehension.

While the atrocities emerged, Hitler's regime crumbled. On April 25th, the Soviets reached the Elbe River. United Press correspondent Ann Stringer scooped the press corps by making the first contact with the Soviets. Ordered to return to Paris for violating safety rules, Stringer instead went to the front and flew over the Elbe in a Piper Cub. Seeing smoke, her pilot landed and they made contact with the Soviet Army in a jubilant meeting.

The war was almost over. On April 30th Hitler committed suicide. Lee Miller raced to Berchtesgaden in Bavaria and arrived in time to photograph Hitler's mountain retreat in flames. The next day, the Germans in Italy surrendered and Berlin fell to the Soviets—"their true revenge for Leningrad and Stalingrad," Virginia Irwin wrote. On May 8, 1945, Germany surrendered. The war in Europe was over.

Lee Miller (above) in 1942. Fashion model and photographer, in World War II she reported on the war in Europe for Vogue, *taking time when she reached newly-liberated Paris to cover the fashion scene. She was at the front when the Allies took Strasbourg, Cologne and Leipzig. She reported on the meeting of the U.S. and Soviet armies at Torgau. The first photo-journalist to record the horrors at Dachau, her photos appeared in* Vogue *with the title "Believe It."*

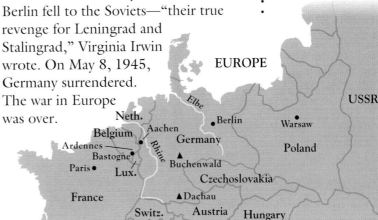

Reporting from the Pacific

In the Pacific, the U.S. military deemed the hard-fought tropical island assaults too dangerous for women, and did not allow female correspondents near the front for most of the war. Instead, a number of women covered the action secondhand from Hawaii. Yet female reporters had been in war-ravaged places in Asia throughout the 1930s, beginning with the Japanese attack on Shanghai, China in 1932. A number were still in Hong Kong and the Philippines in December 1941 when the Japanese attacked Pearl Harbor and began their offensive in the Pacific. Women reported from the Philippines until February 1942, shortly before the U.S. surrender. By then Japan occupied virtually all of Southeast Asia. In late 1944, after the U.S. recaptured most of the Pacific islands, the navy could no longer deny accreditations to women for reasons of safety. From hospital ships and island bases, female correspondents reported from Guam, Iwo Jima, Saipan and Okinawa until war's end.

Peggy Hull was the first U.S. woman accredited war correspondent. She gained her accreditation in September 1918, so late that World War I ended before she could reach her post in Siberia. In the 1920s and 1930s, she and a handful of female journalists covered China for U.S.-owned newspapers and wire services. Peggy Hull, Irene Corbally Kuhn, Helen Foster, Agnes Smedley, and Edna Lee Booker sent in firsthand reports of the Japanese attack on Shanghai in 1932. All except Hull were still in China when full-scale war erupted in 1937. In December of that year, the Japanese Rape of Nanking—a binge of rape, looting and murder that killed over 40,000 Chinese—etched for Westerners an indelible view of the Japanese as barbarians.

As the war ripped through China, a number of women ventured in to get the story. Anna Louise Strong, Martha Gellhorn, Betty Graham, Barbara Finch and Sonia Tomara traveled to the front lines or covered the action in Chungking. *Life* photo-reporter team Carl and Shelley Mydans spent hours in Chungking's damp, sandstone tunnels in early 1941, sheltering from air raids.

The Mydans were to see more bombing in Manila on December 8, 1941 when the Japanese devastated U.S. defenses in the Philippines and launched an offensive throughout Southeast Asia. As Japanese troops advanced on Manila, disorganized U.S. and Filipino forces withdrew to the Bataan Peninsula to wait for reinforcements. Shelley Mydans watched U.S. hopes turn to despair as the army retreated and Manila became an open city. Her editors at *Life* cabled her, requesting a story on "Americans on the offensive." Amazed, she cabled back the first intimation that the U.S. was losing the Philippines, "Bitterly regret your

Dickey Chapelle's widely reproduced photo (below) spurred blood donations across the U.S. Corporal William Fenton survived in spite of near fatal wounds sustained at Iwo Jima.

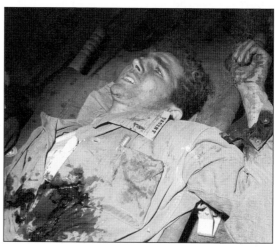

Map labels:
Manchuria
Korea
China
Japan
Chungking
Shanghai
Bonin Islands
Okinawa
Iwo Jima
Formosa
French Indo-china
Hong Kong
Marianas Islands
Philippines
Saipan
Thailand
Bataan
Corregidor
Manila
Guam
Malaya
Caroline Islands
Sumatra
Borneo
Celebes
New Guinea
Solomon Islands
Dutch East Indies
SOUTH PACIFIC
Australia

request not available here." The Japanese took Manila, and the Mydans were interned with American civilians. In 1943, the two were among the few repatriated to the United States.

Also in Manila during the attack were Annalee and Melville Jacoby. They had fallen in love in China, where Annalee worked for United China Relief, and Mel for *Time*. Married just weeks before the Japanese assault, they were loath to separate in the midst of danger. On New Year's Eve they escaped to Corregidor. From the island fortress, Annalee reported for *Liberty* magazine on the conditions in this "subdivision of hell." She and Mel crossed to Bataan for *Life* and photographed the wounded in the jungle hospitals. In the next few months, many of these men would die on the brutal Bataan Death March or in Japanese prison camps. By mid-February the Jacobys realized relief was not coming. Eluding Japanese patrols, they escaped by boat to Australia. Mel was killed on an Australian airfield in April when a fighter went out of control at takeoff.

The fall of the Philippines in May 1942 completed the Japanese conquest of Southeast Asia. During the next three years, the U.S. fought an offensive war of bloody campaigns up through the Solomon, Gilbert, Caroline, Marianas and Philippine islands. As the U.S. secured bases, the military's policy of denying women access to the Pacific came under pressure. In late 1944, the navy finally issued accreditations to women correspondents. Among the first were *Woman's Home Companion* reporter Patricia Lochridge, Barbara Finch of Reuters, and *Cleveland Plain Dealer* correspondent Peggy Hull Deuell, now widowed and in her mid-fifties. Bonnie Wiley (AP) and Shelley Mydans soon followed to Guam and from there to Saipan, Iwo Jima, or Okinawa.

The big action was at Iwo Jima where U.S. marines fought a hellish battle against 20,000 dug-in Japanese. For the first time, the navy allowed women in the combat zone. Patricia Lochridge reported from the hospital ship, *Solace*. "The wounded came on and on. Some still had their rifles; others were naked except for their battle dressings. Most were in pain. All were terribly brave."

By 1945, the Pacific war was nearing its conclusion. Throughout the spring, Shelley Mydans watched B-29s fly out of the Marianas to firebomb Japanese cities. Their napalm-filled incendiary bombs killed some 400,000 Japanese. Still Japan did not surrender. Fearing projected American casualties of over a million in an invasion of Japan, on August 6th and 9th, 1945, the United States unleashed its newest weapon over Hiroshima and Nagasaki—the atomic bomb. The blasts killed an estimated 180,000 Japanese. Five days later, on August 14, 1945 Japan surrendered.

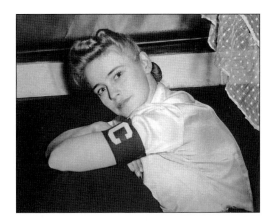

Iwo Jima: Dickey Chapelle

Six days into the assault on Iwo Jima, photojournalist Dickey Chapelle (above) arrived on the hospital ship *Samaritan*. Assigned to report on the use of whole blood, her photos vividly captured the benefits of transfusions. One marine, Pfc. Johnnie Hood, was so revived by the 14 pints of blood he received that she didn't recognize him the next day. His before and after photos ran side by side and aided blood drives throughout the U.S. for years.

After *Samaritan* took its casualties to Saipan, Chapelle flew back to Iwo Jima to photograph blood treatments at a makeshift field hospital. She longed to report on combat, and when two marines agreed to take her to the front she was exultant. They drove her to a distant sand ridge. Chapelle climbed to the top, set up her tripod and photographed a panorama while the air buzzed with the sound of wasps. When she came down, the marines screamed that the "wasps" were sniper fire and she had been a standing target!

Chapelle went on to Okinawa where she made one more foray into the battle zone, against direct orders. During her week of firsts—first woman reporter on Okinawa, first to spend the night on an island during battle—she photographed the field hospitals and endured a major kamikaze attack. On her sixth day ashore, military police arrested her. The navy revoked her credentials and sent her home. Nevertheless, her photographs of Okinawa ran in *Cosmopolitan*.

Entertainment

Fifty thousand dollar kisses, golden legs and short coiffures were just a few of the weapons female Hollywood stars used to help win the war. When Uncle Sam came calling, entertainers from Broadway to Los Angeles responded enthusiastically, lending their talents and their glitter to hundreds of wartime causes. Plays, movies, songs, and radio shows broadcast morale-lifting messages and patriotic themes. Women celebrities rallied the public with blood drives, knitting campaigns and scrap collections. They sang to wounded soldiers in hospitals and held "dream parties" for lucky GIs. At the popular Stage Door Canteen in Manhattan and the Hollywood Canteen, superstars mixed nightly with service people, providing food and diversion. Star-studded tours like the Hollywood Bond Cavalcade crisscrossed the country, raising billions of dollars to finance the war.

Overseas, adorning the insides of tanks, submarines, and the noses of bombers, pin-ups and hand-painted images of glamorous women stars rode with the soldiers for good luck. Entertainers with the USO, the United Service Organizations, traveled to U.S. bases and frontline camps to bring cheer to soldiers far from their homes. Braving plane crashes, air raids and frostbite on the "Foxhole Circuit" they put on thousands of shows, with tremendous impact. For a few long-cherished hours, with laughter, songs and dazzle, they banished the ugliness of war for the men who fought.

The Copacabana All Girl Review (opposite) performs in France to an audience of 10,000 Allied servicemen and women.

Stars for the War Effort

Veronica Lake
(above) cut her long
hair when she learned
that women war
factory workers who
copied her hairstyle
were getting their hair
caught in machines.

Marlene Dietrich
(below) visits soldiers
in a Belgian hospital
in November 1944.

When the Japanese attacked Pearl Harbor, Hollywood mobilized its talents, creativity and star appeal to help win the war. Actors, musicians, writers, and directors of every political stripe banded together to raise money and morale. Seemingly overnight, organizations like the Hollywood Victory Committee and the War Activities Committee sprang up to coordinate aid efforts.

This was a switch from the prewar years when studios tried to silence actors who spoke out against fascism. After she raised the alarm among fellow actors about Hitler's threat to usurp Austria, Czechoslovakia and Poland, actress Myrna Loy of the *Thin Man* movies, received a letter from Metro-Goldwyn-Mayer, warning her against mixing her career with politics. The letter incensed her, and she found it especially ironic because many of the studio executives were Jewish: "Here I was fighting for the Jews and they're telling me to lay off because there's still money to be made in Germany." After December 1941, she worked ardently to support the war effort. Stage and screen actress Tallulah Bankhead was also an early advocate of bringing the U.S. into the war in Europe. Deeply affected by the Allied retreat at Dunkirk, Bankhead traveled the country giving anti-Nazi speeches.

Once the U.S. joined the war, the stars found hundreds of ways to contribute: they made patriotic films and radio broadcasts, performed for soldiers, lent their names to war bond sales, bandage rolling, and knitting campaigns, and joined the Treasury Department's payroll deduction program, which devoted ten percent of their pay to the war. Actresses mixed with servicemen at the canteens and hosted morale-boosting visits in their homes. In 1944, for *Life* magazine, dancer Ginger Rogers threw a "dream party" for a GI just returned from the Pacific. With seven beautiful starlets, Rogers entertained him with food, dancing, games and a romp in the pool, before sending him off covered with bright red lipstick kisses.

Others stars made more personal sacrifices. Sultry Veronica Lake, whose long, blond hair draped across one eye became the rage with women across the country, cut her "peek-a-boo" tresses for the duration once she learned that 20,000 women war factory workers with her hairstyle were at risk of scalpings in their jobs at turret lathes and other machinery. Ingrid Bergman also promoted the short haircut when she appeared as Maria in *For Whom the Bell Tolls*. Her new short curly "do" soon became the latest across the nation.

Celebrity visits to hospitals brought comfort, laughs and smiles to wounded servicemen, but were not always easy for the stars. Betty Grable became indignant when she came across a life-size cardboard cutout of herself at Halloran Hospital in New York. Myrna Loy, who was with her, convinced her to stay and soon, in Loy's words, she was "putting her lip prints on plaster casts as the men moved joyfully around her." Singer and actress June Allyson recalled singing for men in their hospital beds at an amputee center near San Francisco. "After my performance. . . there was no clapping. They just whistled. I thought to myself, 'Oh, they didn't like me!' Then I saw the explanation. Most of them had lost at least one hand. . . . That's why they whistled."

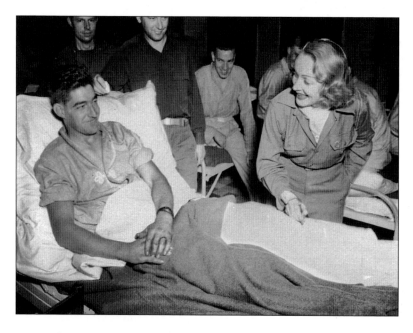

Pin-ups

Almost all female stars in Hollywood posed in swimsuits and low-cut gowns to help launch their careers. Press agents distributed publicity photos widely to newspapers and fans, including thousands of servicemen overseas. In the barracks, on ships, inside of tanks and painted on the noses of bombers, the images of glamorous stars rode with the GIs for good luck. The most famous pin-ups were Betty Grable, with her cheery, provocative over-the-shoulder bathing suit pose, Rita Hayworth, kneeling on a bed in black satin and lace, and the "café-au-lait" beauty Lena Horne, who although a reluctant pin-up, became the favorite of black servicemen. Others included Dorothy Lamour, the "sarong girl" for her south seas poses, Jane Russell in racy "Outlaw" shots, the mysterious, exotic Hedy Lamarr, and "sweater girl" Lana Turner. For far-flung soldiers, pin-ups were reminders of girlfriends and home. "There we were out in those damn dirty trenches," one veteran told Betty Grable, "exhausted, frightened, confused and sometimes hopeless in our situation, when suddenly someone would pull your picture out of his wallet. Or we'd see a decal of you on a plane and then we'd *know* what we were fighting for."

Rita Hayworth (left) contributed her "bumpers" to help publicize the need for scrap metal. Admired as an actress and as a pin-up, army flyers called red-haired Hayworth "the woman we would most like to be cast adrift with."

Betty Grable (above) was the number-one favorite pin-up of GIs. Known as the "Technicolor Blonde," Grable appealed to servicemen and their families alike for her playful sensuality and warmth. So valuable were her shapely legs that 20th Century Fox insured them for 1.5 million dollars with Lloyd's of London.

War Bonds

The Hollywood Victory Caravan (above) was one of the many troupes of actors, singers and dancers that crossed the U.S., promoting war bonds. Left to right: Producer Mark Sandrich, Charles Boyer, Joan Bennett, Desi Arnaz, Eleanor Powell, Joan Blondell, Ray Middleton, Claudette Colbert, Fay McKenzie, Bert Lahr and Frank McHugh.

The power of female stars was never so evident as when it come to bond sales. Using their talents, sex appeal and ingenuity, Hollywood celebrities raised billions to help finance the war. In towns across the nation, civilian volunteers also sold war bonds: at fairs and picnics, at booths on street corners, in banks, post offices, food markets, and department stores—anywhere people gathered. For an investment of $18.75, a Treasury bond would bring $25 in ten years; for $750 it would yield $1,000. With patriotic slogans like "Buy a Share in America" and "Keep 'em Flying," the government urged the public to buy. To keep track of it all, a four-story high cash register in Times Square tallied the war bond sales for the nation.

Recognizing the attraction of the stars, the Treasury Department enlisted the aid of Hollywood early in the war. Celebrities sang, danced, did comedy sketches and signed autographs to promote war bond sales at rallies and on multi-city tours. Some stars made defense bond tours even before Pearl Harbor. Judy Garland, Mickey Rooney and a troupe of entertainers crossed the country on the Metro Bond Train as early as 1940. German-born Marlene Dietrich, appalled by the fascist regime that gripped her homeland, was also an early promoter. "Our tours were exhausting," she recalled, "—six to eight hours a day, and sometimes also an evening performance. I had to go into factories and call upon workers to give a certain percentage of their salaries as a loan to the government. . . . I raised a million dollars, which flowed into the Treasury coffers. All that effort was supposed to contribute—at least in my eyes—to the ending of the war as quickly as possible." After the attack on Pearl Harbor, the public came out in great numbers to support bond sales. In January 1942, when actress Carole Lombard was killed in a plane crash on her way home from a bond drive, the nation mourned her as a casualty of war.

In response to Lombard's death, Hollywood stars launched more bond drives and relief tours. Billed as the "Bond Bombshell," Dorothy Lamour swung through New England, where she exchanged autographs for war bond sales. "I made a deal with the Treasury Department that I would not take pledges, only cash. That way I got the money before they got the autograph. I was extremely proud that in the first four days, I brought in $30 million." In the spring of 1942, the Hollywood Victory Caravan train crossed the country to raise money for the families of men killed overseas.

Madison Square Garden in New York, where most of the stars gathered. That night they raised $86 million in war bond sales. Myrna Loy, of *The Thin Man* fame, did what she called a mock "strip tease," removing her hat and gloves for the cause. "My hat brought $30,000, and a pair of elbowless crimson gloves $25,000."

Certain celebrities found special ways of selling. Jeanette MacDonald sold encores for relief fund contributions. Hedy Lamarr offered kisses for $25,000 each, and racked up $17 million in bond sales in a single day. Lana Turner charged $50,000 for her kisses and found many takers. "I'm told I increased the defense budget by several million dollars," she said. Marlene Dietrich, a prolific bond seller, once even pledged to wash all the windows in the house of anyone who

Carole Lombard (below) kicked off the first big Hollywood bond drive of the war in her hometown of Indianapolis in January 1942. Dazzling the crowds in a black velvet gown, she sold two million dollars' worth of war bonds in a single day. On her return to Hollywood to be with her husband, Clark Gable, her plane crashed near Las Vegas. Her death shocked the nation. Many regarded it as a sacrifice for the war effort.

Hedy Lamarr offered kisses for $25,000 each, and racked up $17 million in bond sales in a single day. Lana Turner charged $50,000 for her kisses. "I'm told I increased the defense budget by several million dollars," she said.

Featuring headliners like Claudette Colbert, Bing Crosby, Olivia de Havilland, Cary Grant, Frances Langford, Bob Hope and more, this was the largest group of Hollywood stars assembled up until that time. Desi Arnaz, who was on the tour, remarked, "If that train had been wrecked, Hollywood would have been out of business."

Another major war bond tour, the "Stars Over America," included seven groups of celebrities that split up to cover nearly 350 American cities in the first eight months of 1942. Among them was the persuasive Bette Davis, who in Tulsa, sold her autograph for $50,000, and a photo from the film *Jezebel* for $250,000. In two days' time she sold $2 million worth of bonds.

War bond sales were in full swing. In just the month of September, 1942, a new tour, featuring seven groups of celebrities, covered 353 towns and raised $775 million. The drive ended in a major rally at

bought bonds. "I've still got the sore back to prove it," she said.

The commanding Kate Smith was one of the most successful bond sellers of all time. In 18 hours, on September 21, 1943 on a CBS Radio marathon appeal, she sold more than $39 million in bonds. Known for her stirring "God Bless America," she also sang such favorites as "The Last Time I Saw Paris" and "The White Cliffs of Dover." During the war, she traveled 520,000 miles, crossing the country hundreds of times. She appeared on stage in a long black dress, and electrified the audience with her resonant soprano. Introducing her to the King and Queen of England at a reception at the White House, President Roosevelt said, "This is Kate Smith. This *is* America."

By 1945, 85 million people, over half of the U.S. population had purchased war bonds, raising more than $100 billion for the war effort.

On the Air

The top Oscar winners of 1942 appear together after the motion picture awards ceremony. Left to right: Van Heflin, on leave from the U.S. Army, best supporting actor in Johnny Eager; Greer Garson, best actress in Mrs. Miniver; James Cagney, best actor for his portayal of George M. Cohan in Yankee Doodle Dandy; and Teresa Wright, best supporting actress in Mrs. Miniver. A home front saga set in wartime Britain, Mrs. Miniver swept the awards ceremony with a total of seven Oscars.

In early 1942, to mobilize the public, the government established the Bureau of Motion Picture Affairs to oversee the production of wartime films. Although some considered this to be censorship, Hollywood studios cooperated enthusiastically, and soon movies infused with patriotism, heroic battle scenes, wartime love stories, and uplifting musical numbers made their way to theaters.

Motion pictures covered a range of themes during the war. Action movies like *Destination Tokyo* and *Objective Burma*, populated almost exclusively by men, portrayed the might and courage of Allied forces in battle. Some epics included subplots about the women back home. In the 1943 film, *Action in the North Atlantic*, Ruth Gordon and Julie Bishop coped with life on the home front, while their men risked German attack with the Merchant Marines. The mix of love, separation and war provided potent material for a number of dramas, including the acclaimed 1942 film, *Casablanca*.

Not all wartime love stories were serious, however. Lighthearted romantic comedies

with musical numbers also filled the marquees. In the 1942 musical, *The Fleet's In*, Dorothy Lamour and Betty Hutton starred as singers who entertain the fleet in San Francisco and fall in love with two sailors. Other musicals, such as *Thank Your Lucky Stars* (1943), *The Gang's All Here* (1943), and *Star Spangled Rhythm* (1944) showcased the song and dance power of Hollywood in all-star extravaganzas that featured such female vocalists as Dinah Shore and Carmen Miranda. The all black 1943 musical, *Stormy Weather*, with Lena Horne, Bill Robinson, and Cab Calloway was one of the few films to record the talent of African American singers and dancers during the war.

A number of movies portrayed the role of women in the military during the war—some based on real events. The 1943 picture, *So Proudly We Hail*, with Claudette Colbert, Paulette Goddard and Veronica Lake told the idealized story of U.S. Army nurses trapped with the troops on Bataan. Pictures also celebrated women on the home front. *Swing Shift Maisie* (1943) and *Rosie the Riveter* (1944) built stories around aircraft assembly line workers. *Since You Went Away* (1944) showed the struggles of women holding together house and home while the men went off to war. The 1942 Oscar winning hit, *Mrs. Miniver,* starring Greer Garson

Boy" and "Don't Sit Under the Apple Tree." Swing was the music of the day, typified by large ensembles like the Benny Goodman Orchestra and the Tommy Dorsey Band. Big Bands often spotlighted female vocalists such as the "soft and

as an indomitable British housewife whose family is broken by war, was so influential in persuading Americans to come to Britain's aid that Prime Minister Winston Churchill wired the Metro-Goldwyn-Mayer studio: "*Mrs. Miniver* is propaganda worth 100 battleships."

While at the theaters, moviegoers caught up on progress of the war through newsreels shown at the start of every picture. In an age before television, these contained the only actual war footage the public saw. As in entertainment films, producers crafted newsreels to show the war as just and patriotic.

The Office of War Information (OWI) controlled the dissemination of war news to U.S. and overseas media, including radio, newspapers, and magazines. The OWI not only encouraged publication of certain government messages (such as the promotion of scrap drives or women workers), but also scheduled their frequency in order to increase the public's receptiveness. For radio, the OWI produced patriotic shows and established the Voice of America, to broadcast overseas. Another government broadcaster, the Armed Forces Radio for service people, aired star-studded programs such as *Command Performance* and *Mail Call,* in which celebrities sang songs and read GI letters.

One Armed Forces Radio regular was the popular singing trio, The Andrews Sisters. Patty, Maxene and LaVerne Andrews sang cheerful vocal harmonies and swing hits like "Boogie Woogie Bugle

cool" Peggy Lee, who sang with the Benny Goodman Orchestra or Helen O'Connell of the Jimmy Dorsey Band. As the men went off to war and big bands lost their musicians, "all girl" bands sprang up around the country.

Throughout the war, female singers like Dinah Shore, Frances Langford, Jeannette MacDonald, Ella Fitzgerald, Marlene Dietrich, Judy Garland, Doris Day and Lena Horne entertained the troops and the public with songs that carried wartime themes. The incredibly popular Kate Smith made Irving Berlin's "God Bless America" into a wartime anthem. Other patriotic numbers like "Remember Pearl Harbor" and "Praise the Lord and Pass the Ammunition" rallied public sentiment. And always, the music of love and longing filled the airwaves. "I'll Be Home for Christmas," "It's Been a Long, Long Time" and "You'll Never Know Just How Much I Miss You" caught the emotions of many couples separated by war.

"The war years were full of big band music—songs of exhilaration, of longing, of loss," remembered Stella Suberman, a young Miami resident, "and they were very much a part of our lives."

Stage and screen star, Lena Horne, (below) talks with Harry Torczyner, Chief of the Office of War Information Belgian Desk, in an interview on the Voice of America "Radio Actualities" show. Voice of America, the official government radio service of the United States, aired news and entertainment overseas.

Canteens and Service Clubs

On March 2, 1942, in the basement of the 44th Street Theater in New York, the Stage Door Canteen, offering food and entertainment free of charge, opened its doors to members of the armed services. Sponsored by the American Theater Wing, a war service organization founded by prominent Broadway theater women, the cabaret and dining room captivated GIs with performances from some of the biggest names on Broadway. In its first year, the Canteen entertained 720,000 servicemen from around the world with acts from such theater stars as Gertrude Lawrence, Helen Hayes, Katherine Cornell, and Ethel Merman.

In Hollywood, inspired by the success of the Stage Door, actors John Garfield and Bette Davis decided to start a West Coast canteen. Davis ran with the idea, and within three weeks mobilized the money and talents of influential people in Hollywood and renovated an abandoned nightclub near Sunset Boulevard. The Hollywood Canteen opened in October 1942 to almost instant success. Three thousand sailors, soldiers and marines showed up on opening night alone. With a paid staff of only nine, the Canteen depended on about 100 stars and other volunteers each night to entertain, serve

The Andrews Sisters
(above) LaVerne, Patty and Maxene, sing for GIs at the Hollywood Canteen. One of the best selling female vocal groups of all time, the Andrews Sisters cheered soldiers with boogie-woogie, swing, and be-bop harmonies. During the war, they appeared on radio, in musical films, and performed live for troops in the U.S., Europe and North Africa.

Hedy Lamarr
(right) serves coffee and sandwiches to GIs at the Hollywood Canteen. Stars did everything from performing on stage to washing the dishes. Volunteering at the Canteen sometimes brought dividends. On one tired night, Lamarr met her future husband, actor John Loder, while washing hundreds of cups with him in the Canteen kitchen.

and dance with GIs. "No one simply *performed* at the canteens," said Maxene Andrews of the Andrews Sisters trio. "You sang or danced or told jokes or played a musical instrument . . . but you also waited on tables, danced with the guys or gals, and provided a friendly or sympathetic ear."

A different hostess coordinated activities each night. The hostess took responsibility for procuring ice cream, lining up volunteers, acting as MC for the show and conducting the evening's birthday cake celebration. Serviceman Hal Winter recalled the cake ceremony on his 20th birthday at the Stage Door Canteen: "Suddenly the lights dimmed . . . then out of the darkness walked Hedy Lamarr. . . . Before she left, she did one thing that endeared her to us for life. She came down among us, and gave every man who was celebrating a birthday a kiss! . . . I don't know when I came down to earth, but it was a long time before I washed the spot where Hedy Lamarr kissed me."

Scores of junior hostesses also helped each night, dancing and talking with homesick soldiers, many of them away from home for the first time. Edythe Freeman, a hostess at the Stage Door Canteen quickly learned that dancing with hundreds of men entailed some sacrifice. A pair of dancing shoes lasted only two months and stockings might "run to ribbons" in a single night. "The small dance floor was so crowded we couldn't help but get kicked in the shins and ankles," she said. "We'd silently count to ten and then tell ourselves wryly, 'I'm due for my Purple Heart any day now.'"

The aim for hostesses and stars alike was to give the soldiers a break from the war and entertainment to remember. The Hollywood Canteen regularly swung with big band music from the Harry James' Orchestra or Kay Kyser and his band. Movie sensations like Betty Grable, Rita Hayworth, Eva Gabor, Kay Francis and Marlene Dietrich lent sophistication while singing, dancing, signing autographs or serving up sandwiches. Sometimes, however, volunteering at the club had unimagined consequences. After her one appearance at the Canteen, pregnant actress Gene Tierney came down with a case of German measles. Four months later, she was devastated when she gave birth to a blind, deaf and mentally handicapped baby girl. Many years later, by chance, a gushing female fan recounted to her how as a marine she had sneaked out of quarantine even though she had German Measles to see Tierney, her idol, that night at the Hollywood Canteen.

Throughout the U.S. and overseas, 3,000 smaller clubs sponsored by the USO, the nonprofit United Service Organizations, paralleled the canteens with social and recreational activities for men and women of the armed forces. USO clubs, offering lounges where soldiers could talk or rest, play Ping-Pong, or get doughnuts gave respite to 12 million service people during the war. Large and small, canteens afforded diversion and sometimes lasting memories to GIs. Forty years after the war, Bette Davis wrote, "To this day I often meet men who tell me they had been to the Hollywood Canteen and what a thrill it was for them to see and talk to Hollywood stars."

Bette Davis (left), *cofounder of the Hollywood Canteen, offers a bite of cake to a sailor during a birthday celebration. A powerhouse at organizing, in just three weeks Davis mobilized the stars and transformed an abandoned nightclub into an entertainment mecca for men and women in uniform. "There are few accomplishments in my life that I am sincerely proud of," said Bette Davis. "The Hollywood Canteen is one of them." An estimated three million GIs visited the Hollywood Canteen during the war. The studios showcased the songs and comedy acts of the canteens in three films:* Stage Door Canteen *(1943),* Thank Your Lucky Stars *(1943) and* Hollywood Canteen *(1944).*

On Tour with the USO

Dinah Shore (above) performs for GIs on the war front in France in August 1944. In addition to entertaining troops in Normandy and at the Battle of the Bulge, she made over 300 performance broadcasts for the Armed Forces Radio Network, singing such hits as "Yes, My Darling Daughter," "Blues in the Night," and "Buttons and Bows." In recognition of her efforts, she received the USO Medallion.

Air Force service people (top opposite) greet a USO troupe at Poltava Air Base in the Soviet Union, January 1945. USO entertainers traveled the globe to bring concerts, dance routines, comedy sketches and drama to GIs at the war front.

The Andrews Sisters (bottom opposite) at a stop on their 1945 USO tour of Italy.

The USO not only sponsored recreational clubs for GIs, but also brought live entertainment to troops in the U.S. and overseas. During the war, Hollywood stars and thousands of lesser-known performers brought 400,000 USO shows to more than 200 million service people, diverting them from what some termed their real enemies: boredom, mud, officers and abstinence.

Female headliners like Betty Grable, Rita Hayworth, Carmen Miranda, Gloria Grahame and Tallulah Bankhead made frequent USO tours in the U.S., dazzling audiences with skill and glamour. For black performers like Lena Horne and Hattie McDaniel, USO tours meant trips to out-of-the-way camps in the segregated army. At large bases, they gave two shows: the first for the white troops, the second for African American GIs. Seeing black soldiers treated as second class was hard. At Fort Riley, Kansas, Lena Horne was astonished to see a row of white men up front at the black performance. "Now, who the hell are they?" she asked an officer. "German prisoners of war," he replied. Incensed, she left the platform, went to the back of the hall, and sang to the black soldiers.

Seven thousand performers on the "Foxhole Circuit" traveled overseas to almost everywhere troops were stationed. At bases from

Baffin Island to the South Pacific, foxhole entertainers delighted GIs with shows from pickup trucks, barges, airfields and stadiums. They slept in tents, exposed to the same dangers as the men, and traveled on military transports. A number of USO performers were killed in the line of duty. In 1943, Broadway musical star Tamara Dreisen and 20 other entertainers died when their plane crashed near Lisbon. Jane Froman survived the crash with severe injuries. After numerous operations to restore her shattered legs, she was back, singing to troops before the end of the war.

One of the earliest USO tours, in October 1942, became the subject of the book, *Four Jills in a Jeep,* and a film of the same name. Singer Carole Landis, "big mouth" comedienne Martha Raye, actress Kay Francis, and dancer Mitzi Mayfair embarked on a five-week tour of England only to spend five more months performing at the front in North Africa. Actress Paulette Goddard saw another distant war front on her 1944 tour to Burma, India and China. In a stunning dress, she began each show by seductively removing her long gloves, then turning to the whistling GIs to say: "What's the matter? Haven't you guys ever seen a pair of gloves before?" Being the object of so much pent-up affection was wearying, however. By the end of two months she was tired of being "pawed by so many soldiers" and was glad to return home.

The best known of all the USO groups was the Bob Hope troupe with singer Frances Langford, which toured Alaska and the Aleutians in 1942, North Africa and Sicily in 1943, and the South Pacific in 1944. Describing Langford's arrival at Eniwetok, Hope said, "The GIs whistled so much they blew three planes off the runway." Contralto, Frances Langford took it in stride and serenaded thousands of servicemen with ballads like "I'm in the Mood for Love." She said, "The greatest thing in my life was entertaining the troops."

Andrews Sisters Tour

Shortly after V-E Day, in July 1945, the vivacious Andrews Sisters— Maxene, Patty and LaVerne—began an eight-week USO tour to Italy. Spirited out of New York at night in their winter uniforms, they were surprised when their plane landed in Casablanca, Morocco. Within minutes, a major with a jeep whisked them out to the desert to 7,000 screaming GIs. "We put on a show right there, with no notice or rehearsal," said Maxene. After ten more shows in North Africa, the major got a cablegram, and within an hour the trio were on a plane to Naples. Apparently, they had been "kidnapped" during a short refueling stop.

Throughout Italy, the Andrews Sisters livened the troops with their catchy harmonies, serenading more than 180,000 men. The most requested song was "Rum and Coca-Cola,"— "the national anthem of the GI camps." The last day of the tour was in Naples, where 8,000 dispirited servicemen waited to ship out to the Pacific. "It was the unhappiest audience you ever saw," said Maxene. Just as the sisters went on, the commander handed them a paper, announcing V-J Day. Patty read it: "Fellows," she said, "You don't have to go to Japan. The war is over!" The crowd was silent. "They thought it was part of the show," she said. "But my sisters, who were on stage, began to cry . . . then all hell broke loose! It was like the three of us had stopped the war!"

Beyond Entertaining

Josephine Baker

"**J**'*ai Deux Amours*"—"I have two loves, my country and Paris," Josephine Baker often sang as her signature theme. In World War II, she proved that love in the service of the Free French Resistance. A flamboyant jazz dancer and singer, Baker, grew up in poverty in St. Louis, Missouri, and at age 13 ran away with a traveling show. In 1925, leaving behind the racism of the U.S., she arrived in Paris with La Revue Nègre and became an instant sensation. Comedic, sensuous and exuberant, she electrified the French with her audacious style. At the Folies Bergère, wearing only a skirt of brilliant bananas, she sprang onto stage like a cat and shimmied and danced to wild applause. By 1927, she was the most famous performer in Europe. She cultivated an exotic mystique, walking her leopard on a leash down the Champs-Élysées.

"The Parisians gave me their hearts, and I am ready to give them my life."

When the war broke out in 1939, Baker, now a French citizen, rallied to help her adopted country. Noting her easy access to embassy receptions, Jacques Abtey, a military intelligence officer, asked if she would gather information for the French Secret Service. She quickly agreed. "France made me what I am," she said. "The Parisians gave me their hearts, and I am ready to give them my life." Throughout 1939, she passed along intelligence gleaned from Japanese and Italian dignitaries. After the fall of France, on the pretext of going on tour, she carried Resistance papers to British Intelligence in Lisbon. With photos pinned inside her dress and intelligence reports written in invisible ink on her sheet music, Baker traveled easily. On one trip by boat from Marseille to North Africa in January 1941, she breezed through customs with 28 pieces of luggage and a menagerie that included her Great Dane, three monkeys and two white mice.

Working for the Free French from Casablanca, Baker continued to carry messages and to gather intelligence. She also developed a network of influential Spanish Moroccans to secure passports for escaping Jews. In June 1941, she became gravely ill with peritonitis and spent the next 19 months in the clinic. Rumors of her death flashed across the news, but Baker was "much too busy to die." Just out of the clinic in 1943, she traveled 9,000 miles through North Africa and the Middle East, entertaining American and British troops and advancing the cause of Free France. Then the Allies liberated Paris. In October 1944, when Josephine made her return, traffic stopped and a million Parisians lined the Champs-Élysées to welcome her with flowers as she rode triumphantly into the city she loved.

A poster (above) for The Folies Bergère, Josephine Baker's wildly successful Paris revue.

Josephine Baker (right) in uniform of the Women's Auxiliary of the Free French Air Force. For her aid to the Resistance, the French awarded her the Croix de Chevalier de Légion d' Honneur and the Croix de Guerre.

Marlene Dietrich: "The Only Important Thing I've Ever Done"

Of all the Hollywood stars, German-born Marlene Dietrich spent the most time of any performer overseas at the Allied front. Glamorous and sensual, she became a box office success in Germany with the release of *The Blue Angel* in 1930, and soon after went to the United States where she starred in a succession of motion pictures, including *The Garden of Allah* and *Destry Rides Again*. An ardent anti-Nazi, she dedicated herself to helping refugees to escape Germany. "What this woman [was doing] for refugees and for former friends or even foes was unbelievable," screenwriter Felix Jackson said. "I know scores of people she saved without ever talking about it." Even before the U.S. entered the war, Dietrich sold war bonds. After Pearl Harbor, she was named the champion war bond seller of the nation with four cross-country tours. She also performed at hospitals, military bases, and the Hollywood Canteen—on one occasion, making a bombshell appearance with her legs painted gold.

Wanting to do more, she signed on with the USO. "The Germany I knew is not there anymore," she told a reporter. "I don't think of it. . . . If I did I could never do these tours." In April 1944 began the first of three circuits in North Africa and Europe. In her "nude" flesh-colored evening gown, she electrified the troops, singing songs like the German-banned "Lili Marlene," and playing a musical saw. In Algiers, when a bomb struck nearby and knocked out the power during a show, the GIs shouted for more and turned on their flashlights to light up the stage. "We did the show to flashlights," said Danny Thomas, who was on the tour. "They didn't want it to end."

On tour in Italy, Marlene Dietrich and Irving Berlin (below) look at autographs on a chain of short-snorter bills, foreign currency from each country visited.

Back in the U.S. after a bout of pneumonia and two months of shows in North Africa, Sicily, Corsica, and Italy, Dietrich recorded German love songs for the Office of Strategic Services (OSS) to broadcast as propaganda to homesick German soldiers. In September 1944, she embarked on a new tour to France, Belgium and Holland. By Christmas she was at the front with soldiers at the Battle of the Bulge, sleeping in frozen fields, eating K-rations, and washing her hair in snow melted inside her helmet. For the shows, she wore her sequined evening gowns, and sang even as her hands turned blue in the sub-zero cold.

As she neared Germany with the Third Army she felt increasing danger. She told the generals: "I'm not afraid of dying, but I am afraid of being taken prisoner. . . .They'll shave off my hair, stone me and have horses drag me through the streets." General Patton responded by giving her a pearl-handled revolver. "It's small, but it's effective," he told her, making it clear it would be of use for suicide. Dietrich remained in Europe, performing for troops until well after V-E Day. She had suffered frostbite, influenza and a jaw infection on the tour. For her efforts, the U.S. awarded her the Medal of Freedom and the French made her a "Chevalier de la Legion d'Honneur" and "Officier de la Legion d'Honneur." Her service during the war, she said, was "the only important thing I've ever done."

On the Home Front

When the men left for war, women put on hard hats along with their homemaker's aprons and mobilized to keep the nation running. With energy and newfound capabilities they took on work of every kind in factories, offices and on farms. Among the 19 million women who filled out the labor force were new mothers, who for the first time left their young children in day care. Working women balanced home life and jobs, continuing to do the family shopping, cooking and cleaning after a day at the factory. It was demanding work. Food shortages meant waiting in long lines for scarce items. Shopping with complicated ration coupon books required analytical skill and patience.

Women also pitched in for the nation by planting victory gardens and canning vegetables. They salvaged papers, rags, cans, and rubber, and volunteered for everything from civilian defense to blood drives. In many heartfelt and deeply affecting ways they boosted troop morale with letters, care packages and home-cooked meals. It was an intense, exciting period when many people traveled for the first time. Trains packed with camp followers, war workers and troops crisscrossed the country. Couples fell in love and married quickly, lovers said goodbye, and at home, families waited. Women's endurance on the home front generated new confidence. World War II not only reshaped society's ideas about love and work, but also irrevocably changed women's views of themselves and their abilities.

*A **woman worker** (left) polishes the plastic gun turret of a B-29 bomber at the Boeing factory in Renton, Washington.*

Eleanor Roosevelt

From 1933 to 1945, throughout the Great Depression, the New Deal, World War II and Franklin Roosevelt's four terms as president, First Lady Eleanor Roosevelt was the most prominent and influential woman in the United States. An advocate for peace and human rights, a promoter of women and minorities, she was, according to a poll, "the target of more adverse criticism and the object of more praise than any other woman in American history." Reared during the Victorian era, married at 19 to become a mother of six, "It was not until I reached middle age that I had the courage to develop interests of my own," she wrote.

With her tremendous personal energy and the belief that government should be responsive to the people, Eleanor Roosevelt expanded the role of first lady from White House hostess to political activist and leader. She was the first president's wife to hold press conferences and the first to earn her own money (most of which she donated to charity). She gave lectures, broadcast over radio and wrote a syndicated newspaper column, "My Day," sharing with the public her daily activities and her wide political concerns. She answered an enormous amount of mail, often working into the early morning hours to provide personal referrals for even the smallest requests.

When World War II began, Mrs. Roosevelt reevaluated her pacifist convictions and concluded that fascism could not go unopposed. The Nazis' depravity in Europe and Japan's brutality in China horrified her. Now, when she watched her four sons go off to fight, "I had a feeling that I might be saying goodbye for the last time," she said. "I began to look with wonder at all the women in the country who must be feeling this same way and I came to admire their courage."

Characteristically, she threw herself into the war effort. She took the post of assistant director of the Office of Civilian Defense, without pay, but resigned after a few months when criticism at a president's wife holding an official position grew too great. Throughout the war, she was an ardent supporter of GIs, using her influence for them on issues large and small. She fought discrimination against African Americans and petitioned for an end to segregation in the military.

In the fall of 1942 she toured England, then under German bombardment, and observed the many contributions of British women. She returned with a vision of the important role American women could play, and she urged "full participation" for them in the military. She also saw the potential for women in war jobs, and encouraged government and business to provide child-care centers where working mothers could safely leave their children.

As she had during the Depression and the New Deal, Mrs. Roosevelt traveled throughout the United States to factories, day-care centers, and training camps to see conditions first hand. Some called her the "eyes and ears" of the president; she reported her observations to him, advocating issues she felt important. Through these trips she was able to effect many positive changes. However, her influence did not always win her husband's support. Her calls for tolerance towards Japanese Americans could not defuse the public's hostility, nor alter the president's decision to intern West Coast Japanese Americans. Similarly, the president's concerns about sabotage overrode Eleanor's efforts to

open U.S. doors to European refugees. After the war, when the full horror of the annihilation of the Jews became known, her failure to help the refugees deeply disturbed her: "I should have done more," she told a friend regretfully.

In 1943, Eleanor made a good will tour of hospitals and military camps in the South Pacific. Traveling 23,000 miles in unheated, cramped army transport planes, she visited Australia, New Zealand and 17 Pacific islands, and spoke to over 400,000 troops. Her energy and dedication impressed even Admiral Halsey who initially regarded her as an intrusive "do-gooder." In the end, he approved her visit to Guadalcanal, which was still a target of Japanese bombs. "When I say she inspected those hospitals," he wrote, "I mean that she went into every ward, stopped at every bed, and spoke to every patient." Her visit boosted the morale of the troops.

After Franklin's death in 1945, Eleanor served in the United Nations where the struggle for human rights and equality continued her life's work. During her twelve years as first lady, Eleanor Roosevelt accomplished more than most people could in a lifetime. Her vision, willingness to confront unpopular issues, and her activism for social justice changed the lives of millions.

Eleanor Roosevelt walks by a downed Japanese Zero (above) on Guadalcanal during her five week tour of the Pacific war zone. In her Red Cross uniform, she kept up a pace so demanding that Admiral Halsey admired her hardihood: "She walked for miles and she saw patients who were grievously and gruesomely wounded. But I marveled most at their expressions as she leaned over them. It was a sight I will never forget." Deeply moved by what she saw, Eleanor wrote, "On Guadalcanal, as in many other places, I said a prayer in my heart for the growth of the human spirit, so that we may do away with force in settling disputes in the future."

Home Front Leaders

First Lady
Eleanor Roosevelt (top) addresses workers at Boeing Airplane Company in Seattle. Mrs. Roosevelt traveled frequently to observe conditions firsthand.

Frances Perkins,
Secretary of Labor from 1933 to 1945 (below) was the first woman to serve on a U.S. Cabinet.

First Lady Eleanor Roosevelt's leadership inspired women and opened the way for them to rise to positions of influence. With her support, President Roosevelt named Frances Perkins to serve as secretary of labor in his cabinet—a first for women. Perkins had long devoted her energies to improving health and labor conditions. As a social worker, deeply affected by the Triangle Shirt factory fire of 1911 in which 146 women garment workers died trapped in a sweatshop, Perkins believed only legislation could protect workers. In 1938 she pressed for passage of the Fair Labor Standards Act, which established maximum working hours and a minimum wage. Her most enduring contribution, the Social Security Act, provided insurance for the elderly and the unemployed.

These laws were important as more women entered the work force during the war. Their need for union representation also grew. A few women rose to positions in labor. Mildred Jeffrey, a longtime labor activist, became the first director of the women's division of the United Auto Workers. Rose Schneiderman, president of the Women's Trade Union League, advised government agencies on women's issues.

Women in Congress shaped national policy through legislation. Hattie Wyatt Caraway, the first woman elected to the U.S. Senate, cosponsored an early version of the Equal Rights Amendment in 1943. In the U. S. House of Representatives, Frances Payne Bolton, an advocate for education, health and nursing, spearheaded bills to create the Cadet Nurse Corps and to grant military nurses pay equal to that of men of the same rank. Edith Nourse Rogers sponsored the establishment of the Women's Auxiliary Army Corps (WAAC) and authored the 1944 G.I. Bill of Rights, providing educational and financial benefits for veterans. Margaret Chase Smith supported legislation to establish the WAVES, and in 1945, to grant women permanent status in the armed services. Novelist, playwright, and two-term congresswoman Clare Boothe Luce stood out as perhaps the most influential woman conservative of the era. An outspoken critic of Roosevelt's foreign policy, she nevertheless frequently voted on its behalf.

In the field of education, several women rose to prominence. Mary McLeod Bethune was Negro Affairs Director for the National Youth Administration from 1936–1944, a position that allowed her access to President Roosevelt to whom she presented the ideas of other African American leaders. Her unofficial advisory group became known as the "Black Cabinet." Bethune's influence with the U.S. Secretary of War also enabled African American women to become officers in the WAAC. Another educator, Virginia Gildersleeve, dean of Barnard College, distinguished herself in 1945 as the only woman to serve on the U.S. delegation to the San Francisco Conference which drew up the U.N. charter. The *New York Times* dubbed her "Our Academic First Lady."

In diplomacy, influential Washington hostess Florence Jaffray "Daisy" Harriman became the U.S. ambassador to Norway in 1937. When the Nazis invaded neutral Norway in April 1940, she fled to Sweden and from there helped U.S. nationals and the Norwegian royal family escape.

In the period following World War I, the women's pacifist movement gained momentum. In 1919, Emily Greene Balch, along with Jane Addams, founded the Women's International League for Peace and Freedom and worked for disarmament. Hitler's rise in Germany forced Balch to modify her pacifist views to defend basic human rights. "Fascism and national socialism today can be destroyed only through means which are capable of impressing brutal men of fascism," she said. In 1946, for her efforts to bring world peace and support human rights, Balch became the second U.S. woman (Jane Addams was the first) to receive the Nobel Peace Prize.

Lone Pacifist: Jeannette Rankin

"Peace is a woman's job"

Feisty Jeannette Rankin, the first woman to serve in the U.S. House of Representatives, distinguished herself as the only representative to vote against U.S. entry into both world wars. In 1916, two years after women won the right to vote in her home state of Montana and four years before women could vote nationwide, she was elected to Congress. Shortly after taking office, she cast her "no" vote on U.S. entry into World War I. The war sought to preserve democracy, she said, but women were denied the right to participate in the democratic process. She lost her congressional seat in 1919 but remained true to her pacifist beliefs, working for women's suffrage, children's causes, freedom of speech and the anti-war movement. "Peace is a woman's job," she said.

With Europe in conflict in 1940, she ran a pacifist campaign and was reelected. On December 8, 1941, the day after the Japanese attack on Pearl Harbor, when Congress called for war, she was the only member to vote no. Amid shouts of "Sit down, sister," boos, and hisses, she said: "As a woman I can't go to war, and I refuse to send anyone else." Her vote infuriated the public and once again cost her reelection. "Montana is 110 percent against you," her brother told her. Asked if she ever regretted her action, she replied, "Never. If you're against the war; you're against the war regardless of what happens. It's a wrong method of trying to settle a dispute." Rankin remained an outspoken advocate of peace throughout her life. In 1968, at the age of 87, she led a group of 5,000 demonstrators to the Capitol in Washington, D.C. in a protest against the Vietnam War.

Rosie the Riveter

A destroyer-escort work crew at the Charleston Navy Yard (above). Some 3 million women worked in nontraditional war industry jobs during World War II.

We Can Do It *(top opposite). The War Department used posters like this one to encourage women to fill war factory jobs. Inspired by the popular song, "Rosie the Riveter" by Kay Kyser, the image of "Rosie" became a patriotic symbol of working women.*

During World War II, 19 million American women "Rosie the Riveters" served in the U.S. labor force. Posters, songs, magazines and movies celebrated their work in the defense factories. The slogans "We Can Do It" and "Women in the War: We Can't Win Without Them" ignited their energy and transcended rallying cries. Without their efforts, the strained home front economy would have collapsed, and U.S. war production, so vital to Allied victory, would have fallen far short of its goals, perhaps with disastrous consequences.

Although "Rosie" idealized the industrial work of welders, electricians and mechanics, the majority of working women filled non-factory positions vacated by men drafted into the military. Work as bank tellers, police officers, bus drivers, fire fighters and engineers opened up and females filled clerical, sales, domestic, agricultural, service and professional positions of many kinds.

Many women felt going to work was a patriotic duty and believed their efforts could shorten the war and bring home husbands and sons much sooner. The money was also an attraction. With war factory pay at twice the level of civilian wages, and civilian pay at an all time high compared to Depression-era wages, women flocked to jobs. "Like me, they were just trying to get along," said Alice Caldwell, a working mother and merchant marine wife. "They needed the money and they wanted to do their part."

For the first time, many women had money of their own—and it was liberating. No longer were they financially dependent on men. In addition, work brought self-confidence and a sense of accomplishment. "I absolutely felt after that welding job that I could do anything," said Kay Whitney, an employee at the Boston Navy Yard. She, like many, found a sense of camaraderie in working with others. "You learned from other people that you didn't

suffer in silence." War jobs took housewives from the isolation of their homes into a wider sphere. As people from across the nation migrated to defense factories on the coasts, workers of every race and background came together. Geraldine Berkey, who left Ohio to work near her husband's naval posts, first in the East and later on the West Coast, remembered: "These jobs . . . broadened my view, my outlook on life. They made me a better person. I was a narrow-minded girl who lived in a cloistered community, and now after the war and all my experience and everything, I could see the other side."

As the war progressed, the need for women workers grew. Bucking the societal belief that women should stay home with their children, the government encouraged mothers to work. The Lanham Act of 1943 provided federal funds for day care centers. Communities and some large employers also provided child care. These efforts, however, met only a fraction of the need. Working mothers, many of whom had migrated far from relatives, struggled to find reliable child care and to balance the needs of family and jobs.

Work brought more challenges. In the war factories, women trained for shift work and sometimes heavy labor. They put aside their femininity to wear "snoods" or bandannas to keep their hair from getting caught in the machinery, and wore pants—often for the first time. At the Charleston Navy Yard, electrician's helper Alice Caldwell wore coveralls and a hard hat. "In those clothes, I was the cat's meow!" she said.

Female workers in nontraditional jobs faced resistance from men who believed a woman's place was at home. From stares to outright harassment, women coped in unfamiliar surroundings and in many cases, won the men over once they proved they could work hard. At Kaiser Shipyard, Alison Ely, one of two women assigned to keep track of the welding in an all male area, recalled, "The guys obviously had made a pact not to talk to us—to freeze us out. But we were friendly, doing the job, and after a couple of weeks, they not only thawed out but actually enjoyed us and we enjoyed them."

Throughout the war, women in factory jobs faced dangers. Between 1940 and 1945, industrial accidents killed 88,000 men and women, about a fifth as many as the number of U.S. military combat deaths. Long hours, speedups and hazardous conditions led to 11 million industrial injuries, more than 16 times the number of U.S. military wounded or missing in the war.

Child care centers (below) were part of the government's strategy to win the war by attracting mothers to work. By 1945, government day care centers serviced 100,000 children nationwide—only a tenth of the need. Employer-, community- and church-based facilities provided additional care, but most working mothers relied on relatives or private help.

At Work in the War Factories

Chippers at Marinship Corp. in Sausalito, California (right). Chippers used power-driven chisels to remove imperfections from the metal surfaces. Many shipyard jobs exposed workers to the elements. At Kaiser Shipyard in Portland, Oregon, Alison Ely recalled, "The winter of '43 was unusually cold and nasty. . . . Many days I saw women kneeling on the ice to weld when there wasn't a man welding in sight. These were tough ladies [who] really earned their pay."

Shipbuilding

Shipbuilding played a vital role in the U.S. war effort. The attack on Pearl Harbor, the devastating U.S. shipping losses in the Atlantic, and the need for thousands of merchant ships to carry troops and supplies overseas demanded a major expansion of U.S. shipbuilding. Between 1940 and 1943, the industry expanded 15 times—from 100,000 workers to 1.5 million. Manufacturers developed new methods to speed delivery of ships. Using prefabricated bulkheads, decks and hulls, shipyard owner Henry Kaiser streamlined the production of "Liberty ships" from 355 days in 1940 to 60 days in 1942.

Shipbuilders—all-male by tradition—were particularly slow to hire women. In 1939, only 36 women worked in the nation's shipyards. At the government's urging, shipbuilders employed 23,000 females in 1943 and a peak of 150,000 women before war's end. Trading in their dresses for overalls and hard hats, women took up heavy tools for jobs as welders, chippers, lathe operators, mechanics, truck drivers, and electricians.

The work day was long, often with no formal rest breaks and fewer than 30 minutes for lunch. Many shipyards had inadequate restrooms for women. Exposed to the elements, workers labored several stories up on scaffolding or crammed into confined spaces. Noise reverberated in the holds. "There are times when those chippers get going and two shipfitters on opposite sides of the metal wall swing tremendous sledgehammers simultaneously and you wonder if your ears can stand it," said welder Augusta Clawson.

Accidents occurred easily; work in the shipyards brought risks from dirt, noise, heavy equipment and falling objects. "If you hit the wrong wire or cut into something wrong you could get killed," said Alice Caldwell, an electrician's helper at Charleston Navy Yard. High up on the scaffolding one day, she cut into a wire and got a shock that knocked her knife out of her hand. She watched it plummet to the ground. "If I hadn't been sitting down, I probably would have gone down too," she said.

In spite of the hazards, women persevered. By war's end American shipyards produced 87,620 large and small warships and 5,475 cargo vessels.

Aviation

Aviation, a relatively new industry, accepted women workers more readily than older manufacturers. Aircraft companies needed workers who were small and light and had good finger dexterity. Women, long accustomed to detailed work like sewing and embroidery, provided the perfect labor source. In 1941, only one percent of aviation employees were female. Two years later, they numbered over 475,000 and comprised 65% of the aviation work force. At Convair, 90% of the workers were women.

Employees worked in huge hangars and built the aircraft in sections on large conveyors. Noise, vibration, and strained muscles came with the job. Women filled positions as riveters, welders, stamp press operators, electricians, engineers and designers. They installed radio equipment, painted, inspected and test piloted the finished planes. U.S. factories produced 100,000 aircraft a year at their peak, and a total of 300,000 planes by the end of the war.

"We had a foreman who would say, 'You can take ten of my men and give me four women.'"
—Josephine Rachiele, riveter, Republic Aviation

Production aides
Ruby Reed and Merle Judd (top) work in cramped quarters at Grumman Aircraft. Women could squeeze into smaller spaces than men and were especially adept at the delicate installation of electrical components.

A Boeing worker
amid the "dorsal fins" of B-29 bombers (left). At the Boeing plant in Wichita, Kansas, welder Winifred Shaw recalled, "The noise was atrocious. . . . You felt like you were in a world of your own behind those dark glasses. All you could see was your welding puddle of metal."

At Work in the War Factories

A munitions worker at the Firestone Tire and Rubber Company in Omaha, Nebraska (right) checks 1,000-pound bomb cases before they are filled with explosives. Work in ordnance plants exposed women to noise, monotony and risk of explosion. Josephine Von Miklos described her work: "The thousands of rings that pass through our hands are enveloped in the odor of gunpowder, a sweet odor, unlike anything else . . . it penetrates our skin and our clothes and it doesn't fade out."

Munitions

Munitions was the most dangerous of all the war industries. Arsenals sought out women workers for their dexterity and safety-consciousness. African American women, routinely relegated to the riskiest and least desirable jobs, found work in great numbers in munitions factories. Prior to 1941, arsenals employed 30,000 women. Between 1939 and 1943, the number of women ordnance workers increased more than ten times. Dubbed WOWs (Women Ordnance Workers) or "gunpowder girls," they produced shells, small arms ammunition, rifle grenades, bombs, colored-smoke munitions, gel-type incendiaries, and tear gas.

The work was dangerous and precise. The amounts of explosives and their alignment had to be exact. At the same time, the jobs were monotonous and it was difficult to stay attentive; solvents containing ether made workers sleepy. Women knew all too well that the lives of soldiers depended on how well they did their jobs. Most had a brother, husband or son overseas.

To protect against explosion and fire, arsenals were located at remote sites, with low buildings separated by lawns. Employees removed their clothes on arrival each day and gave up such items as cigarettes, matches, jewelry or hairpins, whose metal could spark an explosion, and silk underwear, which could cause static electricity. On the job they wore flameproof clothing and rubber-soled boots. They worked in small groups or in steel booths. Buildings had automatic sprinklers, heavy metal doors and walls three feet thick.

In spite of these precautions, accidents occurred. An explosion in Elkton, Maryland in May 1943 killed 15 and wounded 54 workers. The Chemical Warfare Arsenal in Pine Bluff, Arkansas suffered two explosions in a single year. At another plant, Estrella Montgomery came close to being a casualty and seeing the entire ammunition depot explode when her coworker accidently dropped a fused bomb. Luckily the bomb landed lengthwise. "I never felt more thankful than I did on that day," she said.

Black and Hispanic Workers

Trackwomen on the B & O Railroad (right). In spite of strides made during the war, African Americans and workers of other races often encountered discrimination. At North American Aviation, Tina Hill recalled, "They had 15 or 20 departments, but all the Negroes went to Department 17 because there was nothing but shooting and bucking rivets." As blacks, Mexican Americans and other minorities struggled against racist treatment, hate riots erupted periodically. In 1943 at Baltimore Western Electric, a walkout begun by 22 white women to protest black women in their department ended with federal troops occupying the plant while the company installed separate restrooms.

A Hispanic worker (below) sorts tomatoes at the Yauco Cooperative Growers Association. Hispanic women not only provided crucial agricultural labor in World War II, but also found new opportunities in higher paying war industry jobs, and in some instances, in white collar office jobs that had long been shut to them.

For African American women, World War II brought a chance to rise up from domestic jobs to higher pay in industrial and skilled positions. The urgent need for workers broke down traditional color barriers and drew blacks out of the South to northern and western cities. During the war, 600,000 African American women found jobs, and the percentage of black females in industry rose from 6.5% to 18%. For some black women, wages rose as much as 1,000%.

Working in shipyards, aircraft factories, steel mills and foundries, as well as in canneries, transportation, federal jobs and the service sector, African American women frequently met with racism. Employers consistently ignored anti-discrimination standards. (These war industry rules, however, set a precedent for the postwar years.) Blacks were the last hired and the first fired, and employers routinely assigned them to the most menial tasks and the least desirable shifts. Wanita Allen trained for 500 hours to work at Murray Auto Body in Detroit, but still could not get hired. "They would come in from the plant proper to pick women who'd maybe been there just a couple of days on the training program, and they would put them to work. But they were white women."

When the war came to a close, employers laid off blacks at a rate 2.5 times higher than whites. Although discrimination survived, the opportunities provided by wartime jobs brought lasting economic and social benefits to African Americans.

Taxi Drivers and Engineers

Elizabeth Esty,
log roller (right) at a
U.S. Department
of Agriculture
timber salvage mill
near Concord, New
Hampshire, 1943.
As the war pro-
gressed, hiring
biases gave way to
necessity and
women signed on
for jobs requiring
hard physical labor.
Mothers, grand-
mothers and single
women sweated in
mines, steel mills
and on the rail-
roads. Defying the
stereotype of the
"weaker sex,"
women served as
fire fighters, meat
packers and cargo
loaders.

Although "Rosie the Riveters" of the war factories gained national attention, most women held nonindustrial jobs. With the men gone, the country sought women of all ages and races to maintain the railroads, harvest the crops, police the streets and serve in other vital capacities.

Food was the most essential civilian industry, and during peak harvest season the need became crucial. Skeptical farmers hired city women to work in the fields and orchards, and were surprised to find that "the quality of their work was better than of boys." Women worked conscientiously in all areas and broke stereotypes. Female cashiers, stock clerks, buyers, porters, bakers, gas station attendants and drivers proved themselves in professions long held by men. In sports, the All American Girls Professional Baseball League provided diversion. Hundreds of "all-girl" swing bands entertained civilians and troops in the U.S. and overseas. In 1943, Time Magazine reported, "A granite precedent was shattered, a male stronghold crumbled . . . when a woman went to work on the floor of the New York Stock Exchange for the first time in 150 years."

Although many fields opened up during the war, the percentage of women in professional and managerial jobs did not rise. Employers routinely passed over women for promotion to management positions. In spite of a critical shortage of doctors, medical schools accepted only five percent women.

Low wage traditional female jobs such as domestic work, teaching and nursing suffered major shortages as women secured better pay at the war factories. Schools recruited retired and married "inactive" teachers or hastily certified trainees. Nursing looked to volunteers and suspended restrictions against hiring married women—a change that continued into the postwar years.

Nearly one million women found work in government offices, which desperately needed clerical help. With 3,000 new jobs opening every month, "government girls" flocked to Washington, D.C. and crowded into rooming houses. Their work as secretaries, stenographers and typists reshaped the clerical field as a "feminine" profession. Women also filled civilian jobs for the military, working as flight simulation teachers, military trainers, engineers, and more. Their contributions were pivotal; they kept the U.S. wartime economy alive and they proved that physical strength and gender did not determine fitness for employment.

A trolley operator (left) in Brooklyn, New York. Women worked many jobs in transportation, including as train conductors, truck drivers and "milkmen."

Gisela Gabriel and Laura Cook pack cookies at the American Cracker Company (below). Women filled jobs in canneries, slaughter-houses, factories and farms to meet war-time food demands. Waitresses in their sixties and seventies served in restaurants. Food handling con-sultants sought the best ways to transport food to the army.

Taxi drivers in San Francisco (top).

Engineer Rita Carlin (above) inspects a high power radio transmitting tube at Westing-house. Working as war factory or civilian military employees, women physicists, chemists, engineers, mathema-ticians, architects, and astronomers filled professional positions tradition-ally held by men. Lorraine Gaylord, the first mathemati-cian hired at the Ford Instrument Company, remem-bered the surprise when she arrived on her first day of work. "I walked in there and I was the only woman. One man said, 'She's going to put up drapes?' I'll never forget that. They didn't know what to make of me."

The Changing Job Front

The more women at work
THE SOONER WE WIN!

SEE YOUR U.S. EMPLOYMENT SERVICE

Posters like these (above and top opposite) encouraged women to work for the war effort. Rather than challenging cultural stereotypes by emphasizing the independence and new skills jobs could offer, government recruiters reinforced traditional views of women by portraying them as patriotic heroines. War work remained voluntary. In 1942, Congress considered a bill to draft women for civilian service, but although it had considerable public support, the National War Service Act never came to a vote.

Victory depended on production, and production desperately needed women workers. By December 1942, 14 million women filled war industry and civilian jobs, and an additional 4–5 million workers were needed. With many single women already in the work force, the government looked to housewives as a major labor source.

Throughout 1943 and 1944, the War Manpower Commission and the Office of War Information struggled to break down cultural attitudes about women workers and bring housewives into the labor pool. Stereotypes went deep. Most men (and many women) believed females were too weak to hold jobs outside of the house. Husbands were the breadwinners, and a woman's place was at home with the children (who did best in the care of their mothers). Society might break down if women went to work.

Government-sponsored radio ads, newsreels, magazine stories and posters countered those images by portraying women workers as heroines of the home front. "There's work to be done and a war to be won . . . Now!" one poster exhorted. In fact, patriotism became a driving factor: "My brother went into the army, and now I feel that I'm in the fight too," one woman worker declared. Money also drew women, especially wives who needed to supplement their husbands' small GI paycheck.

War work changed the country. Twenty-five million people of every class and background poured into war industry cities like Seattle and San Diego. The rapid growth overwhelmed schools, sanitation and housing. Families crowded into any available quarters, including tents, trailers and abandoned buildings. In these new locales, working mothers struggled to balance the needs of family with jobs, and to seek out reliable child care. Most did "double duty," managing housework and child rearing in addition to their 48-hour workweeks. With gas rationing in effect, they often had long commutes by bus or carpool.

Yet, in spite of these difficulties, many women found their new experiences uplifting. Joan Wilt, a civil service employee on Bainbridge Island, Washington recalled, "[The war] brought out the best in people. You saw more people than

WOMEN!
There's work to be done
and a war to be won . . . NOW!

Do the job HE left behind
APPLY
U.S. EMPLOYMENT SERVICE

WITH SONS AT WAR
. . . AMERICA NEEDS WORKERS!
BE A "FIGHTER-BACKER"
you can do a lot

you ever had . . . you met marvelous people."

With earnings of their own and new responsibilities, women grew more self-reliant. In Mankato, Minnesota, 19-year-old Jeanne Kaufman independently managed the bookkeeping for a woodworking firm. "I learned how to do everything—the payroll, Social Security—pretty much by myself," she said. Her success at work gave her the confidence to pursue a personal ambition: college. "The biggest thing for me was finding the guts to go to the university. No one encouraged me. I just set my goal and saved my money." In the fall of 1945, she entered the University of Minnesota.

I've found the job where I fit best!

FIND YOUR WAR JOB In Industry – Agriculture – Business

While earnings made women more independent, inequities prevailed at the workplace. In most areas women earned 40 % less than men for equal work. Business owners circumvented government standards by establishing "female" positions with low pay scales. In 1944, the average pay for women in manufacturing was $31.21 per week, compared to $54.65 for men. Although women proved themselves conscientious and hardworking, employers rarely promoted them to higher positions.

Unions offered some recourse. During the war, 3.5 million women belonged to unions. While some unions actively barred females, others were friendly and helped with such "women's issues" as child care, equal pay, and petitions for evening store hours (so women could shop after work). Unions, however, focused mainly on male causes, and championed equal pay only to keep industry from lowering the standard for men's wages. With few women in union leadership, issues like gender-specific pay scales and job lists took a back seat to men's concerns.

Harassment in the workplace was common, although not universal. Many women suffered cat calls, pats on the behind or demeaning remarks, while others never experienced the problem. Mary Todd Droullard, a shipyard employee described the men at work: "Always hitting on me. They kept hanging around me and looking and trying to get me to go out with them. You got the feeling you wouldn't have a job if you didn't go along with them." Taxi driver Mary Pitts remembered, "The hardest thing about the job was to overcome the hostility of men toward women driving." Often, dealing with discrimination proved to be more difficult than the work itself.

In 1945 when the GIs returned, employers dismissed women workers at a rate 75% higher than men and demoted remaining female workers to low status jobs. Yet, as women left the labor force, they took away new confidence and lifelong skills. They had been part of the largest migration in the nation's history, and their wartime service brought change—a permanent acceptance of women as intelligent and able workers.

As the war wound down, the government had a new message for women: give up your jobs and go back to keeping house. News articles and radio reports warned of "psychic harm" to children if mothers did not stay home. Magazines dropped timesaving tips in favor of elaborate recipes and home decorating ideas. For women who saw their war work as temporary, this was a natural course of events, but for many it was a devastating blow to finances and self-esteem. Surveys showed that over 72% of women in the factories wanted to keep their jobs. Industry didn't see it that way. By May 1946, four million women had, voluntarily or involuntarily, left the work force.

Your Baby or Your Job

GIVE BACK THEIR JOBS

Sisters under the apron—
Yesterday's war worker becomes today's housewife.

Women: Do Your Part!

Shortages, blackouts, emergency drills and rationing were the norm. It was an extraordinary time, and on the home front war permeated every aspect of women's lives, down to the most mundane household tasks. Housewives could do their part for the nation by conserving vital materials, boosting morale, keeping victory gardens, and volunteering in hundreds of ways. Government ads appealed to their patriotism, while pushing fear and guilt about everything from fashion to state security, because women's participation was absolutely crucial to victory.

Advertisers joined the fray with war-related promotions. "Millions working for victory have found chewing gum is a real help on the job," a Wrigley's spearmint gum ad declared. Pepsodent toothpaste advised daily brushers to conserve: "Don't let it run down the drain . . . don't squeeze the tube carelessly."

Of all the home front campaigns, national security was most urgent, and the country mobilized its civilian defenses. Urged on by the Andrews Sisters song, "Cooperate with Your Air Raid Warden," women hung blackout curtains and drilled for air raids. Fears of infiltrators ran high and the government counseled families not to disclose the military units, ships or locations where loved ones served. "Wanted For Murder. Her Careless Talk Costs Lives," one poster warned. "Loose Lips Might Sink Ships," admonished another.

Wartime shortages curtailed travel for all but necessity, as troops and war workers filled trains and buses to overflowing. "Is Your Trip Necessary?" posters inquired. Women walked, joined carpools or rode public transit to jobs and shopping. Tire and

Posters like these *exhorted women to help win the war by doing everything from saving bacon grease to buying victory bonds. The war affected almost every aspect of home front life, from the availability of food to the amount of gasoline for transportation. With little available in the stores, women learned to substitute or do without everyday items.*

gasoline rationing began in 1942. Under the restrictions, commuters with important needs (such as emergency workers) could purchase the most. For those without pressing needs, rationing brought an end to pleasure drives and routine car trips. The Office of Defense Transportation mandated a 35 m.p.h. speed limit to make cars and tires last "for the duration."

In addition to gasoline, shortages of metal appliances, food, clothing, soap and heating fuel made daily life a challenge. The government advised consumers: "Use it Up, Wear it Out, Make it Do, or Do Without." In 1942 the first ration books appeared and shopping became a test of perseverance and luck. "If you saw a line you got into it and then asked what it was for," June Schmidt recalled.

Even fashion adapted to wartime shortages. In 1942, the War Production Board issued restrictions to save 15% of yardage on women's and girls' clothing. Flowing sleeves, pleats, and cuffs gave way to tapered styles with narrow belts and fewer pockets. Slacks for women suddenly became acceptable. The shortage of silk and nylon stockings, however, proved problematical. With a choice of heavy cotton or rayon stockings, many women opted to go bare-legged in the summer and apply leg makeup and pencil line "seams" on their legs to give the appearance of stockings. "We had to shave our legs daily for smooth application," said Ruth Carpenter. "Rain made the makeup run like cheap mascara, and I often washed the stuff off my shoes. Still for summer, we hailed it as a lifesaver."

Going without stockings was one of the small sacrifices for the

"All the girls came to the window and kept throwing candy out to us. . . . It was something very special."

war effort. Throughout the country, women felt the excitement of working together to help end the war as soon as possible. In many small but deeply affecting ways they brought comfort and aid to GIs and their families. Mothers and grandmothers "adopted" soldiers, inviting them in for home-cooked meals. Others opened their houses for overnight stays to GI families, sent care packages, talked and danced with lonely soldiers, or took food to troop trains, which had no dining cars. Oscar Rea Mowery, a young marine traveling cross-country on a flat car, guarding guns and living on C-rations, remembered the day his train pulled into Nashville, alongside a candy company. "All the girls came to the window and kept throwing candy out to us. I never forgot the Brach's candy company. It was something very special."

Wartime fashion guidelines cut down on the use of cotton, rayon, silk and wool. The prewar outfit at the top, featuring balloon sleeves and French cuffs, used 6 yards of rayon. The wartime version (bottom), with narrow cuffs, modified sleeves, no sash on the blouse, and slacks with tapered legs without cuffs, used just over 4 yards.

Scrap Drives and Civilian Defense

Boys collect
*newspapers (right)
for recycling.
Mothers and school
teachers organized
newspaper and scrap
drives to salvage
commodities for the
war effort. Industry
needed tin cans,
razor blades, gum
wrappers, alumi-
num, toothpaste
tubes, bottle caps,
old pans, golf clubs
and car fenders to
turn into planes,
tanks, ships and
ammunition. Used
flashlight batteries
provided zinc,
carbon, brass and
copper. War
factories trans-
formed millions of
old tires, rubber
boots and hot water
bottles into tank
treads and new tires
for military vehicles.
With sawmills
producing war
materials such as
plywood, paper was
precious. Mills could
recycle waste paper
quickly and at 50%
of the cost of newly
made paper.*

With world supply lines of raw materials cut off, merchant ships pressed into military service, and a critical need for metal and rubber in war production, salvage and conservation became essential to winning the war. Newspaper articles and posters urged women to scour their attics, closets, and basements for old pots, metal pipes, garden hoses and other salvageable articles. Housewives amassed tons of supplies for the nation by saving in their everyday routines. "Get in the Scrap," "Win with Tin," and "Save, Serve, Conserve" became slogans. The country had a use for everything the home front could salvage.

War factories required metal of all kinds for armaments. Tire manufacturers re-cycled and retreaded existing tires "for the duration." Housewives saved paper, rags and glass bottles for recycling and reuse, and sacrificed nylon and silk stockings to make such valuable equipment as tow ropes for glider planes and parachutes.

Even bones were useful. A block of housewives salvaging bones from meals could supply several tons of material to make glue. A pound of meat drippings and bacon grease saved in cans had enough glycerine to make a pound of black powder explosive. Yet in spite of massive publicity and Mildred Bailey's song, "Scrap Your Fat," waste fat collections fell far short of their goals until butcher shops began to offer two extra food ration points in return.

In addition to conservation, millions of women donated their time for everything from civilian defense to salvage sewing.

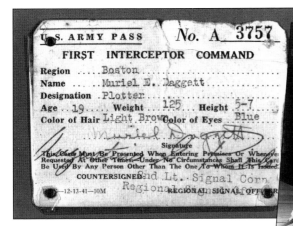

Volunteering was a way to support the war and join with others outside the home. With numerous agencies asking for their time, there was no lack of ways to contribute.

From 1941–1943, the Office of Civilian Defense drew 12 million volunteers to serve in such roles as air raid wardens, ambulance drivers and airplane spotters. In New Jersey, women pilots flew antisubmarine patrols for the army and navy until the Civil Air Patrol absorbed their group and prohibited female fliers. Militia groups arose, and under the direction of retired male officers, uniformed women in groups like the Green Guards and the Powder Puff Platoon drilled, marched, and practiced marksmanship and other "home defense" maneuvers. With the likelihood of invasion low, especially after 1942, many people regarded these groups with scorn.

More immediately useful, perhaps, were the efforts of 3.5 million women of the Red Cross, 124,000 U.S. Cadet Nurse Corps trainees, and thousands of blood bank volunteers. Women donated time to run rationing offices, entertain and serve soldiers at USO and other service clubs, assemble care packages to send to troops, knit (they "Purled Harder")and convert worn donations and textile scraps into usable clothing to send to Europe.

Throughout the war, women's volunteer efforts not only supported industrial production and the soldiers in the field, but more importantly, maintained the country's morale.

The Army used volunteers to plot the positions of aircraft in order to be able to direct air defenses to intercept attackers. The Pinkerton Detective Agency investigated volunteers like Muriel Daggett, whose identification card is shown above, before they were approved for service.

Volunteer plotters (above) worked four or five hour shifts, pushing markers into place on a large map to indicate the positions of aircraft as phoned in by observers. As the war progressed, Women's Army Auxiliary Corps (WAAC) members filled these positions.

Airplane spotters (below) on duty at a tower on the Pacific Coast. Early in the war, the army established the Aircraft Warning Service (AWS) to provide air security. Lookouts phoned or radioed observations in to Interceptor Command.

Rationing

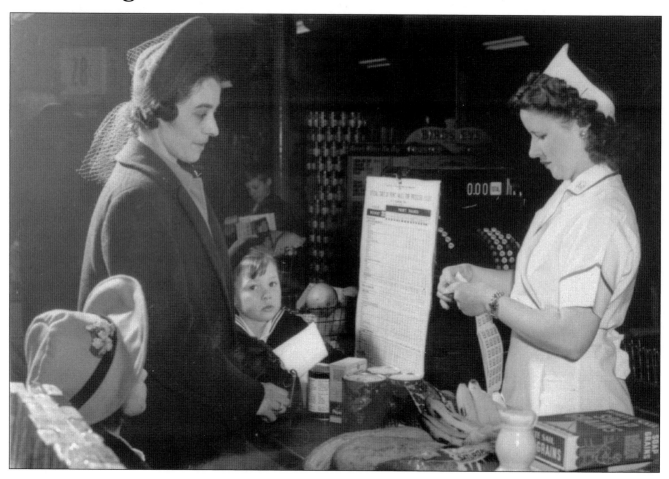

RATION STAMP NO. 1

RATION STAMP NO. 1

RATION -STAMP NO. 1

A shopper (top) uses ration stamps: red for meat, fish, dairy and fats and blue stamps for canned goods. With only 15 percent of the nation's steel supply allotted to the home front in 1943, canned, dried, bottled and frozen foods were severely limited.

In the panic after the Pearl Harbor attack, shoppers bought up food of every kind and sent prices soaring. The scarcities of World War I were still fresh in many minds, and with merchant shipping cut off, conditions promised to be no different this time around. To distribute goods equitably and prevent inflation, the Office of Price Administration (OPA) instituted rationing and price ceilings in 1942, and urged the public to conserve with slogans like "Food Will Win the War" and "Where our Men are Fighting, Our Food is Fighting."

It took considerable skill and extra labor to shop and prepare food under rationing. Women (who almost universally did the family cooking and shopping—even when they worked outside the home) had to wait in long lines for scarce items, calculate purchases using the complicated point system, devise substitutions for unavailable ingredients, and find ways to make meals stretch. Stella Suberman, an

army air force wife recalled, "Grocery shopping was a little like a treasure hunt. If word got around that a shipment of a rare item—canned peaches or tuna fish, maybe—had been unloaded, you waited in line for as long as it took to get the one-to-a-customer item."

The OPA allotted ration books of color-coded stamps to every man, woman and child. To prevent hoarding, stamps were only valid for about a month. Ration stamps carried a value in points, which varied depending on the scarcity or quality of the item. For example, applesauce might require 10 points one month and 25 points a few months later. Good cuts of meat took more points than lesser cuts. "I was very bad at staying within my allowance," Stella Suberman remarked. "On one occasion I used up all my red stamps on rib roast—69 cents, 8 points a pound."

The first food to be rationed was sugar, an essential for home baking and canning.

Ration coupons allotted one pound of sugar per person per week—about a third of the modern U.S. intake of sweeteners. Housewives coped by cutting down the sugar in recipes, substituting honey, molasses or corn syrup, or serving fruit instead of baked desserts. Red meat was also scarce. The military bought up large quantities and much of what remained sold for high prices on the black market. In spite of the two pounds a week ration, butchers' display cases were often empty.

At a time when people wanted meat every night, women served vegetable casseroles, fish when available, chicken (which was not rationed) and even horse meat. They stretched hamburger with fillers, made meatless sausages using oatmeal, substituted white oleo margarine (with its capsule of yellow dye for coloring) for butter and served "Roosevelt coffee" brewed from leftover grounds. Their ingenuity extended to "victory" recipes like War Cake, which used bacon grease for shortening, and spices to cover the flavor. Prepared under difficult conditions, the food was filling and generally nutritious. As M.F.K. Fisher put it in her cookbook, *How to Cook a Wolf,* it was "honest" food.

Victory Gardens

To augment food production, the Agriculture Department encouraged civilians to plant "victory gardens," small vegetable plots in every place from backyards to parks to city rooftops. By 1943, 20 million victory gardens on a total of four million acres supplied a third of the nation's vegetables. Answering the call to "Grow Your Own, Can Your Own," women (like the gardener planting peppers below) supplemented their family meals with fresh vegetables, and canned produce for storage. Because commercial canned goods were rationed, shoppers could not buy many vegetables in the winter. Neighborhoods formed cooperatives to share equipment and help one another with the laborious job of canning, a specialized skill which required proper techniques to avoid food contamination.

Beyond victory gardens, approximately 1.5 million women labored on farms as part of the Women's Land Army. Headed by Florence Hall, the Land Army recruited high school girls, teachers on vacation, college students and servicemen's wives to fill in for agricultural workers. Brought in as an emergency aid to harvest rotting crops in the first year of the war, women volunteers proved essential to the nation's food production. Farmers, who initially feared agricultural work might prove too heavy for females were soon surprised to find "there was almost no part of the work that women did not do."

Until We Meet Again

A child tugs at his father's leg, (right) joining in his parents' embrace.

Young government workers in Washington D.C. share living quarters (below). The nation's capital had such an influx of wartime employees that in some rooming houses, workers slept in shifts; some worked nights, allowing daytime workers a place to sleep while they were gone. This is one of many scenes recorded by photographer Esther Bubley, whose photos capture the loneliness and longing among women on the home front.

"Being by yourself was very lonely. You couldn't plan from one day to the next because life was very precarious." —Shirley Hackett

Separation was a fact of life during the war. Thirty million Americans left home—many for the first time ever—to serve in the military, take war jobs, or follow loved ones. For each of the 16 million GIs who went off to serve, one or two women—a mother, sister, girlfriend, or wife—was left behind.

Many service wives tried to delay the separation by following their husbands from one training post to another. The older generation admonished them not to go, but GI wives went anyway, sometimes pregnant or with young children, traveling thousands of miles and overtaxing the railroad system. "The conditions on the railroads were horrendous," recalled Dellie Hahne, a military wife. "The trains were packed with women following their husbands." Without military priority, women, who up to now had lived sheltered lives, traveled on their own, quickly learning such worldly skills as how to purchase a bus ticket or use a pay phone. This rootless life of frequent moves, high rents and low paying temporary jobs was difficult. When their husbands finally went overseas, wives found themselves alone in unfamiliar cities, having to find housing.

Wherever they lived, women suffered loneliness and anxiety for the safety of their husbands, sons or sweethearts. When her husband shipped out, Shirley Hackett found ways to cope with the separation: "I did everything I could to stay busy. There were always people you could help who were really having a rough time."

The separation was especially hard for young mothers. "It was a very lonely time. I felt buffeted about," said Barbara de Nike, who was pregnant and also had a young son when her husband left with the navy. "I think my children helped sustain me. . . . I felt that if I lost my husband I still had them. That was some support."

Approximately 15 million babies were born in the U.S. during World War II. Frequently, women gave birth alone, while their husbands were overseas. Some children were three or four years old before they saw their fathers.

Wartime separations also deeply affected older children, who worried that their fathers might never come back. Mothers tried to allay their children's fears, meanwhile coping with the duties of both mother and father. In addition to homemaking, women now made home repairs, took out the trash, and handled legal matters—tasks once the province of their husbands. Mary Gardner, a mother of six, who had her hands full when it came to disciplining her sons, recalled, "There were times when it should have been a man's job to do these things. I had to do it."

World War II separated women not only from the men they loved, but also from the longtime protections of men. Living on their own, heading up households and holding down jobs in a time of national emergency allowed them to discover their strengths and capabilities and take pride in new-found self-reliance.

ARMY WOMAN'S HANDBOOK

Official Guide for
The Association of Army Wives

Written for the Woman
Behind the Man
Behind the Gun

CLEL

POWER OF ATTORNEY

If your husband receives orders for a foreign station, or is to be absent for any length of time, it will facilitate your handling any business for the family if he gives you what is known as "Power of Attorney" during his absence. This does not in any way, of course, take the place of the Will, described in a later chapter. However, it gives you the right to sign papers, sell property, make loans, or otherwise do business in the name of and for your husband during his absence. If anything should happen to him and the Will has been properly drawn according to directions given later, you will have perfect continuity of action. Death causes little break in your personal handling of the family affairs. The Will is probated, you are given "letters testamentary" and are empowered to carry on as before.

The Army Woman's Handbook *(above) by Clella Reeves Collins gave practical, if sobering, advice to army wives about wills, finances, and legal matters.*

Private D. N. *Daniels kisses his wife goodbye (right) at the Greyhound bus terminal in Chicago. Typical of thousands of military wives who went long distances to be with their husbands, she traveled from Minnesota to meet him on furlough. (Photo by Esther Bubley.)*

Love and Distance

Romances blossomed quickly during the war. It was an exciting time; no one knew what might happen tomorrow. Soldiers poured across the United States, looking heroic in their pressed uniforms, prepared to sacrifice all for country. A young woman's duty, society made clear, was to support and entertain these soldiers, and to marry one! In service clubs and at gatherings across the nation, young women served up food, dancing and conversation to soldiers far away from home. "There was a kind of fierceness, almost desperation about people meeting each other. . ." remembered Frances Veeder, "that attitude of 'Well, I'm going to be shipping out next week, so let's stay up all night and dance.'"

The uncertainties of war made couples break all the rules. Although society strongly disapproved of sex outside of marriage, pregnancies inevitably resulted. When a quick wedding was impossible, families hustled expectant mothers away to "secretarial school" or to visit a maiden aunt. It was understandable if a young man sowed his wild oats, but women were expected to remain chaste until marriage.

The year 1941 saw the highest marriage rate ever recorded in the U.S. In boom cities like Seattle, the number of marriage licenses increased by 300 percent as couples married impulsively or moved up long-planned weddings before the men shipped out. Often, there was no time for even a honeymoon.

One of these quickly married brides was June Sargent, who appeared older than her 16 years when Ervin Schmidt, a navy submariner, struck up a conversation with her one day at the bus station near Vallejo, California. As part of the home front war effort, June's family regularly invited servicemen in for home-cooked meals, so June invited Ervin to dinner with her family. They got along well. When Ervin shipped out to the Pacific he wrote to her, "Dear June. You're too young for me. Grow up and leave the field open for other women." After a few war patrols, his tone changed. He wrote, "Dearest June. . . ." Time dragged on in the Pacific. His third

While they rode the bus into San Francisco—their third time ever together—he proposed to her. She hesitated, surprised, and two sailors in the next seat said, "Give him a break!"

letter began, "Sweetheart. . . ."

On leave in April 1944, he stopped to see her. As they rode the bus into San Francisco—their third time ever together—he proposed to her. She hesitated, surprised, and two sailors in the next seat turned and said, "Give him a break!" About six weeks later, she did. They made their decision on Thursday and were married Friday night. In 2004, June and Ervin celebrated their 60th wedding anniversary.

Although many wartime marriages were long-lasting, by 1945 the divorce rate doubled to 31 percent. The war also tested the bonds of almost one million GI brides from over 50 foreign countries. With restrictive immigration laws, some had to wait years to travel to the U.S. Upon arrival, they had to adjust to a new culture, a new language, and life with a husband they hardly knew. One war bride, arriving from Britain, recalled, "At first when I saw my husband in civilian clothes, I thought, what have I done? He looked so different. . . . He probably wondered what he had let himself in for also."

Ervin and June Schmidt (above) at a dance hall at the navy base in Portsmouth, New Hampshire in early 1945, shortly before Ervin shipped out for his last submarine patrols of the war. Like many couples during the war, they married after knowing each other only a short time.

Girl of My Dreams . . .
Betty Willett

A chance encounter on the dance floor one night changed Betty Willett's life. It was March 1943, and Betty, a 19-year-old San Diego college student, was helping out at a La Mesa Women's Club party for young marines. That night there was dancing to popular records. Betty recalled, "In the middle of the dancing they said they would have a 'Paul Jones,' where the girls went one way [in a circle] and the boys went the other way and when the music stopped you grabbed the person in front of you. . . . And I grabbed *him*."

"Him" was Oscar Rea Mowery, a 19-year-old marine corporal not long out of basic training, who had recently arrived in town. They danced together. "I thought: I'll just hold onto him," Betty said. "We kind of clicked. We became very friendly." Two months later, Rea (pronounced "Ray") shipped out to serve as a cartographer in the Pacific. They didn't see one another for two years, but they wrote letters. "He wrote every single day and I wrote every single day," Betty said. At one point Rea missed a few days and Betty didn't find out until later he had been hospitalized with malaria and dengue fever. They numbered their letters because they sometimes arrived all at once. "Some days you'd get 12 or 15 and if you had them numbered you could stack them up and have them in sequence," Rea said.

Meanwhile on the home front, Betty graduated from college and worked at the Post Office and later at the County Department of Education. She volunteered for a while as a civilian defense aircraft plotter. And she waited for Rea. "It was very hard. We practically got acquainted through letters. It's funny, you can know a person really well because you're talking to him—only it's written," she said. "We wrote about everything that happened—all the details. We talked about where we wanted to go. What we wanted to do." One time Rea made a record of himself, singing "Girl of My Dreams" and sent it to Betty. "It brought tears to the eyes," she said.

As their relationship deepened, the young couple planned their wedding. Rea sent money to Betty's mother to buy a ring for Betty. On July 16, 1945, just one week after Rea arrived in San Diego from the South Pacific, Betty and Rea were married at the Naval Chapel. Four children, 11 grandchildren and many adventures later, in 2005, they celebrated their 60th wedding anniversary.

Betty Willett *(top) wrote letters to Rea Mowery every day while he was in the Pacific. He sent her* *a record of himself singing "Girl of my Dreams." The two were married (right) in the Naval Chapel in San Diego.*

At Every Mail Call

Use
V-MAIL
...to be SURE

FLY TO HIM IN V-MAIL LETTERS

The government issued posters (top) to spur letter writing, which it considered vital to troop morale.

V-mail letters and greetings (below) saved space on overseas transports by reducing individual letters to tiny photos on a roll of film. Processors near the destination printed each letter and enclosed it in an envelope for delivery.

Mail. It helped to endure the separation. It brought reassurance, love and sometimes heartbreak. Troops on isolated islands, fresh from battle, or still in the U.S., gritting their way through basic training waited for it with longing. With its power to boost troop morale, mail from home was a "military necessity." In 1942 the government gave GIs free mailing privileges and encouraged women on the home front to "Be With Him at Every Mail Call."

Buddies Clubs, posting the names of service people who wanted mail, sprang up around the nation, and home front women enthusiastically obliged with letters and care packages. Josephine Rachiele and her sisters wrote letters almost every

night to GI friends stationed overseas. "Some were from the neighborhood, and they would give our names to other soldier friends and we'd write them too. We used to send them things we baked, like cookies, and cheese and crackers, all kinds of candy, and writing paper and pens. Anything we thought they might like," she said.

Overseas mail increased by 513 percent during the war. From 1940 to 1945, the Post Office handled 200 billion pieces of mail. To save space on overseas transports and speed delivery, in 1943 the government introduced Victory-mail or "V-mail," in which the mail service photographed individual letters and sent them overseas on film where they were developed and printed for delivery. Although it amounted to only a small percentage of the total mail, the over one billion V-mails sent during the war helped to free up precious cargo space.

Censorship was an annoyance to many letter writers. Military censors routinely snipped out references to places, dates of troop movements, units, ships, and branches of service to prevent strategic war information from falling into enemy hands. Sometimes mail arrived so heavily cut up it was hard to figure out what the writer intended to say. "He couldn't really say very much except 'I'm ok' or 'I'm sick' because they were always monitored," recalled Betty Willett, who received frequent letters from her boyfriend Rea Mowery, a marine stationed in the Pacific. For Betty and Rea, whose courtship took place almost entirely by mail, censorship was particularly irksome because one of Rea's censors was a man Betty knew from high school. "I'd get Rea's letters. I'd think, *that guy,* he cut out some good stuff!"

Some people tried to get around the censors by devising personal codes or dropping hints. Sent to Kandy, Ceylon to head up an OSS registry, Julia McWilliams (later better known as Julia Child, the "French chef") tipped off her friends about her whereabouts by ending her letter with the Ogden Nash quote, "Candy is dandy, but liquor is quicker."

Although letters had the ability to lift morale and allay anxieties, they sometimes also carried sad news. Families lived in dread of the telegram announcing a death, war wound or prisoner of war status. Sometimes when GIs were killed, letters to them were returned unopened, marked "deceased." For each telegram with its painful uncertainties, families wrote anxious letters to the Red Cross, the military and to returning soldiers, seeking news, any news, of loved ones missing, captured or dead.

The worry and anxiety took a toll. Everyday letters to GIs reflected the strains felt on the home front. "Darling, this is my third letter to you today," Ethel Wiggins wrote on August 19, 1944 to her husband in the infantry in Europe, "but I'll sleep better if I write you tonight. . . . It's just this strain of waiting . . . Buddy,

take better care of yourself than ever, precious. You just must."

The pressures of the war tested marriages and engagements, and sometimes mail call carried a "Dear John" or "Dear Jane" letter, breaking off relations. Elliott Johnson recalled one time while serving overseas when he was asked to read a Dear John letter for one of the soldiers. "His reaction was complete silence. He got up and walked away, came back and asked me to read the letter again. . . . I could see the lines of grief in his face, the total disbelief."

For every heartbreaker, however, hundreds of thousands of letters brought pleasure to GIs and hope for the time when loved ones could once again be together. On Thanksgiving Day 1942, Edna Golan wrote to her husband, "Dearest, in spite of all this misery and chaos I am thankful to be alive for I love you. . . . My love goes out to you."

At a time when *long-distance telephone calls were rare and telegrams allowed only a few clipped sentences, people wrote letters frequently— sometimes as often as every day. In 1945, the last year of the war, Americans sent 3.5 billion pieces of mail overseas.*

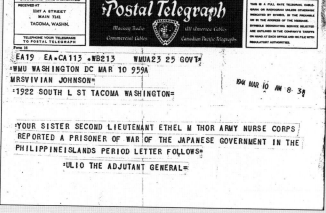

Army nurse Ethel Thor wrote home from her post at a jungle hospital near the front lines on Bataan in the Philippines. "Just like a camping trip. . . ." Her letter understates conditions, no doubt to avoid censorship and reassure her family. Her sister, Vivian Johnson, received this telegram after Ethel was taken prisoner by the Japanese at the fall of Corregidor. Throughout the war, Vivian Johnson wrote letters to the Red Cross and other agencies to try to find out more about her sister's condition. Ethel remained a POW until 1945 when U.S. forces liberated Santo Tomás internment camp in Manila.

The Ultimate Sacrifice

World War II claimed more casualties than any war in the history of the planet. Worldwide, between 50 and 60 million people died. Over 400,000 members of the U.S. Armed Forces died in battle or noncombat situations. More than half a million were wounded. At home, industrial accidents killed 88,000 workers and injured 11 million—more than ten times the total U.S. combat casualties.

Women lived in fear of "the telegram," the terse missive from the War Department informing that their beloved was killed, wounded, missing, or taken prisoner. "We regret to inform you that your husband was killed in action while in the service of his country," a typical telegram began. Whenever possible, Red Cross or military officials delivered the news in person.

News of a death desolated most families. Young wives who had married quickly during wartime grieved to have had so little time with their husbands. Children suffered deeply and often blamed themselves for the loss; mothers had to put aside their own grief to comfort distressed children. Notices about missing soldiers or prisoners of war left families in an ongoing state of suspense. When the military could not return the body or personal effects, families had difficulty finding closure. "There are some things you never find out," Jean Eisen remarked wistfully, fifty years after her brother, Donald Naze, was lost on the submarine, *Seawolf.*

After the initial shock, widows and wives of disabled GIs coped not only with the grief but also with everyday problems of how to manage their families. Widows' pensions and disability payments (ranging from $50 to $115 per month, depending on the number of children or the percentage of disability) were not enough to support a family, and most women had to work. In addition, many women had to nurse husbands or sons who returned home maimed or traumatized. Personal struggles to endure grief permeated the home front. Never at the same time had so many women faced the problems of surviving loss.

"I Can't Give Up Hope . . ."

Many families wrote to returning servicemen and women to ask for news of missing loved ones. Most had received only a telegram and a condolence letter from their husband's or son's commanding officer, and they hungered for eyewitness accounts. Returning service people tried to provide some bit of information or solace to those who wrote, even when they knew nothing about the person. This was the situation for Lt. Ethel Thor, an army nurse POW just returned from the Philippines in March 1945, when she received the following letter from a service wife:

Dear Lt. Thor,

"I am so very anxious to get some news of my husband. . . . The last direct message I had from him was in December of 1941. In May 1942 I received the message that he was 'Missing in Action,' and in December of 1942, I received a message that he was a prisoner of war in the Philippines. In June of 1943, I received a message that he had died in Osaka, Japan.

"I can't give up hope until I know something more definite, but regardless of the outcome, I want so badly to hear some news of him from someone who knew him or something of him, either before of after surrender, or both. It will mean so much to me. If you knew him, or something about him, please write me and tell me when you last saw him, where and how he was and anything else of interest, good or bad. I feel now that I can take anything, so please don't hesitate to tell me things I should know. I pray so hard that his death message is all a mistake and that he will return to me."

Gold Star Mothers

Much attention was given to the wives of servicemen who died, but perhaps the mothers suffered even more. Because the majority of draftees were single men, mothers were four times as likely as wives to experience a war death. The loss of a son or daughter—especially an only child—was a devastating blow for a mother who had devoted a great part of herself and her own life to seeing her child into adulthood. The military did what it could to assure a mother that her child's sacrifice was meaningful. To ease the shock, War Department visitors and letters reassured families (not always accurately) that the death was "painless" and "quick." Esther Burgard, whose son John was killed while serving with the Army Air Force in England, was shattered when she received the telegram. "I think that only a person who has gone through this can really know the feeling that comes over you," she said.

"It was a terrible feeling—he was lost, he was gone." After the war, Burgard joined the American Gold Star Mothers Organization to seek solace with other mothers.

Alleta Sullivan, mother of five sons who died when a Japanese submarine torpedoed their ship, USS *Juneau,* in November 1942, remembered the morning at 7 a.m. when three men came to the house with the news. "In my first blind grief, it seemed as if almost everything I had lived for was gone. I couldn't eat or sleep . . . I did find comfort in one thing they told me. I learned that everything happened so fast that the boys must have died quickly." After the Sullivan tragedy, the navy changed its policy and no longer allowed siblings to serve on the same ship. The Sullivan family became widely known across the country. Their patriotic sacrifice was underlined when their remaining child, Genevieve, enlisted in the Navy as a WAVE.

A cross and a helmet in France (top opposite) mark the grave of a fallen U.S. soldier. About 400 women died while in active service in the U.S. military, Women Airforce Service Pilots (WASP), and the United Service Organizations (USO). Working near the front lines, army nurses experienced the highest casualties of all the women's services.

The government *awarded stars (above) to the families of servicemen and women— a blue star for each son or daughter in the armed forces, and a gold star for each one who died.*

Japanese American *mothers in internment receive gold stars (right). Their sons fought and died in Europe for the Allied cause, even while the United States denied freedom to their families.*

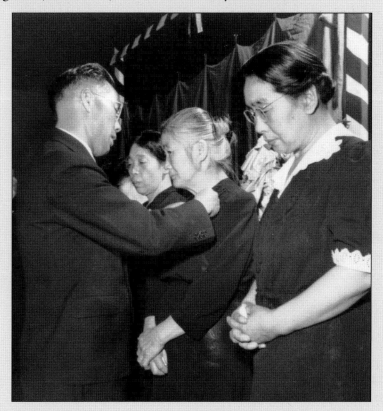

In Uniform

With war on two fronts and limited manpower, the military looked to womanpower to fill the ranks of noncombat jobs. Offering travel, new skills and the opportunity to help win the war, the Armed Forces recruited over 340,000 young American women, including Asian, African, Hispanic and Native American minorities. Enlistees in the Women's Army Corps, Navy Women's Reserve, Coast Guard Women's Reserve, and Marine Corps Women's Reserve filled myriad jobs, from gunnery instructors to filing clerks. In military hospitals perilously close to combat, Army Nurse Corps and Navy Nurse Corps enlistees provided vital medical care to wounded soldiers. Millions more women served in nonmilitary organizations, supporting the armed forces. Women Airforce Service Pilots tested and ferried military fighters, bombers and cargo planes. Undercover agents with the Office of Strategic Services gathered intelligence and worked covertly to undermine the enemy. American Red Cross volunteers on the home front organized blood drives and assembled care packages. In the war zone, with the friendly smiles of "the girl next door," Red Cross women brought food and recreation to GIs at clubs and hospitals. The duties of women in uniform exposed them to risks. Four hundred died in military service and more than 85 were taken prisoners of war. Managing jobs once reserved for men, venturing to distant battle fronts and keeping calm under fire, women in uniform redefined traditional roles and paved the way for future participation of females in the armed services.

Women Airforce Service Pilot, Elisabeth Gardner, (opposite) in the cockpit of a B-26 bomber at Harlingen Army Air Field, Texas.

In Uniform

First Lady
Eleanor Roosevelt with leaders of the women's branches of the U.S. Armed Forces (right) on November 23, 1943, the first anniversary of the Coast Guard Women's Reserve (SPAR). Left to right: Capt. Mildred McAfee, director of the Women's Naval Reserve (WAVES); Col. Oveta Culp Hobby, director of the Women's Army Corps (WAC); Eleanor Roosevelt; Lt. Col. Ruth Cheney Streeter, director of the Marine Corps Women's Reserve; and Lt. Comdr. Dorothy Stratton, director of the SPAR.

A recruitment *poster for the women's armed services (opposite left).*

Cmdr. Thomas *Gaylord (opposite right) gives the oath to three new navy nurses, (left to right) Marion Bendix, Adela Lee Bruce, and Barbara Zeigler.*

American women played a part in all of the nation's wars. As far back as the Revolution and the Civil War, small numbers of determined women served on the battlefront as nurses, undercover soldiers and spies. Starting in 1901 and 1908, respectively, the Army and Navy officially accepted women as military nurses, and during World War I the Navy, Coast Guard and Marine Corps enlisted several thousand women for noncombat service.

While the U.S. Armed Forces were not eager to expand women's roles in the military beyond nursing, the sheer demand for soldiers in World War II made it a compelling option. In 1942, First Lady Eleanor Roosevelt visited war-ravaged London and observed British women working in nontraditional military and civilian jobs. She returned to the United States convinced of the powerful role women could play in the U.S. military and on the home front. With her support, Margaret Chase Smith and other female members of Congress lobbied for legislation to allow women in the armed services. In 1941 and 1942, Rep. Edith Nourse Rogers sponsored a bill to establish the Women's Army Auxiliary Corps (WAAC). Soon afterward, Congress established the Navy Women's Reserve (WAVES), the Women's Coast Guard (SPAR), the Marine Corps Women's Reserve, and the Women Auxiliary Ferrying Squadron (WAFS) and Women's Flying Training Detachment (WFTD)—predecessors to the Women Airforce Service Pilots (WASP).

Barred from combat, enlisted women served as air-traffic controllers, clerks, truck drivers, trainers, parachute riggers and in any other military job that could free up servicemen for duty at the battlefront. By war's end, over 340,000 women had served in the U.S. Armed Forces and millions more in military-related support organizations like the WASP, the Office of Strategic Services (OSS), the Public Health Service Cadet Nurse Corps and the Red Cross.

Recruitment

- **Army Nurse Corps (ANC):** established 1901; 59,000 army nurses served during the war.

- **Navy Nurse Corps (NNC):** established in 1908: 14,000 navy nurses served.

- **Women's Army Corps (WAC):** first established as the Women's Army Auxiliary Corps (WAAC) May 15, 1942; converted to the Women's Army Corps (WAC) on September 30, 1943; 150,000 women served in the WAAC/WAC during WWII..

- **Navy Women's Reserve (WAVES—Women Accepted for Volunteer Emergency Service):** established July 30, 1942; 86,000 women served during the war.

- **Coast Guard Women's Reserve (SPAR— Semper Paratus/Always Ready):** established November 23, 1942; 13,000 women served.

- **Marine Corps Women's Reserve:** established February 13, 1943; 21,000 women served.

- **Women Airforce Service Pilots (WASP):** never officially U.S. military; established August 5, 1943 by merging the Women's Auxiliary Ferrying Squadron (WAFS) and the Women's Flying Training Detachment (WFTD); 1,074 women pilots served in the WASP.

"Share the Deeds of Victory. Join the WAVES," "Be a Marine . . . Free a Marine to Fight," "The Army has 239 Kinds of Jobs for Women," "Don't Miss Your Great Opportunity. The Navy Needs You." The armed services began to enlist women in earnest in 1942. Recruiting slogans appealed to women's patriotism, economic desires, and sense of adventure. On May 27, 1942, the first day of WAAC recruiting, 13,000 women stood in line for as long as eight hours to apply for 440 officer candidate positions. Enlistees to the WAAC had to have a high school education, be between ages 21 and 45, five to six feet tall, and weigh 100 to 200 lbs. Surprisingly, for the time, the WAAC did not require married women to seek their husband's permission to enlist. Young recruits had to overcome the objections of friends and family who viewed the military as "unfeminine" and not a place for "nice girls." Nevertheless, hundreds of thousands answered the call.

The Military Life

Military service offered women something civilian jobs did not—the chance to go overseas. Nurses were already in the Philippines when war broke out, and soon the Army and Navy needed them for service in all combat theaters. The Women's Army Corps (WAC) challenged military tradition and deployed women around the globe. Even the home front military services—the WAVES, SPAR and Marines—offered women a chance to serve overseas late in the war in the territories of Alaska and Hawaii. "I wanted desperately to be where the action was," said Irene Brion, a WAC who secured duty as a code breaker in New Guinea. Wherever they served, military women freed up men for combat, traveled, met people from every part of the country, and had the chance to work in a wide range of traditional and nontraditional jobs.

Although the military required females to be older and better educated than male enlistees, it gave women second-class status. In most branches, women's pay was less than men's, or women held lower ranks than men of similar abilities.

Women in the armed forces contended with harassing wisecracks from male GIs who thought females didn't belong in the service. Female recruits developed thick skins just to get by. In time, women proved their usefulness and the men's attitudes became more accepting.

Basic training for women, however, remained as hard as the men's. A typical day at WAC boot camp at Fort Des Moines, Iowa began with a bugle call at 5:45 a.m. and 6 a.m. roll call, no matter what the weather. A rigorous schedule followed: march to the mess hall, inspection, assignment of extra duties (grounds cleanup or the much despised KP—kitchen police), drills, calisthenics, classes on military history and procedures, hikes, obstacle courses, and after supper a class or film about a topic such as venereal disease or "Loose Lips Sink Ships." By lights out at 2200 hours recruits fell into their hard, narrow cots with the exhaustion of marathon runners.

Regulations dictated everything from their undergarments to the angle of their salute. Hair had to be "above the collar," uniforms spotless, stocking seams straight. As WAC Grace Porter put it, "Army life requires plenty of courage, stamina, and a boiler-plate stomach."

Military service opened new vistas for women. They traveled and gained confidence and worldliness. Women made friends for life and learned flexibility and cooperation, working together as a unit. A few—especially those relegated to mundane jobs—found it disillusioning, but for many it was the high point of their lives.

Life in the military afforded little privacy; women ate together, drilled together, marched with their group, lived in close quarters—often in rugged conditions—and ultimately did their jobs as part of a well-trained unit. (Below) Flight nurses bivouac on Oahu during jungle training. (Bottom right) WACs eat at the mess in their New Guinea camp.

Boot camp was a challenge to even the hardiest souls, with a dawn til dark regimen of classes, drills and discipline. Women experienced the same rigors as men, with a few exceptions: 10-mile hikes instead of 20, and no weapons or tactical training. (Right) WACs on a training march. (Bottom left) WACs exercise aboard ship en route to Hawaii. (Bottom right) Nurses slated for frontline assignments carry heavy combat packs on an 8-mile training hike through the India-Burma jungle.

"Boy, am I tough. I can take everything— putrid chow, no room for my stuff, obnoxious Southerners, pushups, and KP, all in one week." —Ann Bosanko, WAC in basic training

Women's Army Corps

WACs *(right)*
*prepare for takeoff
from the Alaskan-
Wing-Air Trans-
port Base at Great
Falls, Montana,
October 1944.
The WAC was the
only women's
military service,
other than the
nurses, that served
in combat zones.
The first WAACs
overseas arrived in
Algiers, North
Africa in December
1942, after sur-
viving a German
U-boat torpedo
attack that sank
their troop ship.
During World War
II, about 150,000
women served in the
WAAC/WAC,
including Hispanics,
Asian, African and
Native Americans.
Six hundred fifty-
seven received
medals and cita-
tions, including the
Purple Heart (in
some cases for
wounds suffered
from exploding V-1
bombs in London).*

On May 14, 1942, Rep. Edith Nourse Rogers won a hard-fought struggle that challenged 167 years of army tradition. In groundbreaking legislation, Congress established the Women's Army Auxiliary Corps (WAAC) to support the army in noncombat positions. Longtime newspaper editor Oveta Culp Hobby became the first director. An advocate of women, Col. Hobby was among those disappointed that Congress, to mollify opponents, did not make the women's corps part of the army. As "auxiliaries," WAACs received lower pay than male reservists of comparable rank and were not eligible for retirement pay, death benefits for beneficiaries or veteran's medical care.

To add to these obstacles, WAAC recruits met with resistance from male GIs who did not want to be "freed" for combat service and who circulated the groundless rumors that 90% of WAACs were prostitutes and 40% were pregnant. Predictably, WAAC enlistments plummeted. In response, on July 1, 1943 Congress established the Women's Army Corps (WAC) with military status as part of the Army. Over 41,177 enlisted women and 4,600 officers took the option to join the WAC as the WAAC went out of existence.

The previous July, the first group of 439 WAAC officer candidates—including 39 African Americans housed in segregated barracks—began their six-week training at Fort Des Moines, Iowa. The first enlisted women arrived one month later for four weeks of basic training. WAAC training centers soon opened in Daytona Beach, Florida; Fort Oglethorpe, Georgia; Fort Devens, Massachusetts; and at camps Polk and Ruston in Louisiana.

Trained WAACs took up duty with the Aircraft Warning Service, the Army Air Forces, Army Ground Forces, Army Service Forces and the Manhattan Project.

About ten percent of WAAC/WACs served overseas in North Africa, Europe, the Pacific, the China-Burma-India Theater, and the Middle East, providing clerical, administrative, intelligence or technical support. At some overseas posts, WACs lived and worked in tents in rough conditions. Their presence in the war zone often astonished male GIs. Tech Sgt. Mabel Carney, who crossed to Normandy with a group of generals immediately after the D-Day invasion, recalled, "The landing was difficult. . . . Our boys were still coming ashore. They were really surprised to see a WAC there!"

Major Charity Adams and the 6888th

The only African American WAC Unit to Serve Overseas in World War II

Maj. Charity Adams (left) and Lt. Elfreda LeBeau at the 6888th's snack bar in Rouen.

Major Charity Adams (front) inspects the 6888th in Birmingham, England.

Members of the 6888th WACs and French civilian employees sort mail in France.

African Americans comprised only 4,000 of the 150,000 women who served in the Women's Army Corps. Before World War II, the military excluded black women from service. Charity Adams, one of two black women to attain the rank of major in World War II (the other was Harriet West) recalled her arrival at Fort Des Moines in 1942 with the first group of WAAC officer trainees: "A young red-haired second lieutenant stood in front of us and said, 'Will all the colored girls move over on this side.'. . . There was a stunned silence, for even in the United States of the forties it did not occur to us that this could happen."

Adams languished in administrative positions at Fort Des Moines for over two years while the white officers around her quickly moved up to new assignments. WAC units had to be requested, and no one was requesting African American units. Finally, pressure from national civil rights organizations forced the issue. In February 1945 the Army assigned Major Adams to organize the 6888th Central Postal Battalion of 850 black WACs for service overseas.

Adams' arrival in England met with incredulity from U.S. military personnel: "Salutes were slow in coming, and frequently, returned with great reluctance. . . . Accepting any Negro officer in the U.S. Army was hard enough, but accepting Negro women officers was a real burden." The 6888th went to work in Birmingham and later in Rouen, France, redirecting warehouses full of mail to U.S. troops throughout Europe. In three months they moved three million letters and parcels—a crucial boost to troop morale.

The battalion completed its work in Paris after V-E Day. Before leaving port on the voyage home, Major Adams was surprised when the captain, by reason of her seniority, put her in charge of all the women on the ship, including 600 white nurses. Arguments soon broke out; the white nurses did not want to travel home under the command of "a colored woman." Major Adams held her ground, inviting those unwilling to travel under her command to disembark. (No one did.) "After three and one-half years, I was leaving the service facing the same kind of prejudice I had encountered when I entered," she said. Segregation remained U.S. Army policy until 1948.

Women's Army Corps

The various army forces employed WACs for diverse duties. Women handled almost any job that could free up male GIs for combat. (Left:) Cpl. Margaret Gurry drives a jeep at the 12th Replacement Control Depot in England. (Below:) T/5 Catherine Hardy works at a quartermaster supply depot in Australia. (Bottom:) WAC air traffic controllers at Randolph Field, Texas.

When WAAC/WACs completed basic training they took up a wide range of duties. The first group to graduate manned Aircraft Warning Services stations along the U.S. East Coast. Initially, WAACs filled clerical, administrative and driving positions with the Army, but over time as the forces found them capable, they received more diverse assignments. About 40 percent served with the Army Air Forces in positions such as weather observers, cryptographers, parachute riggers, sheet metal workers, bombsight maintenance specialists, radio operators and control tower operators.

The Army Service Forces utilized another 40 percent of WAAC/WACs in key areas. In the Ordnance Department WACs computed the velocity of bullets, measured bomb fragments, loaded shells, and worked as draftswomen, electricians, and mechanics. In the Transportation Corps women processed men for overseas duty, worked as boat dispatchers and performed clerical duties on board hospital ships. WACs with the Signal Corps served as switchboard, telegraph, or radio operators and as photograph or map analysts. In the Army Medical Department women functioned as lab, surgical or x-ray technicians, medical secretaries, and ward clerks. The Chemical Warfare Service assigned WACs as glass blowers and field equipment testers, while the Quartermaster Corps used women to track supplies.

The Army Ground Forces (AGF) employed 20 percent of WAACs in routine office jobs and motor pools. AGF staff officers did not always welcome WAACs and underutilized them to the extent that when the Women's Army Auxiliary Corps converted to the Women's Army Corps, many women assigned to the AGF declined to reenlist.

Finally, about 400 WACs served as clerical support, cryptographers, chemists, metallurgists, and electronics technicians for the top secret Manhattan Project, which developed the atomic bomb.

Camp Life in New Guinea

New Guinea

"There were no floors for the tents, and trenches had to be dug around them to keep the rain from turning dirt into mud. The tents leaked. . . . There was no electricity."

—Irene Brion, WAC codebreaker
Base G, New Guinea

In 1944, the Army began to send WACs to Australia, New Guinea and the Philippines in the Pacific. In all, 5,500 WACs served in the region, most of them in administrative and clerical capacities.

WACs stationed in New Guinea found island life beautiful, but rugged—palms, tropical birds and wild orchids mixed with searing heat, humidity and disease-laden mosquitos. WACs lived in tents or thatched huts. To guard against malaria, the women took Atabrine, which turned their skin yellow, a state they jokingly called their "Atabrine tan." Long-sleeved shirts, men's khaki pants and high boots gave further protection.

In these remote camps, requisitioned food and supplies often did not arrive. Meals consisted of canned and dehydrated foods, C-rations, and coconuts, mangoes, and limes scrounged from around the island. Not everything was in short supply, however. With a ratio of about 25 men to every woman, dating was easy.

Parties and dating helped to balance the dangers that were always close at hand in the jungle. In May 1945, a C-47 carrying seven WACs and 14 airmen crashed on a flight over uncharted territory, killing all but three. Badly burned and with legs becoming gangrenous, Cpl. Margaret Hastings and two airmen survived six weeks in the jungle with the help of natives and army medics who parachuted in. When sufficiently recovered, they hiked to a valley for rescue by glider.

WACs take their first taste of chlorinated water from a lister bag (above) at their New Guinea camp. Hanging in the tropical heat, the water was clean, but tasted warm and brackish. "We preferred to wait until mealtime and drink 'battery acid,' a synthetic lemonade that was usually cool,"

remarked WAC Irene Brion.

WACs in their New Guinea tent barracks (right). The women used mosquito nets over their cots at night. With snakes, spiders and rats "the size of house cats" in the nearby jungle, the nets afforded some protection.

Navy WAVES

Draped with belts of 50-caliber ammunition (below), gunnery instructors Florence Johnson and Rosamund Small walk to the target range. WAVES provided aerial gunnery training, simulated flight instruction, and pilot instrument training to navy airmen. In the last two years of the war, WAVES conducted some part of the training for every naval aviator sent into combat.

A WAVE spins the propeller of an SNJ training plane (right). WAVES served in aeronautical positions as control tower operators, aviation metalsmiths,

meteorologists and aviation machinist mates; in communications assignments as watch officers, radio operators and decoders; in administrative positions as storekeepers, air transport supervisors, secretaries, clerks and mail handlers; and in medical capacities as x-ray technicians, therapists and pharmacist's mates. Many duties placed women in hazardous situations near machinery, explosives and heavy equipment. Sixty-nine WAVES died while on active duty during the war.

A WAVE carto- grapher works on a map (top opposite).

"They taught us to set an example. . . . They taught us discipline, especially at boot camp at Hunter College in the Bronx."

—*Regina Podolski, WAVE decoder*

In December 1941, while her bill to establish the WAAC was still under debate, the persevering Rep. Edith Nourse Rogers approached Rear Admiral Chester Nimitz with the idea of drafting similar legislation for the U.S. Navy. Seven months later, on July 30, 1942, in spite of navy foot-dragging, President Roosevelt signed the bill into law.

Unlike the WAAC auxiliary, the WAVES (Women Accepted for Volunteer Emergency Service) was made part of the Naval Reserve, with the same ranks as the men. Women received equal pay for equal rank, but unlike male reservists were not eligible for retirement, veteran's medical care, or—if killed on active duty—a death gratuity for beneficiaries. Eighty-six thousand women served in the WAVES, performing "shore duty" in the Continental U.S. (and in U.S. territories after

1944). Mildred H. McAfee, the respected president of Wellesley College, became director of the WAVES and the Navy's first commissioned woman officer. Perhaps because of her education background, many WAVES training centers were established on college campuses. WAVES officers trained at Smith College and Mt. Holyoke College, near Northampton, Massachusetts.

Enlisted women trained at the University of Iowa, Cedar Falls, and after February 1943, at the large boot camp established for all navy women at Hunter College, the Bronx, New York. The first thing "boots" learned was to speak the navy way: they didn't enter a building, they "went aboard," and when they left they "went ashore." The floor was a "deck." They stowed their gear, chowed in the mess, and turned in for sack check at 2310.

Over the course of the war, WAVES worked in nearly every stateside non-combat position in the Navy and released 50,500 men for sea duty. By 1943, women reservists filled not only jobs formerly done by men, but many new positions that paralleled the technical developments in weaponry. In some parts of the service WAVES made up the majority; at the Washington Communications Center, WAVES comprised 75 percent of the staff. Likewise, WAVES performed 75 percent of jobs at the Bureau of Naval Personnel, 55 percent at the Navy Department, and 80 percent of the Navy's mail services.

Grace Hopper: Computer Scientist

Lt. Grace Hopper with members of the navy crew at the Harvard Computation Lab, 1944.

Grace Hopper was an unlikely candidate for the Naval Reserve in 1943. At age 37, 105 pounds, a Ph.D. from Yale, and an associate professor of math at Vassar, she was overage, underweight and working in a civilian job considered crucial to the war effort. But she wanted to serve in the Navy: "There was a war on! … it was the only thing to do," she said. By special permission she entered the WAVES and was assigned to the Bureau of Ordnance Computation Project at Harvard University.

There, Hopper and a small crew programmed the Mark I, the first large, fully automatic digital computer in the U.S. At fifty-one feet long and eight feet deep, they used the room-sized Mark I to find a way to quickly calculate crosswinds, temperature, air density and weight to accurately aim new navy guns. The team worked 24 hours a day and often slept at their desks. "There was a rush on everything, and we didn't realize what was really happening," she said. "All of the sudden we had self-propelled rockets, and we had to compute where they were going and what they were going to do. The development of the atomic bomb also required a tremendous amount of computation, as did acoustic and magnetic mines."

On a hot day in August 1945 while building the Mark II computer, the machine stopped and the crew discovered a moth inside the relay and removed it with tweezers. "From then on," Hopper recalled, "when anything went wrong with a computer, we said it had bugs in it." After the war, Hopper helped to develop the first compiler and to invent COBOL, the first computer language to use words rather than binary code. In 1986, she retired from the Navy with the rank of rear admiral.

SPAR—Semper Paratus Always Ready

SPAR cadets in training (above). Over 11,000 women served in the Coast Guard SPAR, performing shore duty in the continental U.S. (and after 1944, also in Alaska and Hawaii). The only SPARs allowed to work on the water were those with the rating of surfman, trained as small boat instructors. The SPARs supplied emergency personnel for the Coast Guard from November 1942 to July 1947.

"The thought that we were participating in a system that was playing such an important part in winning the war gave us a feeling of being as close to the front lines as was possible."
—Lt.(jg) Vera Hamerschlag, SPAR, Loran Monitoring

In November 1942, four months after the creation of the WAVES, Congress established another navy women's service to free up men for sea duty: the U.S. Coast Guard Women's Reserve or SPAR. Directed by Dorothy C. Stratton, former dean of women at Purdue University, the SPAR took its name from Coast Guard motto: *Semper Paratus*—Always Ready.

SPAR officers trained at Smith College and at the Coast Guard Academy in New London, Connecticut. The first enlisted SPARs attended boot camp at Oklahoma A & M, Iowa State Teachers College or at Hunter College. In June 1943, the newly established training center at the Biltmore Hotel in Palm Beach took over as SPAR "boot school," enticing recruits with the slogan, "Train Under the Florida Sun."

The Coast Guard, whose mission was to patrol and protect U.S. ports, used SPARs to fill most of the shore jobs at its U.S. stations. Women decoded shipping messages, operated radios, radar, and teletype machines, provided air/sea rescue support for plane crashes at sea, and assisted patrol planes in identifying the locations of U.S. submarines en route to the Pacific. They also worked as storekeepers, clerks, drivers and pharmacist's mates.

A small number served in top secret LORAN monitoring stations along the East Coast. LORAN (long range aid to navigation) used special radio signals to help ships calculate their exact location in blacked-out coastal waters. "LORAN was so 'hush-hush' that not even the training officer had any conception of what the duties of these SPARs would be," said Vera Hamerschlag, who commanded an all-woman LORAN monitoring station in Chatham, Massachusetts. The Chatham station was believed to be the only all-female station of its kind at the time.

Aboard the CGC Assembly: Muriel Daggett

Born into a New England sea-loving family, it was only natural that Muriel Daggett would join the Coast Guard Reserve. Her grandfather was a lighthouse keeper, and her father and all of her uncles had gone to sea. So at the age of 20, in March 1943, she joined the SPAR. After an abbreviated 3-week boot camp at Hunter College (the last boot camp held in the Bronx before moving to Palm Beach), she shipped out to Seattle where the commander "wanted all the SPARs he could get."

Daggett traveled across the country on a troop train with a group of 30 SPARs. The SPARs were kept in a separate car with guards at each end. "The only men you saw was when the train went around a curve," she recalled. At twenty years of age, "the boys" in the other cars were very much on their minds.

In Seattle they were billeted in the top two floors of the Hotel Assembly, referred to in Coast Guard terms as the Coast Guard Cutter *Assembly.* There, she roomed with three other SPARs from Massachusetts, and took up a position in cost accounting, allowing the male Coast Guard accountants to transfer to sea duty. Seattle, with its military bases, was bustling with young sailors, and the SPARs had their choice of dates. "All of the sudden I was very popular. Anyone that asked me out, I said 'yes.' I was having the best time!" she said.

While stationed in Seattle, Daggett took the qualifying exam to move up to first class rating. She studied *The Bluejacket's Manual*, memorizing facts. "This old chief who had been in 30 years was giving the test—waiting for me with bated breath," she said. "Well, I have a mind that hangs onto trivia. About the third question he asked me was what was the orlop deck. And I knew! I knew it. That was it, my God. He went running through the office [telling everyone] that I knew it. So, I made seaman 1st class." Reflecting on her experiences, Daggett saw her service as a rite of passage. "I can't even think of having done anything else. When you go into the Service, it defines you for the rest of your life."

SPAR seamen 1st class *Anita Giardino and Muriel Daggett (left to right) on the steps of the Seattle Courthouse in 1943.*

SPAR Soundings (below) *newsletter for the SPARs at the Hotel Assembly. Daggett wrote a gossip column for the paper.*

Marines

Male Marines (right) with full packs march off on their way to the battle front, while women marines, trained to take noncombatant jobs march in to Camp Lejeune, North Carolina. Women marines performed hundreds of essential jobs, including gunnery instruction, radio operation, truck driving, meteorology, celestial navigation, drafting, map making, stenography and clerical work. In addition, 43 women from prominent music schools across the country entertained troops, gave concerts on the radio, and performed at official functions as part of the Marine Corps Women's Reserve Band.

Even though 300 "Marinettes" served with the Marines in World War I, the Marine Corps of the 1940s was very resistant to the idea of admitting women. Urgent wartime necessity forced the decision however, and on February 13, 1943, the corps with the reputation of being the bravest, toughest and most selective of all services accepted females to its newly created Marine Corps Women's Reserve.

Although the public waited for a catchy nickname like WAMS, Femarines, Glamarines, or Leather-neck Aides, Gen. Holcomb put an end to the idea, stating in *Life* magazine on March 27, 1944: "They are Marines. They don't have a nickname and they don't need one. They get their basic training in a Marine atmosphere at a Marine post. They inherit the traditions of Marines. They are Marines." Ruth Cheney Streeter, an active civic leader, commercial pilot and mother of four became director of the Women's Reserve, or WR as it was commonly called. With the slogan, "Free a Marine to Fight," the WR enlisted over 21,000 women from March 1943 to September 1945.

Initially, enlisted women trained at Hunter College, and officer recruits attended Smith College and Mt. Holyoke. In July 1943, the Marines consolidated all basic training for women at Camp Lejeune, North Carolina. There, along with other basics, WRs observed the men in field demonstrations of hand-to-hand combat, mortars, flame throwers and other weapons, to inspire them to the traditions and spirit of the Marine Corps.

One "tradition" the women found hard to bear was the disrespect and open hostility of the men toward the WRs. Crude language, mean-spirited remarks and the derogatory label, "BAMS" (broad-assed marines) took a toll on the morale of even the toughest women. By August 1943, the problem reached such proportions that the commandant sent orders to unit commanders making them responsible for stopping the harassment. The situation slowly defused, especially as the women's competence proved their worth.

By war's end, WRs performed duties in 225 specialties and filled the positions of one-half to two-thirds of all permanent personnel on major marine posts. Most of the Marine Corps Women's Reserve was demobilized on September 1, 1946.

Dear Molly . . .

Dearest Molly
Rained this evening. And
rain in Guadalcanal is R-A-I-N!

Well Molly of the Marines
There is nobody I would rather
"steam off" to than you

Two months after Pearl Harbor, Detroit radio personality Molly Carewe volunteered to help Marine recruitment in a big way. Over the next 14 months, she became liaison, mother, sister, friend and sounding board to marine recruits and their families. Dubbed "Molly of the Marines," her interviews, pep talks to new recruits, and Michigan Radio Network program, featuring letters from marines, earned her the admiration of the leathernecks as they struggled through basic training, lived in rugged camps, or suffered the terror of seeing their buddies killed. She answered every letter. To Pvt. Lloyd Trutna who wrote, "I have been so lonely since I left home," Molly wired: "Your welfare and happiness of paramount interest. Have started ball rolling on your behalf. Chin up until letters and things reach you. Remember I am banking on you to hold a true course. Don't let me down. A heart full of love to Molly's leatherneck." Molly also wrote to the marines' mothers and read their letters on the air. Mrs. Teresa Gidley wrote, "I suppose I felt like all mothers do when they see their sons go to war—brokenhearted and fearful, but so proud. "

One third of women in the Marine Corps Reserve served in aviation at Marine Corps air stations. Their duties included such jobs as control tower operator, aircraft instrument technician, aviation supply and flight simulation instructor. Top: a marine rigs a parachute at Cherry Point, North Carolina. Above: Sgt. Grace Wyman practices aerial photography. Right: marine airplane mechanics learn about hydraulic systems.

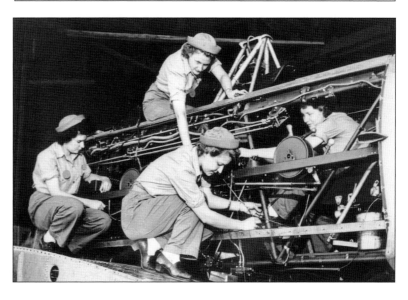

Women Airforce Service Pilots

Although they wore uniforms, lived in barracks, marched and drilled during training and flew military aircraft, the Women Airforce Service Pilots (WASP) never officially became part of the armed forces during World War II. Yet from 1942 to 1944, more than 1,000 female pilots provided essential military air support in the United States and flew every kind of military aircraft, from cargo planes to fighters and bombers. For many young women pilots it was the high point of their lives. "We had the best of all worlds," said Barbara Erickson, who was in the first group of women ferry pilots. "We had all these beautiful airplanes to fly, all these great people that we were associated with . . . and we worked hard."

The WASP was the vision of two women with independent, but similar ideas: Nancy Harkness Love, a charter pilot and employee at the Air Transport Command; and Jacqueline Cochran, a nationally known pilot and winner of the 1938 Bendix Transcontinental Race. In May 1940 and July 1941, respectively, Love and Cochran each proposed the use of women pilots in the Air Corps Ferrying Command. With the U.S. not yet at war, General H. H. "Hap" Arnold, head of the Army Air Forces, turned them down.

In early 1942, Cochran took 24 U.S. women pilots to England, then at war, to observe and work with British women pilots of the Air Transport Auxiliary, ferrying aircraft from factories to squadrons. While Cochran was in England, Gen. Arnold gave Nancy Love the go-ahead in the U.S. to form up the Women's Auxiliary Ferrying Squadron (WAFS).

The WAFS, whose sole objective was to ferry airplanes, began in September 1942 with a handpicked group of 28 licensed pilots. Standards were high; each pilot had to have at least 500 hours of flying time on a minimum rating of 200 horsepower. The first group of 12 at New Castle Air Base near Wilmington, Delaware had an average 1,200 hours and were among the most experienced pilots (male or female) in the nation. Among them were Evelyn Sharp, a barnstormer and

"One day I would be flying a P-51 and the next day a B-17 or a B-25. They were all marvelous . . . every airplane was just a glory and a joy to fly." — *Barbara Erickson, WASP ferry pilot*

transport pilot with 2,900 hours of flying time, and Cornelia Fort, who had successfully evaded the attacking Japanese at Pearl Harbor. After just 40 days of orientation, including two weeks of learning to fly the "army way," the WAFS went to work, ferrying airplanes to training schools and overseas shipping points.

Meanwhile, Jackie Cochran returned from England convinced that women pilots without extensive experience could be trained to do much more than ferrying. She proposed her ideas to General Arnold and he authorized her to create the Women's Flying Training Detachment (WFTD). The WFTD recruited women with 200 hours of flying experience—a bar that was lowered to just 35 hours in April 1943. In August 1943, the WAFS and the WFTD combined to form the Women Airforce Service Pilots (WASP) with Jackie Cochran as director and Nancy Love as head of the ferrying division.

Avenger Field near Sweetwater, Texas became the training base for the WASP. Word traveled quickly about the beautiful women pilots and within the first week over 100 young male pilots made "forced landings" at Avenger to see for themselves. The base command quickly put an end to this practice. At Avenger, WASP trainees lived six to a room in barracks and received basic training similar to male aviation cadets, including calisthenics, marching, inspections and classes on military protocol. Training was divided between a half a day of ground school and half a day of flight practice.

At ground school, WASPs studied Morse code, navigation, engine assembly, radio communications and weather theory. They practiced flying blind in storm conditions or deep fog using LINK instrument trainers (flight simulators).

Flight training, first with an instructor and then solo, included practice with takeoffs, landings, spins and stalls. WASPs trained on a succession of aging aircraft, from open cockpit primary trainers (PT-17s or PT-19As) to basic trainers (BT-13 Vultee Vibrators) to advanced army and navy trainers (AT-6s) to dual-engine planes (AT-17 twin-engine Cessnas). To graduate, trainees had to successfully learn to fly single-engine and twin-engine planes and become proficient in night and instrument flying. A civilian check pilot and an army check pilot tested the WASPs after each level of training and "washed out" anyone who could not meet the standard. "I would sit by the hour in the cockpit blindfolded (on the ground, of course), touching various things in the 'busy' cockpit as one of my classmates tested me," recalled Bee Falk, a twin-engine utility pilot. "We would do these things in our free time so we were proficient in locating any item in the cockpit without having to look down."

After seven and a half months of training and over 200 hours of training flights, the WASPs graduated. Success was well-deserved; of the 25,000 women who applied to the WASP, only 1,830 were accepted for training and 1,074 earned their wings.

Nancy Harkness Love (top), *founder of the Women's Auxiliary Ferrying Squadron (WAFS). When the WAFS merged into the WASP, Love became the head of ferrying division.*

Jacqueline Cochran (above), *head of the Women's Flying Training Detachment (WFTD), became director of the Women Airforce Service Pilots.*

Women Airforce Service Pilots

WASP Wilda
Winfield (right) with an instructor flies on a photographic mission at Frederick Army Air Field, Oklahoma.

Barbara Erickson
(below, in cockpit) and Evelyn Sharp, two of the original WAFS. Erickson was awarded the Air Medal for ferrying aircraft 8,000 miles (40 flying hours) in just five days—as much as most ferry pilots flew in a month. Sharp, the WAFS pilot with the most flying hours, died in April 1944 when the engine of her P-38 failed on takeoff. Her hometown of Ord, Nebraska named its airport Evelyn Sharp Field in her honor.

After graduation, WASPs went on to specialized training and a wide range of air support jobs. About a quarter of the graduates worked in Nancy Love's ferrying division, delivering military aircraft to training bases and overseas shipping points. One day a woman might fly a B-26 bomber, the next day a single-engine fighter with a cockpit so tiny she could only carry a small bag of necessities.

Florene Miller found a way to cope: "I always liked to turn into a girl any chance I could," she said, "so I would put a shoe in one of the ammunition boxes out on the wings. . . I'd carry a Phillips screwdriver in my pocket, unscrew the lid, fill it up . . . another shoe over here . . . another skirt over here."

Among other tasks, WASPs had the hazardous jobs of flying aircraft to repair depots and taking war-weary planes to the junk yard. On these flights, worn tires could suddenly explode on the runway or decaying fuel could cause a fatal stall.

WASPs were often the first to fly new aircraft from the factory. With the possibility of inexperienced workmanship or sabotage from traitors or disgruntled employees, the women inspected each plane carefully, opening the plates and checking the cables before taking off. "We learned never to trust gauges, and never trust the flight line attendant," recalled Kay Gott, who shuttled P-51 fighters from the assembly line at Hensley Field. "Planes were always coming and going. . . . It was *your* life."

A few WASPs discovered sabotage by chance. After flying a P-38 from Dallas to Amarillo, Ruth Dailey stopped overnight in Denver, where it snowed. The next day "the head man on the flight line said I wasn't going anywhere. They found the sump frozen solid. . . investigators said it was water in the gasoline."

Troop training support was another WASP duty. Flying in A-24 Dauntlesses, women pilots towed target sleeves for anti-aircraft gunners to shoot at with live ammunition. Women also flew smoke-laying raids, nighttime search and tracking missions, and simulated bombing and strafing runs. To train glider pilots, WASPs in 6-pilot crews flew huge C-60s, towing and releasing gliders. At training schools, they worked as instructors and instrument trainers for male cadets. They also served as transport pilots for cargo, weapons and non-flying officers.

Thirty-eight WASPs died during the war—11 in training and 27 on active duty. Even the most experienced pilots did not always make it. Cornelia Fort, who had dodged the Japanese at Pearl Harbor, crashed in March 1943 after a male pilot came too close in formation and clipped her wing. As civil service employees, women pilots were not eligible for military death benefits; fellow WASPs sometimes had to chip in to send their bodies home.

The lack of status and benefits angered Jackie Cochran, who wanted the WASP militarized as part of the Army Air Forces. In 1944, Gen. Arnold submitted legislation to Congress, but the bill was voted down. Public support was lacking; male pilots were returning from Europe and would be sent to the Pacific for infantry if their pilot skills could not be utilized.

With this defeat, Hap Arnold issued a surprise order to deactivate the WASP as of December 20, 1944. The women were stunned and unprepared for the news. Most believed the program would run until the end of the war. "It was such a traumatic thing to get dismissed, disbanded when we were so useful, so needed," said pilot Kay Gott. The WASPs went home—most to non-flying jobs. Airlines offered them work as stewardesses, not pilots. And although they went on to active and interesting pursuits, those two years of challenge, camaraderie, freedom and flight were glittering days—the most fulfilling time of their lives.

Air Emergency: Florene Miller

"I was flying at night with a sick airplane, low on gas, not knowing the status of my gear, no radio, the first day I had flown on the plane, and never having made a night landing before."

Florene Miller, one of the original 25 WAFS, was attracted to flight since childhood. At the age of eight she rode in a barnstormer, and by the time she was in college she was piloting her family's two-seater Luscomb. When her father and brother were killed in a plane crash, she decided to keep on flying. By 1943, Miller was at Love Field in Dallas, commanding a small contingent of WAFS who ferried everything from trainers to bombers.

One Sunday, while learning to fly the large, heavy P-47 fighter, she came close to meeting the same fate as her father and brother. Approaching the landing strip with the setting sun in her eyes, she struck a utility pole and felt a violent vibration. "The nose of the plane shot up and the plane started to roll on its back," she said. She quickly righted the fighter and found herself hurtling straight toward a hangar. With power just above stall speed, she cleared the top of the building and headed out of the city.

The P-47 climbed slowly and she had to cross the controls to fly straight. One wing was damaged, part of the tail was gone and she had no radio contact. She started to bail out, but hesitated because the plane was still functional. She tested the controls and thought she could land. By now it was dark and she was low on fuel. She flew back to Love Field, but it had vanished! (She had knocked out the lights at the airport when she hit the pole.) "I had a sick, desperate feeling," she said. Just then a repairman at Love Field picked her up on the radio. He telephoned the control tower and got car headlights aimed at the ends of the runway to guide her in. "I pulled the throttle back . . . and the plane landed like a big rock," she said. When she got out she discovered that high voltage wires had melted part of the propeller, and the belly of the plane was ripped open from nose to tail.

Red Cross Relief Efforts

Red Cross women *in Seattle (right) prepare gift boxes of dried fruit, candy, gum and cigarettes for GIs stationed overseas. During the war, volunteers prepared millions of gift and food packages for refugees, soldiers, POWs and civilian internees.*

After the attack on Pearl Harbor, civilians across the country flooded Red Cross chapters, wanting to do something to help. With a critical demand for its services, the Red Cross, a nonmilitary relief and disaster response organization, gladly signed on seven million volunteers—more than half of them women—for everything from driving for the motor corps to providing first aid training for Civilian Defense workers.

On the home front, the Red Cross Production Division amassed great quantities of medical and comfort items for distribution. Red Cross women rolled an incredible 2.5 billion surgical dressings. In assembly plants in the East and Midwest, in community halls and around kitchen tables, women made clothing for refugees, sewed and filled 16 million "ditty bags" with comfort items like food, candy, gum, cigarettes and hand-knitted sweaters for soldiers, and assembled life-sustaining food packages for POWs and civilian internees in enemy hands. Margaret Sherk, an internee at Santo Tomás in the Japanese-held Philippines, remembered with joy the 48 pound Red Cross food packages

she and her children received in late 1943—the first of two allowed them during the war: "There was every good thing imaginable to eat . . . chocolate, coffee, cheese, jam, Spam and a kind of butter that was wonderful," she recalled. "I wonder if anyone who was not there can realize what that much food meant to us. I am positive, had we not received that comfort kit, many hundreds of us would have been dead long before the Americans returned."

The Red Cross not only provided parcels, the Home Service Division also handled important messages and provided financial assistance to service people and military families in trouble. Some 42 million Red Cross messages advised service members of births, weddings, deaths or illnesses in the family. Families received word through the Red Cross about wounded sons or daughters, and about conditions in POW and internee camps. They also, on occasion, received brief messages from POWs. One cablegram from 21 U.S. airmen in a POW camp in Germany had the same message for each of their wives: "Now a prisoner of war. Has the baby come yet?"

For GIs on mandatory leave and soldiers in isolated military posts throughout the country, the Red Cross set up canteens and organized parties, baseball games and dances for entertainment. Organizers called on local young women to round out the activities. In Miami Beach, Red Cross coordinator Billie Banks Doan reported, "If you were going to have a dance you ordered so many girls, so many cases of beer."

On a more serious mission, the Red Cross Nursing Service recruited nurses throughout the war, and certified qualified individuals for service in the Army and Navy Nurse Corps. As home front nurses joined up, the newly created Nurse's Aide Corps filled the shortages in civilian hospitals by performing basic tasks to free up nurses. In addition, Gray Ladies helped hospital staff, cheered patients, and arranged games and recreation in U.S. military hospitals.

Blood drives were perhaps the most vital of all Red Cross services. Through its Blood Donor Service, the Red Cross collected 13.4 million units of blood in cities and rural areas across the United States. Over six million Americans donated their blood, an act that made some feel they were contributing directly to the welfare of loved ones. One navy wife who donated blood five times arrived home to the news that her husband was seriously wounded in the Pacific, and his life had been saved by five successive blood transfusions.

The Red Cross processed large amounts of blood into dried plasma, an easily portable, long-storing dried powder that medics in the field could reconstitute with distilled water. Plasma was a tremendous lifesaver on the battlefield where medical corpsmen used it on the wounded to prevent shock. Field hospitals and hospital ships then administered whole blood transfusions to seriously wounded GIs.

Red Cross volunteers provided many important services during the war, but the real test of their disaster preparedness in

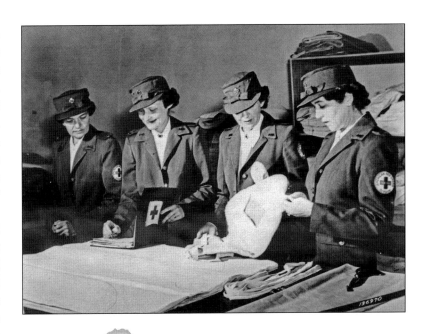

The Hawaiian Islands

the U.S. came on December 7, 1941, when the Japanese attacked Pearl Harbor. Within 24 hours of the attack, the Hawaiian Red Cross registry marshalled 1,000 nurses and first aid team workers—most of them women—to staff first aid stations and treat the tidal wave of casualties that flowed into the civilian and military hospitals. Red Cross volunteers quickly set up canteens at key locations to feed refugees and disaster responders. During the initial blackout they served sandwiches and hot coffee by flashlight; later they furnished full meals to thousands in 24-hour shifts.

In addition, women of the Motor Corps delivered surgical dressings and medical supplies to the hospitals, and evacuated civilians trapped in bombed areas around Pearl Harbor and Hickam Field. Driving family cars in Hawaii's first total blackout, corpswomen traversed streets so dark that they risked head-on collisions. The city buzzed with tension and jittery guards fired at the slightest sound, adding to the dangers on the roads. On the night of the attack, the Motor Corps worked until 3 a.m., transporting 3,000 refugees to safety.

Red Cross workers (above) in Hawaii inspect gas mask hoods in April 1942. After the Pearl Harbor attack, the Red Cross distributed gas masks on Oahu, as protection in the event of a further Japanese strike.

Overseas with the Red Cross

Red Cross women served overseas in more than 50 countries during World War II. Traveling to troop encampments, clubmobiles (right) staffed by two to four women, cranked out coffee and an amazing 1.6 million fresh doughnuts during the war for hungry GIs. Similarly, cinemobiles, with projectors and a fold-down stage, brought movies and live entertainment to isolated units. Red Cross women drove in daylight, darkness and pouring rain, sometimes dangerously close to enemy lines, to bring food, music and a touch of "the girl next door" to soldiers in the field.

Servicemen (opposite) make Christmas cards at a Red Cross club in Kunming, China. Clubs provided food, games, activities, and sometimes overnight accommodations for GIs.

PACIFIC
Bataan — Manila
Philippines
Australia

While volunteers worked feverishly in Hawaii, Red Cross personnel across the Pacific in the Philippines scrambled to respond to the destruction of the Japanese attack there. On December 30, 1941, with U.S. and Filipino forces in retreat to Bataan, and Manila Harbor blasted and burned, the American Red Cross quickly outfitted the only craft available, the decrepit interisland steamer *Mactan*, as an escape vessel for wounded soldiers left in Manila. Without detailed charts or a guarantee of safe passage, *Mactan*, its small staff of Red Cross nurses and doctors and 224 wounded GIs, journeyed 25 days through enemy waters to safety in Australia.

Disaster responders in the Philippines and Hawaii were among the first Red Cross women to face dangers in the war zone. During World War II, some 12,000 to 13,500 Red Cross women served overseas, many of them in field hospitals and clubmobiles harrowingly close to the front. Fifty-six Red Cross women died during the war, the first at Anzio, when German bombs struck the hospital tents.

With a minimum age of 25 and college education, women who went overseas with the Red Cross not only furnished recreational and hospitality services, but also symbolized "home" to soldiers in the field. "Wherever we were sent," clubmobile worker Rosemary Langheldt recalled, "we were expected to be the friend, the girl next door, the kid sister, the funny aunt, mom, adviser, sympathizer."

To provide leisure to GIs, the Red Cross staffed and supplied 1,800 recreational sites and rest homes overseas. Service clubs ranged from large, spacious facilities in major cities with meals, entertainment, and accommodations to smaller canteens on the outskirts of military camps, or even tiny recreation huts in places like New Guinea. The giant Rainbow Corner Club in London served 60,000 meals a day. In contrast, in Kunming, China, which recreation workers reached by flying four hours at 14,000 feet without oxygen over the jagged peaks of the Himalayas, service club staff scrounged the countryside for food to serve in the airfield canteen.

Clubmobiles and cinemobiles, converted half-ton trucks and buses fitted out as canteens or traveling entertainment centers, took food, music and movies to soldiers in the field. Women traveled to where the troops were bivouacked, fired up their coffee and doughnut-making equipment, turned on the record player, and passed out hot refreshments. They often worked beyond their jobs, for example, staying late on the docks in England at Christmastime to laugh and listen to soldiers shipping out to the Battle of the Bulge; or following troops all the way to the front in Italy, because there wasn't enough time to serve the *entire* division in the safe zone.

Working near the battle front was also part of the job for Red Cross workers at evacuation and field hospitals, who provided social work, medical aid, recreational activities and comfort items to wounded soldiers. Frieda Wolff, posted in an evacuation hospital in France, met every litter coming in from the battlefield: "I stayed up for four days without going to bed . . . to talk to them as soon as they came in and offer to write a letter or send word or something they'd want."

The hours were long, the experiences life-changing. In the end, the women of the Red Cross overseas remembered the "laughter and tears, camaraderie and loneliness" and, as entertainer Eileen O'Leary put it, the feeling of being part of a family "doing all we could to win the war."

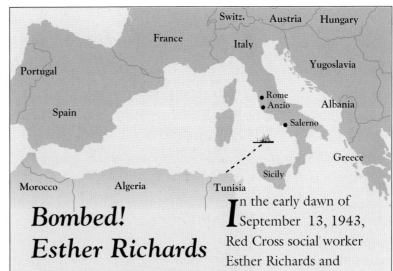

Bombed! Esther Richards

In the early dawn of September 13, 1943, Red Cross social worker Esther Richards and medical personnel aboard the HMHS *Newfoundland* (below) scrambled for their lives. The German *Luftwaffe* had just bombed the hospital ship, despite its clear medical insignia. Richards, a former World War I nurse in her mid-fifties who served with the American Red Cross in North Africa, was in transit to the Italian front when the bomb struck. Thrown out of bed by the blast, she crawled with bleeding cuts on her forehead and an injured back, through the debris of crashing walls to escape.

After recuperating in North Africa, Richards requested to return to the front and was sent to the besieged Anzio beachhead to help wounded GIs at the 95th Evacuation Hospital. Working among the casualties, she provided not only medical aid, but also counseled wounded soldiers who had lost limbs and were anxious about the reactions of their wives and families. In addition, she sometimes took on extra duties, helping recreation workers.

Within days of her arrival at Anzio, the Germans shelled the hospital. On February 7, 1944, a bomb struck the medical tent, critically wounding Esther Richards. Medical personnel rushed her to surgery. She died on the operating table, the first American Red Cross woman in World War II killed in action. Secretary of War Henry Stimson awarded her the Purple Heart posthumously.

Army and Navy Nurses

African American nurses (right) arrive in Scotland after their voyage across the Atlantic. In June 1944, 63 black nurses were sent to England to care for German POWs at the 168th Station Hospital. The Army Nurse Corps maintained quotas for "colored" nurses and accepted only 479 during the war. Black nurses served in segregated units in the United States, Liberia, Burma, England and the Pacific. The Navy Nurse Corps did not accept African American nurses until 1945.

Fire rages along Battleship Row at Pearl Harbor (top opposite) just after the Japanese attack on December 7, 1941. The hospital ship, Solace, was moored not far from these ships.

A wing from a Japanese "Kate" torpedo bomber (bottom opposite) shot down in the first attack wave on December 7th. The plane crashed on the grounds of the U.S. Naval Hospital at Pearl Harbor.

More than any other women's service, army and navy nurses experienced the intensity and the danger of combat, serving at frontline hospitals, on medical ships and evacuation planes in every theater of war. Caring for grievously injured soldiers, staunching shrapnel wounds, working to save torn limbs, treating "jungle rot," and delivering psychiatric care to men suffering battle fatigue, they saw the devastation and the cost of war with indelible sharpness.

Headed by Col. Julia O. Flikke (Army Nurse Corps) and Capt. Sue S. Dauser (Navy Nurse Corps), military nurses served in many capacities, including as surgical nurses, anesthetists, and psychiatric nurses. Also with military medical teams were dieticians, physical therapists and occupational therapists. From a force of fewer than 2,000 in 1941, the nurse corps grew to 59,000 army nurses and 14,178 navy nurses before war's end. Their service brought them satisfaction and a closeness that came from working together under difficult conditions to save lives. In spite of their crucial role, however, military nurses did not receive commissioned officer rank

or benefits until 1944.

In contrast to the nurses, fewer than 100 female doctors served in the military during the war. Although male physicians were in short supply and 3,000 women were eligible, the military refused to enlist women doctors for medical combat teams and limited women to attending to female WAC and WAVES units. Opponents feared that female surgeons would be "too emotional" under pressure, or that male soldiers might feel embarrassed if examined by a woman doctor.

Apparently this was not a concern for the tens of thousands of female nurses who regularly treated male soldiers at base hospitals and POW camps in the U.S. and overseas. Working under wartime shortages, nurses relegated non-nursing chores to corpsmen and took on increased responsibilities, often performing procedures formerly done only by doctors. Their rise in status brought long lasting value and respect to the nursing profession. More than 250 military nurses died on active duty in World War II and 84 nurses—five on Guam, 78 in the Philippines and one in Germany—were taken prisoners of war.

Nurses at Pearl Harbor
"We were too Busy to be Afraid"

On December 7, 1941 when the Japanese attacked Pearl Harbor, 119 army and navy nurses were stationed at five military hospitals on Oahu. As the first bombs struck, army nurses at Hickam Field, Schofield Barracks and Tripler General Hospital, and navy nurses at the Naval Hospital and the hospital ship, *Solace*, raced to their posts. For the next three days, alongside civilian nurses and doctors, they worked ceaselessly to save the lives of over 1,100 men. At the Naval Hospital on a point overlooking the harbor, a flaming Japanese bomber flew directly toward the main hospital building, then swerved and crashed outside the laboratory. Casualties began to flow in: men with gunshot wounds, legs torn off by explosions, burned bodies covered with black oil. Amid the stench of charred flesh, nurses and doctors worked feverishly to assess the injuries in triage, give morphine, blood transfusions, and operate on the seemingly endless stream of blast victims. In the harbor on *Solace*, launches went out to pick men out of the burning waters while the bombs were still falling. Fortuitously, the hospital ship was not hit, and nurses worked through the night to care for more than 300 burn victims.

OAHU
HAWAII

Schofield

Solace

Naval
Hospital • • Tripler
    • Hickam

Nearby, at heavily-bombed Hickam Field, seven army nurses struggled to give first aid to hundreds of casualties. Most were sent on to Tripler, where the entry stairs were spattered with blood and wounded men lined the corridors, awaiting surgery. Here the wounded suffered mainly from shock and hemorrhages. Nurses gave morphine and tetanus shots, and with no time for paperwork, marked M and T on patients' foreheads. Up island, at Schofield Barracks, meanwhile, a Japanese plane strafed the hospital. An "inexhaustible" number of wounded streamed in from Schofield and Wheeler Field, and nurses struggled to separate the living from the dead. Nine operating rooms worked nonstop. "I kept hearing planes overhead," said nurse Mildred Clark, "but we were too busy to be afraid or to ask what was happening."

"We heard a plane coming down . . . between the two wards. I rushed to the window. . . . There were big, red, round [Rising Suns] on the wings and on the body of the plane. . . . He crashed right there."

—Lenore Terrell, navy nurse
Naval Hospital, Pearl Harbor

Angels of Bataan and Corregidor

PACIFIC

Luzon
Philippines

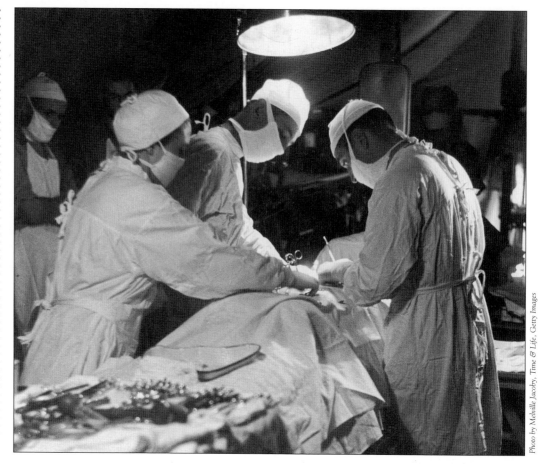

Army nurse Ethel Thor, Dr. Jack Schwartz and Dr. Paul Roland (left to right) operate on a wounded soldier in a tent at Hospital No. 2 on beleaguered Bataan. The surgical arena had only minimal shelter. Most of the 6,000 patients had no cover at all and lay on cots in the open jungle. Without serum to treat gangrene, doctors sliced open and cleaned the wounds, and let the sun and oxygen kill the bacteria. Medical teams did what they could with scarce supplies and little food. "Within yourself you felt angry, because we didn't have more to make them comfortable when we were working on them," said nurse Ethel Thor, "anesthetic . . . anything to relieve the pain." (Photo by Melville Jacoby.)

Malinta Tunnel hospital lateral (bottom opposite) on Corregidor.

The 88 army nurses and 12 navy nurses in the Philippines awoke to the news of the assault on Pearl Harbor only to find their own island, Luzon, under Japanese attack by midday. For the next three weeks, Japanese war planes pounded the airfields and Manila. Army nurses at Ft. Stotsenberg, Camp John Hay, Ft. McKinley and Sternberg General scrambled to treat the river of casualties. At Cañacao Naval Hospital, navy nurses dived into foxholes while bombers flattened the Navy Yard.

The invaders advanced quickly, and on Christmas Eve U.S. forces retreated to Bataan and Corregidor, taking the army nurses and one navy nurse. Japanese attackers besieged the troops on Bataan. Working from two jungle hospitals, nurses and doctors treated a nightmarish flow of patients with head wounds, abdominal trauma, amputations, gangrene, malaria, dysentery, and malnutrition. Japanese bombs struck Hospital No. 1 twice, killing and wounding hundreds of patients. At Hospital No. 2, a jungle clearing where snakes hung from the bamboo and mango trees, patients lay on cots in the open and nurses worked continuously, on half rations and with almost no anesthetics, to treat the mangled combatants.

Japanese shells were coming closer. With Bataan about to fall, the nurses evacuated, through roads choked with retreating troops, across the channel to Corregidor. Underground, in the stagnant air of the hospital lateral of Malinta Tunnel, they cared for new wounded while a constant Japanese bombardment shook Corregidor. Even the "Impregnable Rock" could not hold out indefinitely. Under cover of darkness, the army sent out 31 of the nurses on two PBY seaplanes and the submarine *Spearfish*. On May 6, 1942 Gen. Wainwright surrendered to the Japanese. Among those taken prisoner were 55 army nurses and 15 American civilian women. Gen. Wainwright called the nurses the "Angels of Bataan and Corregidor."

Besieged in the Jungle: Ethel Thor

Clark Field □
Ft. Stotsenberg

Japanese Advance

Sternberg

BATAAN

MANILA BAY

Manila

• Limay

Hospital No.1 □ □ **Hospital No. 2**

Mariveles

Cañacao

Corregidor

When Ethel Thor, a 29-year-old army nurse from Tacoma, Washington took up duty at Sternberg General Hospital in Manila in 1939, the relaxed, tropical post was a plum assignment. All that changed on December 8, 1941. Within hours after the first Japanese bombing raids, casualties overflowed the hospitals. At Sternberg General where Ethel worked in surgery, the number of wounded appeared endless. "We were so busy we didn't have time to be worried," she said.

On Christmas Eve, the nurses evacuated from Sternberg. In the dark hours before daylight, Ethel and 18 other nurses crossed Manila Bay to Bataan on a ferry carrying medical supplies to set up Hospital #2. Just after their ferry reached the wharf and the nurses scrambled ashore, Japanese bombers attacked. When the raid ended, their ferry was sunk. The next evening they arrived at the site for Hospital #2, a primitive clearing in the jungle near the Real River. As casualties surged in, bulldozers cleared new sections of the jungle for wards. Patients lay in the open forest on cots or mats under the trees. Supplies of food were critically short, with only enough for two meals, and later, one meal a day. Ethel did her best to adjust. With the other nurses, she slept outside under mosquito netting and bathed in a nearby creek (". . . a godsend. We didn't care who was looking!") At times there were

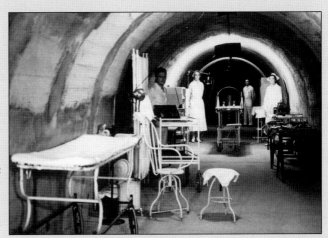

Ethel Thor

snakes or rats. "One day we had flying ants. You couldn't even see anything in front of you," she said. Thousands of wounded flooded the rustic hospital. With scarce medicine, the nurses and doctors worked amid the sounds of exploding bombs and artillery fire. Sometimes shrapnel and stray bullets struck the hospital and the nurses dashed for foxholes. "You were working and trying to do the best you could," said Ethel. "You had to sterilize things. You'd just wonder how you'd get through it all."

On April 8, 1942, the Japanese came within three miles of Hospital #2. Bataan was about to fall and the army ordered the nurses to evacuate to Corregidor. It was devastating to walk away, leaving the patients, doctors, and corpsmen behind. "It was really heartbreaking," Ethel said. "You just feel that awful pain within yourself. Nothing you could do to help." Refugees and soldiers clogged the roads. Explosions lit the night. "There was so much confusion," she said. It took Ethel's group all night to travel the few

miles to the bay. When they arrived, the boats had gone. The surrender of Bataan was official. After two hours, a launch came and they crossed, zigzagging, under attack by planes, with bombs exploding around the boat.

One month later, Corregidor fell. In Malinta Tunnel, Ethel and other American women, fearing they might be killed, wrote their names on a piece of cloth (see p. 1) before the Japanese came in. "We wondered what was going to happen," she said. She did not foresee then that she would spend the next three years as a prisoner of war.

(see p. 1)

Tending the Sick in Captivity

Navy nurse, Margaret Nash, (right) attends to a patient in the hospital at Santo Tomás Internment Camp.

"Most of us were sick with malaria and dysentery, and lived in a crowded room where our beds were about two inches apart. We just worked and did the best we could day by day."

Evelyn Whitlow army nurse, Santo Tomás

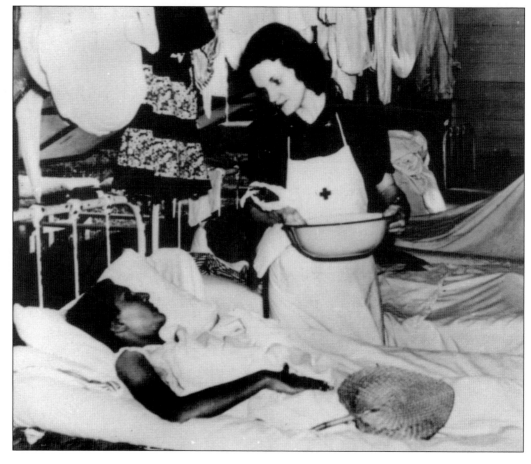

When the last army nurses evacuated from Manila to Bataan and Corregidor, 11 navy nurses were left in the city. The 11 nurses, who had been stationed around Manila after the bombing at Cañacao Naval Hospital, gathered at Santa Scholastica College and waited for evacuation orders, but none came. On January 2nd, the Japanese took the city, and within days arrived to inspect the hospital set up at Santa Scholastica. "They really didn't believe we had patients," said navy nurse, Mary Rose Harrington, "and we had to take the dressings off to show them the wounds." Under the eye of Japanese guards, the nurses continued to care for patients for the next two months. The occupying army could not decide what to do with them. Finally, in early March, the Japanese sent them to the civilian internment camp at Santo Tomás University where the nurses quickly volunteered their services at the camp hospital.

Meanwhile, in April, on besieged Corregidor, 31 army nurses and Ann Bernatitis, the one navy nurse with the army, escaped on two PBY seaplanes and a submarine. Only 21 of the nurses reached Australia, however. On a stop for refueling in Mindanao, one of the PBYs hit a rock on takeoff, leaving ten of the army nurses stranded. Eleven days later, the invading army captured the women and took them to a military hospital. There, the nurses cared for patients until September, when the Japanese shipped them to Santo Tomás.

In addition, two other army nurses, Ruby Bradley and Beatrice Chambers, were not with the main group on Corregidor. They were stationed 200 miles north of Manila at Camp John Hay in Baguio—the first place the Japanese bombed. On December 22nd, they evacuated with the army for Bataan, but U.S. cavalry was no match for Japanese tanks, and at Balete Pass they were forced to scatter. Chambers, Bradley and a doctor took off together. "There were sawmills in the mountains and we tried to hide in them, but the Japanese were like ants up there, and after four days they found us," Chambers said. "They took us on a three-day march back to Camp John Hay, without food or water. It was terrible. They put us in a school, lined us up to execute us, then changed their minds." Eventually, they herded them into internment with about 500 civilians.

At overcrowded Camp John Hay and later, Camp Holmes, the lack of food, water and other necessities made basic sanitary procedures paramount. Doctors, the two army nurses and civilian nurses established a rudimentary hospital, and with homemade soap and smuggled surgical instruments, treated everything from dysentery to an appendectomy. Among the doctors were two women: Dr. Dorothy Kinney Chambers and Dr. Beulah Ream Allen, an expectant mother with a young toddler. Dr. Allen was successful at coaxing vital hospital supplies from the Japanese command.

Back in Manila, conditions at the poorly equipped hospital at Santo Tomás were also difficult as the 11 navy nurses struggled to provide care. On July 2, 1942, the Japanese shipped the 55 army nurses, two dieticians and one physiotherapist captured on Corregidor to Santo Tomás. The exhausted army nurses spent their first six weeks in isolation. "I guess the Japs thought of it as a silent debriefing period," said army nurse Hattie Brantley. "They wanted us to forget all the horror and atrocities we'd seen, and not mention them to the internees in the camp."

Once they entered the main camp in August, the formidable chief army nurse, Maude Davison, persuaded the Japanese to allow the nurses to establish a new 65-bed hospital to treat the growing population of up to 4,000 internees. With rationed medicines supplied by the Red Cross, the hospital treated the illnesses of captivity: plague, pellagra, beriberi, dengue fever, malaria, tropical ulcers, and

near the end of the war, starvation. The nurses came down with many of the diseases they treated. Food was scarce, living conditions crowded. "Every year it became worse," said army nurse Madeline Ullom. "Our rations were cut back whenever the U.S. took over another island." Bertha Dworsky recalled, "If you gave up hope, you would have just folded up and died."

By May 1943, the population of the camp had grown beyond capacity. When the Japanese established a new, rustic camp in the country at Los Baños Agricultural College, the navy nurses, led by Lt. Laura Cobb, volunteered to set up a hospital there. They shipped out with 800 men, crammed in boxcars in the stifling heat, and arrived to find nothing but empty cottages and a hospital stripped of medical supplies. "We started improvising," said Margaret Nash. Nurses boiled and cut up old mosquito nets for dressings, and an internee tapped a rubber tree for adhesive. Men made basins from beaten corrugated tin, and bed frames from iron pipes. Under extreme conditions, the nurses cared for the sick and malnourished. By early 1945, starvation was widespread and the interned nurses and civilians waited, wondering if they would survive until liberation.

Army nurses (below) and the chief navy nurse, Laura Cobb, in a Japanese photo taken at Santo Tomás in early 1943. Back row, left to right: Laura Cobb, Earleen Allen Francis, Edith Schacklette, Anne Wurts, Rita Palmer, Sallie Durrett, and Inez McDonald. Front row: Jeanne Kennedy, Helen Gardner, Adele Foreman, and Ethel Thor. Without adequate medical supplies, the nurses reused and improvised, unraveling hemp to make sutures and laboriously sterilizing surgical sponges.

Stations on the Lifeline

Navy hospital ship, Solace *(right). Nurses on hospital ships cared for as many as 500 to 800 wounded men at any given time. Serving in the waters around Europe and in the Pacific, hospital ships risked aerial and torpedo attacks. Although clearly marked with red cross insignia, German planes bombed Allied hospital ships in the Mediterranean, and a Japanese kamikaze struck USS* Comfort *in the Pacific near Okinawa, killing 26, including six army nurses.*

*L*ike the nurses in captivity, army and navy nurses who followed the troops in combat zones, needed skill, adaptability and "guts" as they worked the chain of evacuation that treated the wounded from battlefield to recovery.

Closest to the fighting, in tents, were nurses at mobile field hospitals and evacuation hospitals. These were the first stops for casualties after the battlefield aid station. Just behind the troops, often within the sound of artillery fire, a typical field hospital had 18 nurses caring for 150 patients. Doctors and nurses met the incoming wounded in triage to determine priority, and sent critical patients directly to the operating tent, and those strong enough to travel to the evacuation hospital a few miles farther from the front, near transportation. An evac hospital might handle as many as 750 patients at any given time. Here, surgeons, supported by 40 to 53 nurses, operated on men with stomach and chest injuries, and evacuated patients needing specialized treatment to station or general hospitals.

Station hospitals, located farther to the rear, had electricity and running water, and were often set up in abandoned or bombed out buildings. Nurses had to scrub and scrounge to make these locations ready to receive wounded. Varied in size, these facilities could hold 250 to 750

patients for as long as six months. Farthest to the rear, non-mobile general hospitals had 1,000 to 5,000 beds for specialized treatments such as orthopedics or facial reconstructions. Nurses at these facilities also cared for GIs with non-battle related illnesses like dysentery and tropical diseases. From here, patients either returned to duty or were sent to the U.S. for long-term care.

Most army and navy nurses worked at home front hospitals, caring for wounded soldiers and enemy POWs sent from overseas, and treating service people and their dependents. This last link in the chain of evacuation would have been impossible to reach, however, without the medical trains, ships and air evacuation planes that transported the casualties from the battle zone.

Army and navy hospital ships served the wounded in two ways: as transport vessels to rear area hospitals, and as floating emergency centers for casualties at amphibious assaults such as the D-Day invasion of Normandy and the Pacific island campaigns. At the outbreak of war in 1941, the U.S. Navy had only two hospital ships: *Relief* and *Solace*. By 1945, the navy hospital fleet numbered 15 ships—including three staffed by army medical personnel—and the army had 29 hospital vessels. Painted white, with large red

Patients await transport under the wing of an evacuation plane in Sicily (left). Flight nurse training included crash survival, parachute drills, simulated strafing attacks, and skills such as how to stabilize patients at high altitudes, or treat air sickness in men with jaw injuries.

A navy nurse (below) tends a patient on the hospital ship, Solace, at Saipan.

The physio-therapy clinic at the 113th General Hospital in Ahwaz, Iran (bottom). Located at least 70 miles from the front lines, general hospitals were able to perform difficult diagnoses, laboratory tests, therapy, and specialized surgeries not available at smaller hospitals near the combat zone.

crosses, and lit up day and night, medical ships were protected from attack by the Hague and Geneva conventions, although as with the red cross marked field and evac hospitals, enemy bombers did not always respect these agreements.

Hospital trains shuttled the wounded on overland routes. Trains usually had one nurse for a car of 32 beds, or one nurse for several cars of ambulatory patients.

Air evacuation planes, staffed by a nurse and a corpsman, flew into battle zones under risky conditions to pick up as many as 25 wounded. Flying without medical insignia (because they also carried in cargo), evac planes had to contend not only with rough weather, but with the bombs and bullets of enemy attackers. Nurses and corpsmen could load an evac plane and be in the air in ten minutes. The first army air evac flights began in the North Africa campaign in February 1943. Navy nurses first flew air evacuation flights in early 1945 in the Pacific and were a critical lifesaver during the Okinawa campaign. All told, 500 army and navy flight nurses served in 31 air transport squadrons worldwide during the war. Of 1,176,048 patients evacuated, only 46 died in flight. Seventeen flight nurses died on duty.

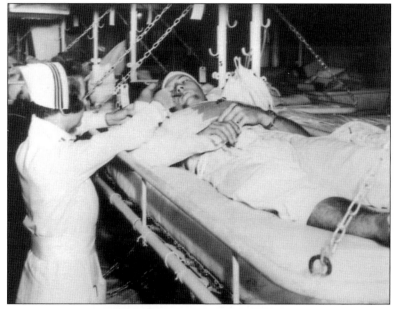

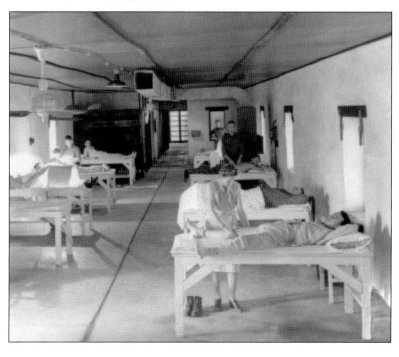

Frontline Nurses: North Africa and Italy

NORTH AFRICA CAMPAIGN

ITALY

Nurses debark on Pantelleria, (right) an island off Sicily. Lessons learned in North Africa led to improved medical techniques in Italy and later campaigns. New treatments included the use of whole blood (instead of plasma) for shock victims, and of the antibiotic, penicillin, for infection.

At dawn on November 8, 1942, in the waters off Oran, Algeria, 60 army nurses of the 48th Surgical Hospital became the first and only U.S. nurses to land with invasion forces. It was the start of the North Africa campaign, a proving ground for troops and medical units alike. The lessons nurses learned here—how to pack and move field hospitals, how to operate under fire—would write the guide for medical care in later campaigns.

Dr. Edward Rosenbaum was with six army nurses that morning. Descending the rope ladder to the assault boats, an artillery shell suddenly blasted a hole above them, and he saw a shocked mirror of his own feelings in the eyes of nurse Vilma Vogler, beside him on the ropes: "At that moment she and the other nurses ceased to be 'the women.' We were all comrades on equally dangerous footing, trying to survive the insanity of combat."

Coping with supply shortages, sandstorms and strafings, the 48th followed Allied troops as they advanced eastward into Tunisia. Each battle tested the new medical evacuation chain as frontline units passed the wounded on to station and general hospitals. In seven months, nurses treated over 3,200 U.S. casualties.

With success in North Africa, Allied troops landed on Sicily on July 10, 1943. Held back from the initial assault, nurses waded ashore three days later under a roar of navy guns. The five-week campaign for mountainous Sicily was marked by intense heat and malaria amid the battle casualties.

Next came southern Italy. On September 13, 1943, en route to invasion beaches near Salerno, 103 U.S. nurses escaped into lifeboats when a German bomber destroyed the British hospital ship, *Newfoundland*. For the nurses it was the dark prelude to the Italian campaign, which from Salerno to Anzio, Monte Cassino to Rome, would expose them to some of the most dangerous combat of the entire war.

At Anzio, pinned to a 15-mile wide beachhead behind German lines, conditions at the hospitals, especially "Hell's Half Acre," were so harrowing that patients went AWOL from their beds to return to the "safety" of frontline foxholes. German opposition was unrelenting. On January 24, 1944, two days after the first 200 nurses landed, *Luftwaffe* bombers sank three clearly marked British hospital ships as they evacuated the wounded. Clinging to the wreckage of the *St. David* was army nurse Ruth Hindman, a survivor of the bombed *Newfoundland*.

German artillery shells rained down on the well-marked hospitals on the beachhead as well, where battle wounds, frostbite and trench foot kept nurses working 15-hour shifts. On February 7th, German antipersonnel bombs devastated the 95th Evac Hospital, killing three nurses and 28 others. Three days later, when German shells hit the operating tent at the 33rd Field Hospital, Mary Roberts and her fellow nurses stayed on, under artillery fire, to help patients. "I just did not have the time to stop working," Roberts said. A total of six nurses died at Anzio. In four months at beachhead, U.S. field and evac hospitals treated 33,128 patients.

Escape from Albania

"After three hours I realized the pilots were lost."
—Agnes Jensen, flight nurse en route to Bari, Italy

Army nurses' endurance was put to the test when a 90-minute flight from Catania, Sicily turned into a 800-mile, two-month-long trek for Agnes Jensen and 12 fellow nurses of the 807th Medical Air Evacuation Squadron. On November 8, 1943 en route to Bari, Italy with a group of army medics, their C-53 ran into a winter storm and strayed into enemy territory. Battered by turbulence, pursued by German Messerschmitts, and without radio contact, they crash-landed on a remote, muddy lake bed in the mountains of Albania. Within minutes, Albanian partisans appeared and helped them to an isolated house. That night the flight crew burned the damaged plane to keep it from the Germans.

The partisans guided them to the town of Berat where they split up and hid in various houses. When German Stukas bombed the town, the group fled, inadvertently leaving behind three nurses. Learning of British intelligence agents in eastern Albania, they decided to seek help there. For two weeks they hiked over snow-covered passes, surviving a blizzard, and staying in mountain hamlets. Many in the group suffered from dysentery, pneumonia and frostbite. On December 1st, they reached the British camp and sent a radio message for help. Planes could not land there, so they started for the coast, fortified by British wool socks and army boots. Two weeks into the rugged hike, they had to retreat because of fighting. They radioed for air rescue and waited ten days in a mountain village, but with Germans nearby, the rendezvous had to be aborted. "We watched from our hiding place as a British Wellington bomber and two C-47s circled," said Agnes Jensen. "Watching them leave was just terrible."

Once again, they headed for the coast. On January 8, 1944, in darkness, they hiked the final mountain pass to the sea and rowed out to meet their rescue launch. The next day, they reached Bari. The three nurses left behind remained hidden in Berat until March. Dressed in Albanian clothing, they traveled by car, and then on foot over the mountains to the coast, where they escaped by boat.

Above (left to right) nurses Frances Nelson, Elna Schwant, Agnes Jensen, Lillian Tacina, Jean Rutkowski and Ann Kopsco arrive in Italy after two months trapped in German-occupied Albania. The nurses wore out their boots (right) on their 800-mile trek to escape the country.

Frontline Nurses: France and Germany

EUROPEAN INVASION

Army nurses wade ashore in Normandy (right) in July 1944. During the D-Day invasion, the Army held back nurses, reluctant to expose them to combat dangers. Within a week, however, it was apparent that nurses were vital to the functioning of field hospitals, so the Army ordered them across the English Channel. By summer's end, 6,500 nurses were ashore in Europe. Their presence in the war zone raised morale among the men. As Pfc. Millard Ireland, an infantry soldier wrote to the nurses in a letter to Stars and Stripes, "We men were not given the choice of working on the battlefield or the home front. . . . We are here because we have to be. You are here merely because you felt you were needed."

The sick and wounded soldiers "they would say 'Are you real?' or 'You are wonderful' or 'You are here in hell with us!' "

—Mary Ferrell, army nurse, northern France

On June 6, 1944, D-Day, the Allies landed in northern France and began the massive invasion of Europe. With fierce German resistance, casualties were high. On the first day of fighting alone, nearly 10,000 Allied soldiers were killed, wounded, or captured. Army nurses arrived onshore in Normandy on D-Day plus four. At Utah Beach, nurses of the 45th Field Hospital and the 128th Evac Hospital waded past floating bodies through waist-deep water to the beaches and went to work, stabilizing the wounded and sending them back to England.

In July, while Allied forces fought their way inland through the hedgerows, more medical units arrived in Normandy. Living in tents, nurses followed the army, packing and moving their hospitals frequently. Delays in transport and misdirection of equipment sometimes left nurses sleeping out in the open without supplies. Boredom and long waits alternated with adrenaline-filled scrambles to handle incoming

casualties. The Normandy campaign ended in late July with 125,000 U.S. dead and wounded.

Allied troops pushed eastward through France toward the Siegfried Line, a defensive wall of pillboxes, observation posts, and concrete "dragon's teeth" that extended from The Netherlands to Switzerland. As the battles continued into late fall, cold rains flooded fields and turned the roads to mud. Medical personnel slogged knee-deep through muck, following the troops. Shortages developed, especially in forward hospitals, and exhaustion and exposure took a toll alongside the wounds of war.

With bad roads hampering overland evacuation of the injured, air evac became imperative. Flight nurse Reba Whittle of the 813th Medical Air Evacuation Squadron was en route to the Belgian-German front to pick up wounded on September 27, 1944 when German anti-aircraft fire struck her C-47. The transport plane nose-dived and crashed near Aachen,

Germany. With the plane on fire, Whittle and the crew escaped through a top hatch. German soldiers with rifles surrounded them. They had "surprised look[s] on their faces when they saw a woman," Whittle said. The Germans sent Whittle to a POW camp, where she cared for sick inmates at the prison hospital.

In December 1944, in the thick Ardennes forest along the Belgian border, the Germans launched a huge offensive at the center of Allied line. The attack was so rapid and unexpected in this "Battle of the Bulge" that the 44th and 67th Evac hospitals had to evacuate immediately to stay ahead of the advancing enemy. With 200 of the patients too weak to travel, five nurses of the 67th volunteered to stay overnight while German guns drew nearer. The next day, just hours before the arrival of Axis forces, the army successfully rescued the patients. Battle of the Bulge casualties quickly overwhelmed medical units. In the icy cold, troops were losing limbs to frostbite and trench foot, but more soldiers than ever before were living, thanks to penicillin, the new wonder drug. "As fast as we could evacuate them, more were brought in," recalled army nurse Virginia Grabowski. Nurses took on new responsibilities. "When there wasn't a doctor there to do it, the nurses did it," said Grabowski. "I did blood transfusions, intravenous medications, and even sewed up secondary closure wounds."

By late January 1945, the Germans were in retreat. Allied troops marched swiftly into Germany, with field and evac hospitals relocating every five to ten days. In April 1945, the 96th Evac Hospital became the first to move forward by air. As the war wound down in Germany, hospitals and nurses began to care for survivors: displaced persons, liberated POWs, and local civilians. Throughout the mud and carnage of the Allied invasion, the dedication, skill and the mobility of nurses and their medical units kept casualties in the European Theater to a remarkably low 3.2 percent.

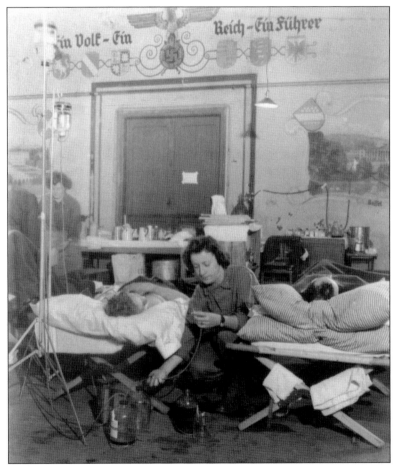

Nurses of the 51st Field Hospital (top) were the first to cross the Rhine in Germany after the U.S. First Army captured the crucial bridge at Remagen.

2nd Lt. Elizabeth *Weston (above) adjusts a surgical drain on a wounded soldier at the 60th Field Hospital in Saint-Max, France, October 1944. Field hospitals frequently occupied buildings vacated by the retreating Germans.*

Frontline Nurses in the Pacific

The Hump (Himalayas) China India Burma
CBI THEATER

The first U.S. Army flight nurses arrive in Kunming, China, December 2, 1943. With the Burma Road cut off by the Japanese, flight nurses flew over the treacherous "Hump" in the Himalayas to pick up Chinese and American wounded in China, and transport them to station and general hospitals in India and Burma. Working in the China-Burma-India Theater required stamina and perseverance as nurses coped with stifling heat, monsoon rains and jungle isolation. Along the Ledo Road, the women lived in bamboo huts with little protection from wild animals. Nurses in remote jungle hospitals struggled to control tropical diseases, and experienced cultural clashes with wounded Chinese soldiers who refused to follow western medical rules.

In contrast to nurses serving near the front lines in Europe and North Africa, "angels of mercy" in the Pacific were held back from combat zones until late in the war. The military kept the women in fenced, guarded compounds near their hospitals, ostensibly to protect them from danger and to discourage sexual harassment or fraternization with the men.

While the Allies fought their way north toward Japan, nurses at station and general hospitals in Hawaii, New Zealand, Australia, Fiji, New Hebrides and New Caledonia treated patients evacuated from the island battles. Only after the Allies secured a combat area did the nurses move forward to those islands. Arriving in March 1942, the first army nurses in New Caledonia were trailblazers for conditions in the South Pacific: tent living, mud, intense heat, and insects. Here, as on most of the islands, admissions for tropical diseases such as malaria, dengue fever, and scrub typhus outnumbered battle wounds five to one.

In October 1942, the first army and navy nurses arrived on secured areas of humid, jungle-laden New Guinea. Conditions were rugged. At the 35th General Hospital barracks at Lae, nurse Clara Wynick recalled, "There were earthquakes and a typhoon, but mostly I remember the mosquitoes and rats. The rats were almost as large as rabbits and we could hear them scurrying over the tops of our mosquito nets."

In late 1944, during the campaign to retake the Philippines, the military finally allowed nurses into the battle zone to care for the wounded. The lifting of restrictions did much to improve nurses' morale, and prompted some who were due for rotation to the U.S. to stay on in the Pacific. Army nurses of the 1st and 2nd field hospitals arrived on Leyte Island in the Philippines on October 20, 1944, just nine days after the invasion.

By the end of 1944, nurses and hospitals had moved on to Saipan and Guam in the Marianas. Arriving on Saipan, shortly after marines secured the island, army nurses of the 369th Station Hospital operated in tent hospitals set up on muddy, rain-soaked earth, and propped up mattresses to protect patients during the many air raids. In early 1945, they treated casualties from the desperate battle at Iwo Jima. Wounded men arrived in severe shock, hemorrhaging, or with devastating burns from kamikaze attacks. "They came in such terrible shape," said Julia Polchlopek. "We just worked until we couldn't move, took a rest somewhere, then went back and worked some more."

Casualties from the fierce, bloody fighting on Okinawa, the last major island in the advance to Japan, also flowed in to Saipan, Guam and Tinian hospitals on evacuation ships and planes. Risking attack during evacuations were army and navy flight nurses who flew long hours to pick up wounded at Iwo Jima or Okinawa and take them to station hospitals. They flew in C-46s, C-47s, or C-54s which doubled as cargo planes, carrying in airmail, ammunition, and other supplies. "Most people don't know that many of the flight nurses carried side arms," said nurse Charlotte McFall. "We were told it was against the Geneva Conventions, but the reason was that flight nurses were in forward areas . . . within hours of the actual fighting. Our planes weren't marked by a red cross and we could have been shot down and had to protect the patients."

Standing just offshore in the Okinawa campaign, army and navy nurses on hospital ships also worked overtime in surgery and in the wards to handle the flood of critically wounded men the small boats brought to them. On April 28, 1945, a Japanese kamikaze plane smashed into the well-marked, 700-bed hospital ship, *Comfort*, while it evacuated a full load of wounded from Okinawa to Guam. The blast drove a fiery hole into the ship's three operating rooms and killed at least 26 people, including six army nurses—the worst disaster in a single day for U.S. nurses in World War II.

Army flight nurse Bernice Harrington of the 801st Air Evac Unit (below), directs the unloading of wounded at Guadalcanal.

Aboard a C-54 medical evacuation flight (bottom) from Guam to Hawaii. Army and navy flight nurses worked 18–20 hour shifts as they flew in from bases on Guam or Saipan to the island battles of Iwo Jima and Okinawa, picked up patients, and returned with a plane load of men with head wounds, chest injuries, burns or emotional trauma. In addition to risking enemy fire, some flight nurses also survived air crashes or flew in hazardous C-46 cargo planes, dubbed "flying coffins" because faulty heaters sometimes caused midair explosions.

PACIFIC
Japan
Okinawa
Iwo Jima
Philippines
Saipan
Guam
New Guinea
Australia

OSS

Embassy spy
Betty Thorpe Pack (above) stole the naval cipher from the Vichy Embassy, providing key advantage to the Allies in North Africa.

The OSS staff
(below) in Kandy, Ceylon included 12 women staffers who served in Research & Analysis, Communications, Special Operations and other positions. Front row, third from right is Cora du Bois, head of the Southeast Asia Command, which organized Resistance movements against the Japanese. Du Bois was one of a few women to attain high ranking positions in the OSS.

Spies, cryptographers and organizers of secret files, the women of the OSS, like army and navy nurses, served in the U.S. and the war zones overseas. The Office of Strategic Services (OSS), headed by William J. "Wild Bill" Donovan, began operations as the U.S. central intelligence office on June 13, 1942. Of the 21,642 staffers in the OSS during World War II, about 4,500 were women. Recruited and trained in secret, the OSS drew its staff from trusted friends, writers, linguists and academics. Although many women recruits had advanced degrees and spoke foreign languages, discrimination within this civilian organization limited most females to low-level secretarial, filing and communications duties. Even so, a number of outstanding women rose to administrative positions, setting their skills to research, analysis, counterintelligence, propaganda, cryptography, mapmaking and the daring work of espionage.

The basement of the OSS building in Washington, D.C. housed the nerve center of the organization. Here, women worked in the secret communications area, coding and decoding messages that supported all OSS operations. In an age with only fledgling computer capabilities, the organizational skill of manually cross-referencing and retrieving information from index cards was of monumental importance. At OSS registries in such places as Ceylon and China, talented women like Julia McWilliams (later known to the world as Julia Child, the French chef) became experts at managing rooms full of top secret intelligence on index cards. In London, the largest overseas station, Katherine Keene and other OSS women experienced wartime shortages, blackouts and bombings while correlating bits of information gathered behind enemy lines. "We painstakingly traced, through factory markings and serial numbers, the production of airplanes, half-tracks, tanks, self-propelled guns, large ammunition and vehicles of all sorts," she said.

More spine-tingling, perhaps, was the work of women espionage agents who risked their lives to obtain covert intelligence. Posing as a pro-Vichy journalist, Betty Thorpe Pack, known as "Cynthia," seduced a Vichy French embassy press attaché and recruited him for the OSS. On successive nights, the two entered the Vichy Embassy in Washington, D.C. for love trysts on a divan in the chancery, while attempting to crack the safe which held the Vichy naval cipher books. After three nights of failed attempts, a guard became suspicious and approached during the operation. Quick-thinking "Cynthia" threw off her clothes and stood naked at the divan in her high heels and pearls. When the guard's flashlight played over her, he fled, embarrassed, affording them the time they needed to steal, copy and replace the naval cipher. With the ability to intercept Vichy messages to the Axis, the Allies successfully launched Operation Torch, the invasion of North Africa.

A very different kind of work took place at OSS Cover and Documentation in London. There, Evangeline Bell and 20 others outfitted undercover agents to go behind enemy lines. With a tailor shop, engravers, and retouch artists, they invented cover stories, forged documents, and provided agents with clothing to fit their new locale. Every detail was important: agents sent to France got shirt buttons sewn with French-style parallel threading. "One mistake and our people could be executed," Bell said. "Their lives depended upon what they wore or carried."

Behind Enemy Lines: Virginia Hall

"The woman who limps is one of the most dangerous Allied agents in France. We must find and destroy her."
— Gestapo communiqué, Lyon, France, 1942

Virginia Hall received the Distinguished Service Cross for "extraordinary heroism" in the OSS.

One of the few OSS women to work behind enemy lines, Virginia Hall, daughter of a wealthy Baltimore family, began her foreign service as a clerk in the U.S. Embassy in Warsaw, Poland in 1931. An ardent sportswoman who had studied in Europe and spoke four languages, Hall was a natural for the foreign service. While stationed at the consulate in Izmir, Turkey she suffered a life-changing accident. On a hunting trip with friends, her gun discharged unexpectedly and she lost her leg below the knee. Within a year she was back at work, serving at the consulate in Venice and walking with a wooden leg. After years of clerical work, however, she found little chance for a woman to move up in the diplomatic service. Denied advancement in 1939 due to her "amputation," she quit and went to Paris.

In September, when war broke out, Hall became an ambulance driver and worked at the front until the Germans invaded France. Battle-hardened and repulsed by the violence against Jews, Hall resolved to somehow continue to work against the Nazis. She traveled to London, then under Blitz bombardment, where one night at a party she made a chance remark about wanting to go back into France. Within days, the British Special Operations Executive (SOE) approached her for undercover service.

In August 1941, she traveled openly to Lyon in unoccupied France, posing as a newspaper stringer for the *New York Post*. Trained in weaponry and evasion tactics, her real mission for the SOE was to set up clandestine Resistance networks to oppose the Nazis. Over the course of 14 months, she located safe houses, secured sites for parachute drops of money and weapons, and helped POWs and downed airmen to escape to England. In November 1942, the Germans occupied Vichy France. With the Gestapo at her heels and her network betrayed by a collaborator, Hall fled over the Pyrenees, hiking a numbing 30 miles over rugged mountain passes, deep with winter snow.

Back in London, she transferred to the OSS, and at age 38, in March 1944, returned to France by boat, landing at night on an isolated Brittany beach. Her identity was well-known to the Gestapo, so she disguised herself as an old peasant woman, with thick woolen skirts, gray hair pulled up in a tight bun and a shuffling gait to cover her limp. Working on farms, herding cows and goats in central France, she reconnoitered the fields for drop zones and radioed observations on German troop movements. Her radio made her especially vulnerable to Gestapo direction finders, and she had to move frequently.

After the Allies landed on D-Day, Hall went to the Haute-Loire district to organize and arm Resistance cells into a unified network. There, with a force that grew to 1,500 fighters, she directed sabotage that blew up bridges, derailed trains, cut communication lines, attacked and killed German troops and captured 800 soldiers. With the Germans in full retreat, Hall had the pleasure of seeing France liberated.

Resistance and Survival

Women caught in war-torn countries faced desperate challenges to survive and evade captivity. Diplomatic repatriation ships extricated a few lucky U.S. nationals from occupied lands, while thousands languished in enemy internment camps. A number of women, through luck or circumstance, eluded capture. Risking death if discovered as they moved from place to place, mothers with children sought ways to escape across enemy lines. Some women stayed and resisted. Under Japanese tyranny in the Philippines, a handful of courageous U.S. women acted to save the lives of hundreds of prisoners of war. In Europe, struggling to thwart Nazi genocide, Resistance women gambled their lives to harbor Jews, act as couriers, spy on troop movements and smuggle Allied airmen out of the country on secret escape routes.

Meanwhile, in spite of restrictive U.S. immigration policies, a handful of American women worked to save the lives of endangered refugees in Vichy France and Italy. When the war came to a close, female correspondents in Europe were among the first to enter the concentration camps and see the inhuman suffering of the Holocaust. Battle-hardened army and navy nurses cared for death camp survivors, liberated POWs, and displaced civilians. As the "rising sun" set in the Pacific, liberated civilians prisoners rejoiced in their freedom. Cities lay in ruins. The war was over. Stunned, weary and elated, the survivors savored this long-awaited day.

A mother (opposite) *seeks refuge with her children during the German invasion of Belgium in 1940.*

Repatriation

The Swedish diplomatic ship, Gripsholm, *(top) was one of two U.S. chartered ships that conducted international exchanges of citizens trapped behind enemy borders. In addition to transporting diplomats and other repatriates, the ships carried desperately needed Red Cross food and medicine packages to civilian internees and prisoners of war.*

"All of us had waited for months for the day of repatriation. . . . Utter strangers made friends of one another at sight, all alike, jubilating in the thought: 'At last we're going home!'"

—Etta Shiber, repatriated prisoner

Caught in Europe and Asia behind enemy lines, U.S. and other Western civilian internees and prisoners of war pinned their hopes on the slim possibility of repatriation on a diplomatic ship. To rescue its trapped nationals, the U.S. State Department chartered the liner *Gripsholm* in 1942, and Britain and the U.S. jointly chartered SS *Drottningholm* from neutral Sweden for use as exchange vessels. Assisting the cause, the International Red Cross took authority for the ships and opened negotiations between opposing countries for the exchange of diplomats, prisoners and internees.

Exchanges began in mid 1942 with Swedish crews operating *Gripsholm* and *Drottningholm.* The ships, traveling under safe conduct arrangements without a convoy, were brilliantly illuminated at night to avoid attack. Each vessel displayed the words SVERIGE (Sweden) and DIPLO-MAT or PROTECTED in bold lettering

along the hull. During the war, *Gripsholm* and *Drottningholm* made 26 voyages as exchange ships and carried over 45,000 passengers. In addition, the ships carried desperately needed Red Cross medicines, concentrated foods, vitamins, blood plasma supplies and mail to Allied internees and POWs.

Gripsholm sailed to Europe and the Orient, conducting exchanges in Göteborg, Sweden and at the neutral Portuguese ports of Lisbon, Lourenço Marques (Mozambique), and Mormugao, Goa (on the west coast of India). *Drottningholm* traveled to European ports as well as to Istanbul and Bombay. For its part in the exchanges, the Axis used *Teia Maru, Asama Maru, Tatsuta Maru, Kamakura Maru* and the Italian ship, *Conte Verde.*

Typically, the ships picked up repatriates at collection points, rendezvoused with the enemy diplomatic ship at a neutral port, exchanged passengers and made the return voyage to their countries.

Each nation negotiated for its desired repatriates. Topping the list were diplomats and high profile prisoners. Others included sick or wounded prisoners, journalists, nurses, missionaries, and businessmen.

One such repatriate, United Press International correspondent Eleanor Packard, left Rome on May 13, 1942 on the last diplomatic train bound for Lisbon. After several months in "polite confinement" in Italy with other American reporters, she was elated to board *Drottningholm* bound for New York.

Aboard the same ship of journalists and diplomats, Etta Shiber had a different story. An American widow in Paris, imprisoned by the Nazis for helping 150 downed British airmen to escape occupied France, she was exchanged for the notorious German "hairdresser" spy, Johanna Hoffman. Ill and semi-starved from harsh treatment at the hands of the Nazis, Shiber traveled by train to the border under the guard of Gestapo agents. "I felt that I was really safe at last when I crossed the gangplank from the dock in Lisbon to the deck of the *Drottningholm*," she said. "The bar, the salons were noisy with the jubilations of men and women. . . . I could feel their elation more strongly perhaps than they did, for, so far as I know, I was the only one who had reached this haven from a Nazi prison cell."

The first exchange with Japan saw U.S. citizens traveling in both directions. Gwen Terasaki, the American wife of a Japanese diplomat at the foreign office in Washington, D.C. chose love and loyalty over personal safety. Unwilling to leave her husband when the United States interned and then exchanged Japanese diplomats, Gwen and her daughter accompanied her husband to Japan. Aboard *Gripsholm* as it left New York in June 1942, Gwen reflected on her parents. "[I] knew it would be years until we could contact them again or they would have news of us." The ship traveled to Rio de Janiero to pick up Japanese diplomats in South America, then crossed the Atlantic to Lourenço Marques, Mozambique where they boarded *Asama Maru* to travel on to Singapore and the austerity of Tokyo. Once in Japan, in addition to enduring the privations of war and surviving Allied bombardment, she was seen as a foreigner from an enemy nation—at best an outcast.

Meanwhile, in China, at Chapei internment center, U.S. journalists Shelley and Carl Mydans, were among the fortunate few selected for repatriation in the second and final exchange with Japan. "We left Chapei on a hot, bright, Chinese morning and rode out the gate to freedom—the luckiest people in the world looking back at the unlucky," Shelley recalled. From Shanghai they sailed on *Teia Maru* to Hong Kong, where more Western internees, including journalists Emily Hahn and Gwen Dew, came aboard. Repatriates from Santo Tomás in Manila and from Saigon joined the passengers, bringing the total to 1,236. After being exchanged in Goa for 1,330 Japanese repatriates, they sailed home to the U.S. on *Gripsholm*.

Repatriates (below) disembark the diplomatic ship, Gripsholm.

"As the two [Japanese] ships eased in next to our Gripsholm I realized my last contact with America was about to be ended. . . . It would be years, if ever, before I would see New York or my home again." —Gwen Terasaki, en route to Japan

Civilian Escapes

"Never shall I forget the faces of those American navy men . . . looking down at us as we approached the submarine in our little native boats."

—*Clara Lindholm, mother of four, escaping the Philippines*

Not all American *expatriates in Europe and the Pacific were willing to surrender to occupying armies. Risking capture and even death, some individuals and families went into hiding or discovered ways to escape. Not all survived; there are no records of the number of U.S. civilians who escaped from behind enemy lines, but some of those who did wrote books, telling their stories.*

When the Japanese attacked on December 8, 1941, most of the Americans in the Far East were concentrated in the Philippines. With its harbor in flames, transport out of the Philippine capital, Manila, was all but impossible. The Japanese advanced with a swiftness that stunned island defenses, and on Christmas Eve the U.S. Army retreated to Bataan and Corregidor, leaving Manila an "open city." Civilians tried to escape but there was little time. In the chaos, a few determined individuals broke out.

On New Years Day, just hours ahead of the Japanese, two American couples, Marjorie and George Colley, and Betty and Harry Weber escaped from Manila in a native boat. They sailed over 600 miles to Sandakan, Borneo, where seasick and with frayed nerves, they rested a short time. With a Japanese landing imminent, they put to sea again, but were betrayed by their crew and captured. They spent the war in internment in Borneo.

On the smaller islands of the Philippines some Americans went into hiding, believing U.S. forces would soon defeat the Japanese. When the Philippines fell, families in hiding risked death if they did not surrender. On Mindanao, Harriet McKay with her husband, young daughter and other families from Mindanao Mother Lode Mines fled inland to the remote Gomoco Goldfield camp in the mountains. There, living on supplies from the mine and bartered vegetables, they survived for two years until rescued by a submarine sent to supply guerrilla fighters. In their isolated camp, rumors of approaching Japanese brought panic and fear. "We live each day poised for change," Harriet McKay wrote in her diary in August 1942.

"Horror stories of their atrocities and cruelty to the gentle Filipinos . . . filter up here to us. Many of the stories are unbearable and unrepeatable. I try not to think about it—maybe I can't think about it."

Americans in hiding had great reason to fear. When Japanese troops discovered a group of missionaries concealed on Panay, they burned their camp and slaughtered the group with bayonets—even the children. Missionaries from Silliman University on Negros Island fared better. After over two years in hiding, missionaries, sugar families and other evacuees escaped to Australia on the submarines *Narwhal* and *Crevalle*. In all, U.S. submarines evacuated over 300 American civilians from the Philippines and the Solomon Islands in 19 separate missions.

Across the globe in Europe, Americans who did not depart at the outbreak of war in 1939 were often left to find their own way to neutral countries. After the U.S. entered the war, they became "enemy aliens" subject to internment. Margaret Vail (who recorded her experiences under this pseudonym) remained in France with her young daughter in 1940 even after her French husband was taken prisoner with the army. In July 1941 when the U.S. Consulate left Paris, she crossed surreptitiously into unoccupied France, affecting an innocent country stroll through the demarcation line. In November 1942, the Germans invaded the unoccupied zone and closed the frontiers. Threatened with internment, she and her four-year-old daughter crossed the Pyrenees—an arduous two-day trek over snow-covered mountain passes 8,000 feet up—to Spain, and from there traveled to the U.S.

Submarine Rescue: Clara Lindholm

The day the Japanese attacked the Philippines, Clara Lindholm, a missionary wife and Silliman University teacher, was giving birth to her fourth child, Janet, at the hospital in Dumaguete City, Negros Island. With invasion of the island likely, she and her husband, Paul, and children, Beverly (8), Dean (6), Jamie (1) and Janet (9 days) and other Silliman University families evacuated to the hills.

In mid 1942, the Japanese landed on Negros and ordered Americans interned. Over the next two and a half years, the Lindholms lived in a succession of rustic hideouts in the Pacuan Valley behind Guihulngan. Aided by Filipino church members who warned them when troops approached, they moved frequently, traversing steep trails by horse or native oxen. Their hideouts included thatched houses on stilts—one that Clara thought looked like "a giant wicker basket"—and two dripping stalactite caves, where the children developed chronic colds. Far from medical care, Clara nursed her children through Dengue fever, infections, and bacillary dysentery. The family bartered for corn and local vegetables, and even ate pigweed and leaves after a horde of locusts destroyed the region's rice crops. Clara spent hours patching and hand-sewing clothing for the family from bed sheets and an old canvas tent.

In April 1944, with the chance to escape on a U.S. submarine, the Lindholms left Pacuan, fortuitously, one day before the Japanese raided the valley. With guerrilla guides, they walked 100 miles through the mountains on steep jungle trails, a trek marked by leeches and hornet stings. After ten days, they arrived near Basay on the Sulu Sea, where they rendezvoused with the submarine, *Crevalle*. Clara felt a deep emotion as she said goodbye to her husband on the deck of *Crevalle*. Paul had decided to remain on Negros to continue his ministry. The realization that she would have to care for the children alone weighed on her.

Forty evacuees, including 21 children, crammed into *Crevalle* along with a full crew. En route to Australia near Bangka Strait, a Japanese destroyer depth-charged the submarine. Explosive concussions threw down passengers, shattered light bulbs and tore open gaskets. In the forward torpedo room, Clara and 11-year-old Beverly watched water pour in. "Are we sinking, mother? Will we all drown?" the girl asked. "I could only admit, 'I really don't know,'" Clara said. She prayed that Paul would not lose his whole family. Five days later, the *Crevalle* arrived in Darwin, Australia.

The Lindholms (bottom) with other evacuees on Crevalle, *outside Darwin Harbor, Australia, May 19, 1944. Front row from left: Clara, Beverly, Dean, Jamie and Janet.*

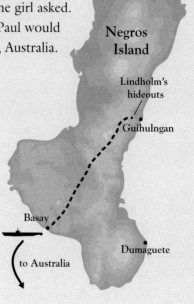

Resistance in the Pacific

Claire Phillips
(left, below) with an
unidentified woman,
possibly Gladys
Savary. Claire
Phillips, owner of
the Tsubaki Club,
gathered military
intelligence from
Japanese officers
between drinks
and elaborate floor
shows. Gladys
Savary smuggled
money and news
to prisoners. The
Japanese had "so
little regard for
women that they
never understood
that women could
do any harm," she
said. "It was always
women and girls
who made the best
contacts with the
military prisons."

In the Philippines, where the Japanese imprisoned Western civilians and U.S. and Filipino POWs under starvation conditions, the efforts of a small group of American women who evaded internment saved the lives of hundreds of prisoners.

Margaret Utinsky, whose resistance began by refusing to go into internment, aided large numbers of POWs in spite of grave risks. "For the life of me, I could not see what use I would be to myself or anyone else cooped up there," she said. When the Japanese took Manila, Utinsky hid in her apartment, undiscovered. After ten weeks, she ventured out, reinvented as Rosena Utinsky, a single Lithuanian nurse, born in Kovno and brought up in Canada.

With the help of Elizabeth Kummer, the American wife of a German, and others, she obtained false papers and went to Bataan with a Red Cross medical unit to look for her husband, a civil engineer. There, horrified by the carnage of the Death March and the appalling treatment of the surrendered armies, she, Dr. Romeo Atienza, his wife, and nurse Josefa Hilado began to smuggle medicine and food to POWs imprisoned at Camp O'Donnell near Capas. Supplies went into the prison hidden in the Red Cross ambulance with notes from Utinsky signed "Miss U."

Soon the "Miss U" network grew, aided by many others—Filipinos, the priests at Malate Convent, members of the Italian, Spanish, Chinese and Swiss communities, and nuns at the hospital in Manila—who passed messages, provided funds, and risked their safety, transporting supplies and making contacts.

When the Japanese moved the men from Camp O'Donnell to Cabanatuan, Utinsky, who learned that her husband had died, found new ways to help the thousands of POWs imprisoned at that camp. With captives allowed to buy food at times in the marketplace, she recruited Naomi Flores and Filipino American Evangeline Neibert, to pose as vendors, and soon established an active trade, in which the POWs purchased food that had hidden money inside so that they could purchase more food. In time, much of the Cabanatuan marketplace was surreptitiously passing messages, clothing, food, medicines and supplies to the prisoners.

In Manila, American Claire Phillips ran yet another Resistance cell. Shortly before the capital fell, Phillips and her small daughter, Dian, fled to Bataan for refuge. There she met John Boone, an American soldier who refused to surrender and was arming guerrillas to fight in the hills. He suggested she help them from Manila. Tanning her skin to pass as a Filipina of Italian descent, she returned to the city and opened the Tsubaki Club, where each night between tropical drinks and lavish floor shows, she observed "how freely the Japanese sometimes talked, particularly when alcohol stimulated their tongues." The club became a center of clandestine activity, with Phillips referred to as "High Pockets," because she hid secret papers in her brassiere. As hostess at the club, she not only extracted intelligence but used the profits to help supply the guerrillas. In addition, she sent food and medicine—on one occasion over 10,000 malaria-fighting quinine tablets—to the POWs at Cabanatuan. Learning of the desperate condition of POWs working at Nichols Field near Pasay, she also smuggled food and money to the prisoners there.

Gladys Savary, a restaurateur and American wife of a Free French soldier, also aided the POWs at Pasay. She remained "outside" throughout the war because the Japanese deemed her French by marriage and refused her the "protection" of internment. As such, she became a lifesaving link to those inside, preparing as many as fifty meals a day for civilian

internees at Santo Tomás, and smuggling in money and messages hidden under her wire hair fox terrier, who rode on the back of her bicycle.

In addition, two Filipino Americans, Josefina Guerrero and Florence Ebersole Smith, distinguished themselves with the Resistance. Early in the war, Josefina Guerrero mapped Japanese mines, fortifications, tunnels and air raid shelters on the Manila waterfront. In 1945, just before the American attack, she walked through enemy lines with the map taped between her shoulder blades and delivered it to the U.S. 37th Infantry Division. Florence Smith, wife of a navy PT boat crewman killed at Corregidor, smuggled food and messages to POWs, and was imprisoned by the Japanese.

As the Allies gained in the Pacific, the Japanese in the Philippines became more brutal. In May 1944 they arrested Claire Phillips, the nightclub owner, and tortured, condemned, and finally imprisoned her at the Women's Correctional Institution. The Japanese also arrested Margaret Utinsky of the "Miss U" network, tortured her, and then released her, battered and feverish with gangrene. After surgery and weeks of recovery, she escaped to Bataan, taking in her care Claire Phillips' four-year-old daughter, Dian. There in rustic mountain camps, frequently on the move, she served as a nurse to the guerrilla army until liberation.

In recognition of their service and sacrifice, the U.S. awarded the Medal of Freedom to Margaret Utinsky, Claire Phillips, Florence Ebersole Smith and Josefina Guerrero.

"After this trip through filth and nightmare . . . I knew that I could not stop until I had given every ounce of my strength to help the men who still lived."

—Margaret Utinsky,
Resistance leader

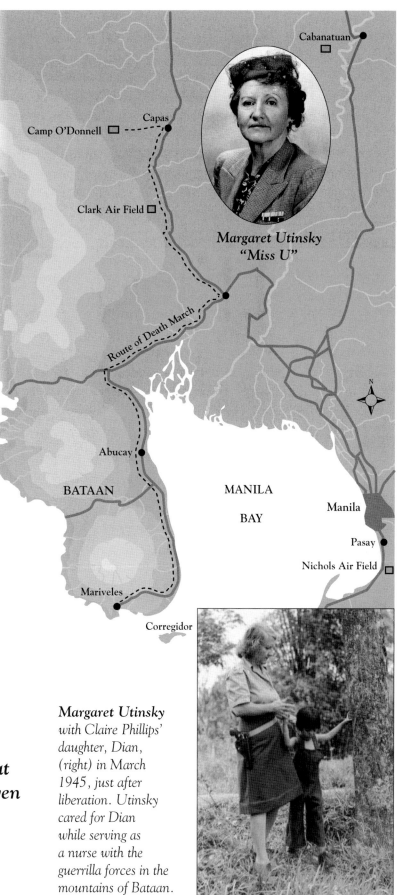

Margaret Utinsky with Claire Phillips' daughter, Dian, (right) in March 1945, just after liberation. Utinsky cared for Dian while serving as a nurse with the guerrilla forces in the mountains of Bataan.

Europe: These are all our Mothers and Sisters

Nazi SS troops (right) round up Jewish women and children in the Warsaw ghetto for deportation to concentration camps. The Germans maintained camps at Auschwitz, Treblinka, Belzec, Majdanek, Chelmno and Sobibor solely for the purpose of efficiently murdering large numbers of Jews and other "undesirables," including partisans, political prisoners, religious fundamentalists, gypsies, mentally ill, prostitutes and homosexuals. An estimated 4.5 million innocent people died at these death camps. So fanatical was the Nazi quest to stamp out the Jews, that even on the brink of defeat in 1944, they diverted vital war resources in order to annihilate the Jewish population of Hungary. In addition, the Nazis sent millions into forced labor camps where inmates worked under extreme conditions, often to death. Ravensbrück, a large women's work camp, imprisoned some 133,000 women, of whom 92,700 died.

In Europe, the people had great reason to resist. On January 20, 1942 at the Wannsee Conference in Berlin, Reinhard Heydrich, head of German security services, outlined the "Final Solution," a plan to murder the entire Jewish population of Europe. This holocaust, which the Nazis carried out with calculated efficiency, annihilated 6 million Jews and more than 5 million other peoples, including Gypsies, Soviets and Poles. Fueled by German dictator Adolf Hitler's obsession with obliterating the Jewish race and others he deemed "inferior," the Nazis killed and buried in mass graves or systematically transported to extermination camps more than 11 million innocent people.

"How can I describe to you our confusion and terror when the Nazis took over?" said Edith Hahn, an Austrian Jew. "We had lived until yesterday in a rational world. Now everyone around us—our schoolmates, neighbors, and teachers; our tradesmen, policemen, and bureaucrats—had all gone mad."

Using race laws, repression and violence, the Nazis mobilized the hatred of anti-Semites throughout Europe. Starting in 1933 with book burnings and a boycott of Jewish businesses, Nazi sanctions escalated incrementally, leaving most Jews unable to escape when the net finally closed. The 1935 Nuremberg Laws stripped Jews of citizenship. Later edicts banned Jews from schools, required them to wear the Jewish star, and to turn over their businesses to Aryans. On November 9, 1938, the night of broken glass (*Kristallnacht*), in a mass organized action, Nazis smashed Jewish houses and shops, and forced over 20,000 into concentration camps.

World War II broke out on September 1, 1939. The Germans pushed through Europe, forcing Jews into sealed ghettos. Warsaw's 1.6 square-mile ghetto housed over 400,000 starving people crowded a dozen to a room. In 1942, the Nazis began mass deportations by railroad cattle cars to death camps like Auschwitz. "Germans would come in the morning, shooting in the air," Zosia Goldberg recalled. "Everybody had to come down."

Many Jews did not resist. "Why did we not fight back?" asked Gerda Weissman, who followed the Nazi order to assemble for transport from Bielitz, Poland. "Because we had faith in humanity. Because we did not really think that human beings were capable of committing such crimes."

The title is from a memorial inscription at Ravensbrück women's concentration camp.

Survival and Design: Alice Dunn

In 1938, Hungarian fashion designer Alice Dunn was at the peak of her success, creating designer gowns for the "most discriminating clientele" in Budapest. That year, the Nazis took over neighboring Austria, and to prevent invasion, Hungary declared an alliance with Germany. As the violence against Jews increased, Alice's family resolved to leave Hungary. In 1939, her brothers left—one for Argentina, the other for New York. Alice and her mother were to follow to New York, but they reached France on the verge of war, and in the scramble for passage could only secure berth for one. And so, on September 1, 1939, the day World War II began, Alice sent her mother off to New York on the *Ile-de-France*.

Unable to obtain passage for herself, Alice left an increasingly hostile France to return to Budapest. There, tightened security prevented any further efforts to reach America, and in time she settled back into her routine. For the next four years her business flourished. Then on March 19, 1944 the Germans moved into Hungary. Police posted a Jewish star on Alice's shop and rioters attacked Jews in the streets. Alice made plans to escape, but in a purge of Hungarian Jews, the Nazis arrested her, and jammed her, exhausted and starving, along with thousands of other Jews onto freight cars bound for Auschwitz.

When they arrived at the camp, German guards forced them off the train and ordered them to strip off their clothes. "The only true reactions were disbelief or horror," Alice recalled. "Many wept in the face of the overpowering shame." For nearly a week—day and night—they stood naked to the elements, relieving themselves as they stood while the Nazis singled out the weak for extermination in the gas chambers. Women reached out and propped each other up; if you could remain standing, you had a chance at survival.

"The only true reactions were disbelief or horror."

Finally the guards took Alice and the other women to a dirty barrack. The dehumanization process was just beginning. In the days that followed the Nazis shaved each woman's head and tattooed her skin with a number. Using a single needle for 600, a doctor injected the women with a sterilization drug to make sure they could never have children. Each new brutality stripped away the women's dignity and identity. "Many gave up," Alice recalled, "became lifeless, emotionless, faceless . . . ."

Trainloads continued to pour into Auschwitz. Alice saw her fate in the moaning mounds of bodies of sick and feeble that awaited the ovens. As a last exercise of individual choice, she walked toward the electric fence to take her own life. But when she touched the fence, the electricity was off, and one of the female guards discovered her and whipped her with a fury.

The next morning at roll call, the same female guard, Margit, called her out of the lineup. But instead of beating her, the guard made a bizarre request. She had discovered Alice's identity. Here in the midst of death and the belching smoke of the crematorium, she wanted Alice to outfit her with designer fashions. And so, with blunt kitchen knives, hairpins for needles, and material from a warehouse of furs, coats and blankets stolen from Jews, Alice stitched fashions for Margit in exchange for an extra slice of bread each day.

One day in November, 1944, Margit told Alice the camp was going to be emptied out. She urged her to sneak out on a transport at dawn. The journey saved her life. The train took her to an aircraft factory at Tchopau, Germany where she was put to work as a forced laborer. Germany was losing the war. In April 1945, the Nazis loaded the slave laborers onto freight cars for transport to an extermination camp. On the way, Alice escaped through a vent at the top of the box car. She wandered in the woods, nearly dead from hunger and exposure until a group of escaped French workers came to her aid. Together they made it to the Allied line. In March 1946, Alice finally reached New York to be reunited with her mother and brother.

Resistance to the Nazis

EUROPE

Denmark
Amsterdam
Neth.
Belgium
Occupied France
Paris
Vichy France
Portugal
Spain
Pyrenees
Gibralter
Ravensbrück
Poland
Germany
Czech.
Austria
Italy

*"We didn't expect to survive.
But we hoped we would."*
—*Rochelle Schleiff, Nalibocka Forest, Poland*

Members of the Maquis (above), a French resistance organization, show how they placed dynamite charges under a railroad trestle to disrupt Nazi rail traffic. Very few women were involved in sabotage activities. Most helped the Resistance in other capacities.

Under the brutality of Nazi rule any show of resistance was an act of extreme courage. The Gestapo (German secret police), the SS paramilitary and their collaborators monitored people's everyday lives and tortured and killed resisters for even the smallest acts. "Whoever helps a Jew shall be punished by death," Nazi posters warned.

In the face of Nazi persecution, resistance sprang up spontaneously. It began with small acts of defiance such as listening to British radio broadcasts or hiding a Jewish neighbor, and grew into extended opposition networks which fought the German occupiers for liberation. In France, Belgium, the Netherlands, Denmark, Norway and other occupied nations, resistance members defied and undermined German forces in hundreds of ways: they hid and rescued Jews, forged papers, scrounged food, operated radios and printed underground newspapers. They also developed escape routes, passed enemy troop observations to Allied forces, sabotaged German military operations and killed collaborators. Women did most of the unheralded but necessary clerical work of the Resistance.

They also frequently served as couriers, because they could move about more freely than men. A pretty dress or a smile at a German checkpoint often allowed contraband to move undetected. In any capacity, their work carried mortal consequences. "It was always exciting, but it was also always dangerous," recalled Diet Eman, who traveled throughout Holland on her bicycle to observe troop movements and carry food and messages to Jews in hiding. "And fear takes a toll finally; when you live in danger from moment to moment, the constant tension becomes very wearying."

While it may be impossible to know the total number of resistance members throughout Europe, records from Germany and France indicate participation of over one million during the 12 years of the German Reich. In France alone, from 1940 to 1944, 150,000 male and female resistance members lost their lives. Women in the Resistance came from every age and background. They resisted for many reasons; some were Jews or intellectuals, already hunted. Others had strong convictions and took action in the face of depravity because it was the only human thing to do.

"I think you have a responsibility to

yourself to behave decently," said Marion Pritchard, a student in Amsterdam who helped save the lives of 150 Jews. Marion's actions were like those of many in the Resistance who aided the Jews. She began by procuring false ration cards and money. When the Nazis started to deport Jews to the death camps, she found hiding places and helpers willing to harbor the intended deportees. On three occasions (twice in five months) she registered newborn Jewish babies as her own so that their papers would show them to be Gentiles.

Although it is often asserted that the Jews in Europe did little to resist the Holocaust, in fact they conducted at least 20 uprisings in the locked ghettos and five revolts inside the death camps. Almost all of these poorly-armed revolts failed; the Nazis crushed the resisters and carried out reprisals against those around them. A few combatants escaped and joined with thousands of partisans—large groups of men and some women—who lived in the forests and conducted raids and sabotage against the occupying armies.

> ## "When you live in danger from moment to moment, the constant tension becomes very wearying."

Partisans became more organized over time and coordinated their resistance with Allied intelligence and other groups. Most women partisans, like Rochelle Schleiff who escaped from the Stolpce Ghetto in Poland to the Nalibocka Forest, cooked and helped with the maintenance of the group. There were exceptions. In Vilna, Lithuania, Jewish partisans treated women and men alike, and women were some of their toughest fighters. Irene Gut, a rescuer of Jews who joined the partisans in the forest near Kielce, Poland, served as a courier, delivering messages, money and ammunition. "The atmosphere of danger and defiance in which we existed made us alive like nothing else," she said. "We lived in the forest and our senses were as sharp as wild animals'. . . . We were fighting for our country."

Early in the war, resistance networks forged out escape routes across the English Channel or over the Pyrenees to Gibralter. Three main lines—the O'Leary, the Shelburne, and the Comet routes—transported Allied airmen, escaped prisoners of war and endangered resistance workers to safety in England. The largest, the Comet Line, started by Belgian nurse's aide, Andrée de Jongh (Dédée) guided nearly 1,000 escapees through Spain to Gibralter. In 1944 the Comet Line came under the leadership of Philippe D'Albert Lake, a French aristocrat, and his American wife, Virginia Roush Lake. Virginia set up safe houses and helped move airmen along the route. On D-Day, while guiding 11 airmen from Paris to a safe camp, the Germans arrested her. She spent nine months in Ravensbrück and other camps before her release in April 1945.

Another American who played a pivotal role in aiding downed airmen was 62-year-old Etta Shiber. An unlikely operative, Etta saw herself as a settled widow, living out her years quietly in Paris with her English friend, "Kitty Beaurepos." Her life changed drastically when the Germans overran Paris. Etta and Kitty fled on roads choked with refugees, but eventually turned back. At a roadside cafe they encountered a wounded British pilot, and with spontaneous resolve, packed him into the trunk of their car and took him to their apartment in Paris. Charged with finding medical aid and a means of escape for him, they soon developed a network of contacts through which they assisted in the escape of over 150 British servicemen.

In its many forms, resistance work carried great risks, and hundreds of thousands lost their lives in the struggle. In Berlin, Mildred Harnack, who provided military intelligence to Russia and the U.S. as a member of the Red Orchestra, had the distinction of being the only U.S. female put to death on Hitler's orders. Arrested after a Soviet intelligence blunder, the Gestapo executed her on February 16, 1943, shortly after the crushing German defeat at Stalingrad.

The Resistance set up clandestine routes (above) to help downed Allied airmen and others to escape from Europe.

Etta Shiber (below), the shy American widow in Paris, who with her English friend, "Kitty Beaurepos," helped 150 British servicemen escape from occupied France. Arrested by the Gestapo, she endured repeated interrogations with the resolve: "Deny everything!" Nevertheless, a German military court sentenced her to three years of hard labor and condemned her friend, Beaurepos, to death. In May 1942, Etta Shiber was repatriated in a prisoner exchange. Her English friend survived the war in prison.

Emergency Rescue Committee

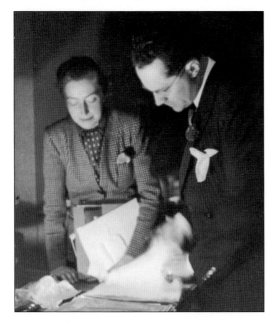

Miriam Davenport and Varian Fry (above) at the Centre Américain de Secours office in Marseille. Miriam Davenport, an American student who fled Paris, signed on as Secretary General of the Emergency Rescue Committee and worked, interviewing refugees. Her knowledge of French, German and art history was invaluable in determining the validity of the claims of refugee artists seeking escape.

Miriam Davenport and Mary Jayne Gold (below; left to right) in a cafe in Marseille. Expatriate American heiress Mary Jayne Gold contributed $3,000 to the Rescue Committee, enabling many more than the initial 200 refugees to escape. She also used her persuasive skills to gain the release of four prisoners.

With public prejudice and restrictive immigration quotas, the U.S. did little to provide asylum to Jews and political refugees facing persecution in Nazi-held Europe. In 1940, an alarmed group of citizens in New York formed the Emergency Rescue Committee (ERC). Through the intervention of Eleanor Roosevelt, they persuaded President Roosevelt to authorize 200 emergency visitor visas for well-known European writers, artists and intellectuals trapped in recently fallen France. Varian Fry, a New York editor, volunteered to go into collaborationist Vichy France for a month to rescue as many as possible. With list of 200 names and cash taped to his leg, he arrived in Marseille on August 15, 1940.

Fry quickly established the Centre Américain de Secours and took on staffers—among them Americans, Miriam Davenport and Mary Jayne Gold—to help, little realizing the rescue would last over a year and aid far more than the 200 on his list. From 8 a.m. to midnight, seven days a week, he and his small staff interviewed refugees and provided general relief, while clandestinely supplying legal and illegal papers and the means of escape—by train to Lisbon, overland through the Pyrenees, or by boat to Africa or Martinique—to hundreds of imperiled anti-Nazis. Police conducted frequent raids. Among those the ERC helped to escape were painter Marc Chagall, political scientist Hannah Arendt, novelist Heinrich Mann, and Nobel prize-winning biochemist Otto Meyerhof. In August 1941, French authorities expelled Varian Fry from France. The ERC continued to help refugees until June 1942. "If I have any regret about the work we did, it is that it was so slight," said Mary Jayne Gold. "In all we saved some 2,000 human beings. We ought to have saved many times that number."

"Our real purpose—and the police understood this—was the exportation, as expeditiously as possible, of people the Gestapo would like to catch."
—Miriam Davenport, Emergency Rescue Committee

Lisa and Hans Fittko: The Escape Route

When the Germans invaded France in May 1940, refugees fled south. The port of Marseille teemed with 40,000 stateless Germans, Austrians, Czechs and other exiles hoping to escape. The armistice with Germany required Vichy France to "surrender on demand" wanted refugees. With the threat of deportation, a tangle of visas to acquire, and virtually no means of passage, panic ruled. Black market forgeries and talk of mirage ships became the currency of the day. Among the refugees seeking a way out were Lisa and Hans Fittko. Lisa, an Austrian Jew from a politically active family, and Hans, a journalist from Berlin, had a long trail of underground resistance and expulsions before their arrival in Marseille.

Thinking it might be possible to cross overland into Spain, Lisa traveled to Port Vendres near the Spanish border to investigate. Through contact with Vincent Azéma, the socialist mayor of the nearby town of Banyuls-sur-Mer, she learned of an old smuggler's route over the Pyrenees. While still in Vendres, philosopher Walter Benjamin appeared at her door, asking for help to get to Spain. The next day she tested the route, guiding the heart-weakened Benjamin up the steep trail and over the mountains to the Spanish frontier. A week later, she was distressed to learn that Benjamin had committed suicide after Spanish authorities told him he did not have the proper paperwork and would have to go back.

Word that she had guided Benjamin over the Pyrenees got back to Varian Fry and the Emergency Rescue Committee in Marseille. Fry asked the Fittkos to serve as guides on the escape route. Putting aside their own plans for departure, they moved to Banyuls with false identity papers, and began guiding Jews, political refugees and downed British airmen over the mountains. To avoid infiltrators, the Committee gave refugees a torn piece of paper and sent the other piece ahead to the Fittkos by courier. Upon the refugee's arrival, the two papers had to match up. "The greatest risk of being discovered by the police or border officials was upon leaving the village and at the start of the ascent," Lisa recalled. "Azéma had impressed upon us: 'Leave before sunrise, mingle with the vineyard workers, take nothing with you except a musette [bag], and don't speak! Then, in the dark the sentries won't be able to tell you from the natives.'" Escorting groups of two or three, as often as three times a week, the Fittkos guided hundreds of refugees to safety. In late March 1941, the Vichy government ordered all border areas cleared of foreigners and the Fittkos left Banyuls. The Rescue Committee helped them to escape by ship to Cuba later that year. In 1948, they emigrated to the U.S.

Hans and Lisa Fittko (left) on the street in Marseille in 1941. At extreme personal risk, they established an escape route over the Pyrenees mountains into Spain and guided hundreds of refugees to safety.

"It was irresponsibly reckless to abandon our plans for departure. . . . Yet, if someone had to take the risk, we couldn't say, 'Let others do it.'"
—Lisa Fittko, escape guide, Banyuls-sur-Mer, France

Refuge for One Thousand

Throughout the 1930s and World War II, isolationist quotas in the U.S. largely shut out refugees seeking asylum. At a time when Jews were desperate to escape the German Reich, an undercurrent of anti-Semitism in the U.S. ensured that even existing quotas were not filled. In 1944, President Roosevelt established the War Refugee Board (WRB) to rescue and provide relief to victims of oppression. In spite of the tens of thousands seeking safety, Roosevelt announced that the U.S. would provide one emergency shelter in the United States for 1,000 refugees.

The shelter, administered by the War Relocation Authority (WRA), would be located at the former army camp of Ft. Ontario near Oswego, New York. Ruth Gruber, special assistant to the Secretary of the Interior, would accompany the refugees and prepare them for life in the United States. In July 1944 Gruber flew to Naples where 982 refugees waited aboard the Liberty ship, *Henry Gibbins*. Representatives of the WRB and others had chosen the assemblage from some 3,000 applicants—each with a painful story of persecution—in an agonizing process that considered family groups, those in greatest need, and those with skills that could make the refugee group as a whole into a coherent community. The refugees, mainly Jews, came from 18 countries, spoke 12 languages, and ranged in age from the infant, "International Harry," born in a jeep on the way to the ship, to an 80-year-old man. Each signed a release agreeing to go back at the end of the war.

The *Henry Gibbins* set sail in convoy through the hazardous waters of the Mediterranean. On the third night at sea, German bombers attacked. Gruber rushed to the refugees and found them stoically enduring the raid. During the voyage, she listened to their fears and concerns. They called her "Mother Ruth," and told her

"For a thousand people it would mean life, not death."—*Ruth Gruber, refugees' advocate*

their stories so that she could make their experiences known to the American public. Some had fled the Nazis over the Alps, been in concentration camps, resisted with the Underground, or been tortured. They peppered Gruber with questions about where they were going and how they would live. To help them adjust, she taught English classes, at the same time impressing the need for military secrecy. "Walking around the ship," she said, "I could hear people reciting to each other in all accents the litany of their first words in English: 'How do you feel? I feel fine. The name of this ship is a secret. We come from the North Pole.'"

On August 3, 1944, they made a joyous arrival in New Jersey. From there the refugees traveled by train to Oswego, New York. At the first glimpse of Ft. Ontario, with its chain link fence topped by barbed wire, a chill swept down the length of the train. "It's another concentration camp!" the refugees cried out. Nevertheless, aided by donations of clothing, toys and other necessities from the people of Oswego and the National Council of Jewish Women, families settled into barracks life. The questions to Ruth continued: "Can we leave the camp? What about jobs? Schools? Freedom to travel?" She had no answers. Gruber could only advocate for them to the decision makers in Washington. Eventually, the WRA allowed 193 children out to attend public schools and 50 men to aid desperate local farmers with the harvest.

Without status under the law, "sanctuary without freedom" weighed on those inside the fence. "Only a major decision could halt the spread of hysteria and depression," Gruber said. In May 1945 the war ended in Europe, and fears of deportation raced through the camp. Most had nothing to go back to. Discussions raged in Washington over whether to return the refugees, until finally, on December 22, 1945, President Truman intervened for humanitarian reasons and allowed them to stay in the United States.

Refugees (below) *pass through U.S. Customs at Ft. Ontario, the only refugee camp in the United States during the war. After escaping concentration camps in Europe, many were upset to find barbed wire surrounding the camp.*

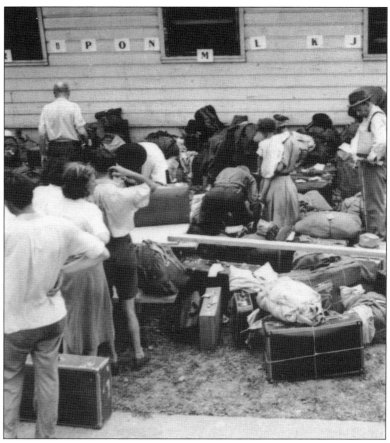

Liberation in Europe

In Europe, the end of the war was near. By January 1945, the Soviets had driven back the Germans into Poland and were moving swiftly toward Germany from the east. In the west the Allies, having regained ground lost in the Battle of the Bulge, now began their push into the German Rhineland. In February, the big three Allied leaders, U.S. President Franklin Roosevelt, British Prime Minister Winston Churchill, and Soviet dictator Josef Stalin met at Yalta and agreed on the division of Germany: Soviets would occupy the territory east of the Elbe River; British, Canadian, American and French forces the area west of the Elbe.

Slave laborers at Buchenwald concentration camp (above) look at their liberators with hope. U.S. troops found 20,000 men, women and children near starvation when they freed the camp on April 11, 1945. Prisoners "were so emaciated and weak that most of them could not raise their voices above a whisper," reported journalist Marguerite Higgins.

War correspondents followed U.S. troops into Germany. Moving toward Cologne in the "wet, raw cold," *Boston Globe* correspondent Iris Carpenter reported, "Every road was an unending column of tanks and supply vehicles." By April 1st, U.S. forces had encircled over 300,000 German troops in the Ruhr and were advancing rapidly across northern Germany. On April 25th, the U.S. and Soviet armies met in a joyous exchange at Torgau on the Elbe River. St. Louis *Post-Dispatch* reporter Virginia Irwin ventured on from there through Soviet lines and was one of the first three Americans to enter Berlin as the Russians took the city. "As we drank our toasts, the battle for Berlin raged only a few blocks away," she said. The Russians showed the Germans no mercy. They were "having their revenge," she noted, for the bitter German destruction of the Soviet Union. On April 30th, with Soviet troops only a quarter of a mile away, Adolf Hitler committed suicide in his underground Berlin bunker.

Just days earlier, the horrors of Hitler's genocidal "Final Solution" became manifest as Allied forces began to liberate the Nazi concentration camps. On April 11th, General Patton's Third Army liberated 20,000 slave laborers at Buchenwald, on the outskirts of Weimar, Germany. *Life* photojournalist Margaret Bourke-White recorded the shocking scene: "I saw and photographed the piles of naked, lifeless bodies, the human skeletons in furnaces, the living skeletons who would die the next day because they had had to wait too long for deliverance, the pieces of tattooed skin for lampshades."

General Patton was so enraged by the barbarity that he ordered MPs to round up a thousand local civilians to look at what their country had done. Over and over, Germans living in sight of the death trains and the camps protested: "We didn't know. We didn't know. But they did know," said Margaret Bourke-White.

On April 29th, Marguerite Higgins of the *New York Herald Tribune* was one of two reporters to arrive at Dachau concentration camp with an advance party from the 42nd Infantry. Seeing the Americans, the emaciated prisoners flooded into the yard, crying, shouting jubilantly, embracing them and lifting them up on their shoulders. Higgins, speaking French, English and German to the prisoners, announced that they were free.

Nurses with army medical units moved in to help the tens of thousands of displaced persons, German POWs and liberated Allied soldiers. At Dachau, the army scheduled nurses on a weekly rotation basis to minimize the psychological impact of working with death camp survivors. The struggle to save tortured, starving victims would continue for several months. Sara Tuvel, one of 85,000 women imprisoned at the Ravensbrück women's camp, who escaped from a death train in the final days of the war, weighed just 44 pounds when American soldiers found her.

On May 8, 1945, the Germans signed the final surrender. Word of the war's end reached *Collier's* reporter Martha Gellhorn while she was at Dachau—a suitable place to hear the news, she reflected, "For surely this war was made to abolish Dachau, and all the other places like Dachau."

EUROPE

▲ Forced labor camps
■ Extermination camps

Neuengamme
Bergen-Belsen
Ravensbrück
Sachsenhausen
Berlin
Treblinka
Chelmno
Poland
Cologne
Germany
Elbe
Sobibor
Buchenwald
Majdanek
Theresienstadt
Auschwitz
Belzec
Czech.
Natzweiler
Dachau
Slovakia
France
Mauthausen
Switz.
Austria
Hungary
Italy
Croatia
Romania
Serbia
Portugal
Bulgaria
Spain
Albania
Greece

Residents of Neunburg, Germany (above) bear victims of SS killings to the town cemetery. U.S. soldiers forced them to exhume the bodies of 161 men dumped in shallow graves and attend funeral rites to give them a dignified burial.

Liberated Jewish children (below) en route to Palestine.

"The minute the two of us entered, a jangled barrage of 'Are you Americans?' in about 16 languages came from the barracks 200 yards from the gate. An affirmative nod caused pandemonium. Tattered, emaciated men, weeping, yelling and shouting 'Long live America!' swept toward the gate in a mob. Those who could not walk, limped or crawled."

—Marguerite Higgins, war correspondent at the liberation of Dachau concentration camp

Liberation in the Pacific

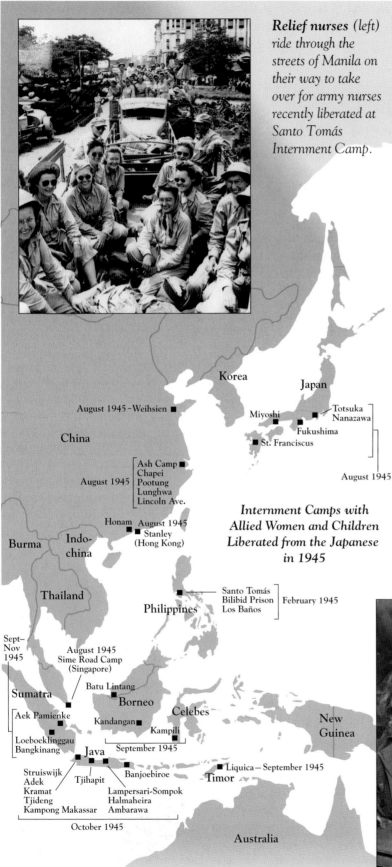

Relief nurses (left) *ride through the streets of Manila on their way to take over for army nurses recently liberated at Santo Tomás Internment Camp.*

Korea

Japan

August 1945–Weihsien ■

China

Miyoshi ■ ┌ Totsuka
Nanazawa

St. Franciscus ■   ■ Fukushima

August 1945 ┤ Ash Camp ■
Chapei
Pootung
Lunghwa
Lincoln Ave.

August 1945

Honam ■ ■ Stanley
(Hong Kong)

Burma   Indo-china

Thailand

Philippines

Santo Tomás
Bilibid Prison ┤ February 1945
Los Baños

Internment Camps with Allied Women and Children Liberated from the Japanese in 1945

Sept–Nov 1945

August 1945
Sime Road Camp
(Singapore)

Batu Lintang

Sumatra   Borneo   Celebes

Aek Pamienke   Kandangan   New Guinea

Kampili

Loeboeklinggau
Bangkinang   September 1945

Java   Liquica—September 1945

Struiswijk
Adek   Tjihapit   Banjoebiroe   Timor
Kramat
Tjideng   Lampersari-Sompok
Kampong Makassar   Halmaheira
Ambarawa

October 1945

Australia

By late 1944, Allied forces had advanced up the island chains of the Pacific to within bombing range of Japan and "returned" to retake the Philippines. As American troops fought their way through the formidable opposition in the Philippines, the army learned of Japanese plans to massacre civilians internees. U.S. forces rushed to Manila where 3,500 Allied civilians and 67 army nurse POWs were imprisoned at Santo Tomás University.

On the night of February 3, 1945, with Manila still in Japanese hands, U.S. tanks crashed through the university gates. Men, women and children internees rushed joyfully onto the plaza. Everyone "was laughing and crying, hanging out of windows and screaming and waving," said army nurse Dorothy Scholl. That same night, U.S. forces moved in on Bilibid Prison in Manila where the Japanese held some 1,300 internees, including 800 POW survivors of the Bataan Death March. There, fighting raged through the night and all of the next day before the liberating forces cracked opened the prison doors.

Word of the liberations in Manila leaked out to Los Baños camp, 42 miles to the south near the shores of Laguna de Bay, behind enemy lines, where the Japanese imprisoned over 2,100 civilians and 11 navy nurses. At dawn on February 23rd, U.S. paratroopers, amphibious forces, and

Filipino guerrillas stormed the camp in a surprise raid. Navy nurse Dorothy Still heard the commotion from the camp hospital, "Everything happened so fast," she said, "Bullets were flying in all directions. Barracks 3 and 4 were burning." With Japanese troops nearby, the rescuers, anxious to evacuate the area rapidly, set fire to the barracks. "I looked around and the whole place was on fire," said navy nurse Margaret Nash, "I didn't even care. We all felt the same way." The internees moved out quickly to the shore of Laguna de Bay, where under Japanese fire, amphibious tractors spirited them across the lake to safety.

Meanwhile, U.S. bombers continued to pound Japan. Gwen Terasaki, the American wife of a Japanese diplomat, who "repatriated" from the U.S. to Japan in 1942 in order to stay with her husband, watched American B-29s fly overhead to firebomb Japanese cities. "Our village sirens wailed all day," she said. "There was to be no let up in the wailing." On March 9, 1945, in the most devastating conventional air raid in history, U.S. incendiaries ignited massive firestorms in Tokyo that killed 100,000 people.

The end of the war was near. On April 12, 1945, U.S. President Roosevelt died of a cerebral hemorrhage and Vice President Harry S. Truman became president. Less than a month later, Germany surrendered and the war in Europe was over. Attention turned to the Pacific and how to overcome the Japanese. On July 24, 1945, in Potsdam, Germany, where Allied leaders gathered, President Truman received word of the successful test of a powerful new weapon—the atomic bomb. The encoded message reported the birth of a "boy." Had the explosion failed, the message would have announced a "girl."

Truman approved use of the bomb the next day, and less than two weeks later, on Tuesday, August 6th, the immense, mushroom-shaped blast of the first atomic bomb ripped through Hiroshima, Japan, leveling 90 percent of the city, and killing 80,000 instantly and tens of thousands more from radiation burns and sickness. On August 8th, the Soviets declared war on Japan, and the next day launched a major assault on Japanese forces in Manchuria. That same Friday morning, the U.S. dropped an atomic bomb on Nagasaki, inflicting more death and devastation.

On August 14th, Emperor Hirohito broke tradition and spoke directly to the populace by radio to announce Japan's surrender. People gathered before their radios and wept as they heard the Emperor's words. "There was a stunned apathy on the faces of the people in the street. Everyone was starving; few had the physical stamina even to express their thoughts coherently," observed Gwen Terasaki. "They waited for what they had to face and seemed resigned to it."

The day the Emperor spoke, news of the surrender also reached navy nurse Ann Bernatitus on the hospital ship, *Relief,* in San Pedro Bay in the Philippines. Bernatitus, who had escaped Corregidor by submarine in 1942 recalled, "[The] bay lit up that night . . . everybody firing something or another. It was beautiful." Nearby on the ship, she heard someone say, "Well, maybe now we can go home."

Freed civilian internees (bottom opposite) eat their first meal following liberation. After years of meager rations, they were overwhelmed by the abundance of food and delighted by the taste of white bread. The much maligned army chow, Spam (a canned spiced ham product), seemed like a delicacy to the half-starved prisoners. "We ate it like it was caviar," said navy nurse Mary Rose Harrington.

Liberated army nurses (below) board the truck to leave Santo Tomás Internment Camp on February 12, 1945 after three and a half years in captivity.

It's Over!

On September 2, 1945, almost six years to the day after it began, World War II ended with the official Japanese surrender at Tokyo Bay. Bells rang out around the earth, and everywhere—in cities and remote villages—humanity rejoiced over the end of destruction and the hopeful beginnings of peace. Europe, the Soviet Union, China and the Pacific lay in rubble. Worldwide, 50 million people had died.

American service women, returning from the bomb-blasted cities and camps of Europe and the Pacific, felt deep emotion as they glimpsed the lights of U.S. cities from their ship railings. War brides from 50 countries stepped onto U.S. shores with trepidation and excitement to start a new life with GI husbands. Malnourished female prisoners of war marveled at the abundance and the new technology in the "land of plenty." As military women ended wartime service, they missed the closeness and camaraderie shared through "hell and high water" with fellow nurses or WACs. They took their discharges in a nation that hardly recognized them as veterans, and went on with their lives.

Women on the home front faced major adjustments too. As factories switched to peacetime production, female workers—voluntarily or involuntarily—left the labor force in large numbers. Wives and sweethearts welcomed home long-serving soldiers and settled to have families. Yet no matter how much women went back to prewar routines, GIs would find their wives and girlfriends changed. In the war, women found confidence, independence, courage, and worldliness. They learned their effectiveness as individuals and their strength in numbers. Through their audacity and service they created an invaluable legacy for their daughters—the foundation of an equitable future.

Cheering U.S. men and women veterans of the China-Burma-India campaigns (opposite) arrive in New York, September 27, 1945, aboard the transport, General A.W. Greely.

Victory for the Allies

The war was over. The nation celebrated. On August 14, 1945, two million people surged into Times Square in New York City, thrilled at the news of the Japanese surrender. Sailors kissed and hugged every woman in sight. In San Francisco, Ann McGhee and a friend tried to walk down Market Street where traffic had stopped. "There was a wave of white coming down the street. We suddenly realized it was all sailors . . . I was swept off my feet, carried on shoulders for blocks!" she said. In New Orleans, Gladys Basile recalled, "It was wild. Just wild. The whistles were blowing, and the church bells were ringing, and everybody was honking their car horns."

Closer to the fronts, other feelings mixed with the joy and relief that the war was over. On V-E Day in Europe, WAC Grace Porter recalled, "I remember no big parties or wild celebrations. We were too close to the war for that. Instead we felt grief for all our friends and loved ones who had died in this horrible war. We felt deep pity for the people of Europe, with their broken cities and families, who now had to rebuild their lives and countries with little or nothing."

In the Philippines during the liberation, Margaret Utinsky, who risked her life to smuggle food, medicine and money to death march POWs, and was subsequently imprisoned and tortured by the Japanese, could not quickly change her feelings. "At that time I was so filled with bitter hatred for the Japanese, after having seen with my own eyes the hideous things they had done to soldiers and noncombatants alike. . . . It was not until I saw pictures of the Yanks stopping in the midst of the fighting to pick up a little Japanese baby and dry its tears, that I began to get back a little perspective."

Utinsky, Claire Phillips and other resistance workers provided "hard-won lists"of Japanese-held POWs and evidence of collaborators to the Counterintelligence Corps. During the next four years, international military tribunals in Tokyo and Nuremberg would hold trials for Japanese and Nazi war criminals.

Covering the Nuremberg tribunal in Germany, correspondent Kathleen

McLaughlin reported for the *New York Times* on the trial of the major Nazi war criminals that began on November 20, 1945: "Four of the world's great powers sit in judgment today on twenty top Germans whom the democratic nations charge with major responsibility for plunging the world into World War II. The twenty-first defendant, tacitly although not specifically named in the indictment, is the German nation that raised them to power and gloried in their might."

Meanwhile, U.S. service people were anxious to return home. The logistics of moving some 16 million service members, however, was staggering. The military

thought she was too weary and numb to feel excited by the Statue of Liberty. But when the great Lady came in sight, "standing proud in the sunshine, her arm raised in greeting," Porter cried, as did most of the rest of the WACs and the GIs on board. On *Lurline*, catching a night glimpse of the lights of San Francisco after a rugged year in New Guinea and the Philippines, WAC codebreaker Irene Brion was similarly moved. The lines of "America the Beautiful" leapt to her mind: "Thine alabaster cities gleam. . . " Arriving in New York in April 1946, Red Cross clubmobile worker Rosemary Langheldt, who sailed from Europe, was amazed by the energy and vitality around her when she stepped

> ### "What bedlam! It was a mass of people, and the sailors were going around kissing and hugging everyone."
> —Helen Wentz, navy nurse, V-J Day in Times Square

discharged and sent home service members on the basis of priority, determined by points accrued for months of service, overseas posting, battle stars and family status (having children). For some it would be a long wait. Stationed in California, WAC Anne Bosanko, who had only twelve points, waited almost a year for her discharge in July 1946.

Some people, in vital positions, stayed on in the former war theaters to do their jobs. While the GIs waited to go home, relief from boredom was essential. USO troupes were in demand, and entertainers like The Andrews Sisters and Marlene Dietrich performed in Europe well after V-J Day. Red Cross workers continued to run clubmobiles and service clubs. Army and navy nurses stayed on duty to provide medical care to displaced persons, death camp survivors and liberated POWs, and to help transport battle casualties home.

For those who served overseas, arrival home to America was sweet. Sailing into New York on the *Queen Mary* in September 1945, after nearly two years in the European theater, WAC Grace Porter

ashore. "Everyone looked fresh and healthy—and alive," she said. "The contrast between this and the war-worn countries I'd just left filled me with wonder."

They threw confetti and kissed anybody in Times Square on V-J Day. Below, Edith Cullen Shain, a nurse from Doctor's Hospital, was surprised when a sailor grabbed her and kissed her during the celebrations. Recalling the moment sixty years later, she said, "The happiness was indescribable. It was a very long kiss!"

Coming Home

The troops were coming home. Amid waving flags and brass bands, wives, mothers and sweethearts lined the docks to welcome returning servicemen. Service women arrived home too, although to less fanfare. Greeting Irene Brion's WAC group as they disembarked from the Pacific was a cluster of professional WAC "wavers." "The fact that only WACs met us was neither surprising nor disappointing," Brion said. "I would hardly have expected to be welcomed by a crowd of flag-waving, cheering civilians. Unlike the men, we service women weren't regarded as heroines."

Returning as veterans, women found little public recognition for their service. Some, like WAC Maria Sally Salazar, who suffered long-term health problems from stress, tropical illnesses and poor diet during her service in the Pacific, came home to find that most army hospitals had no facilities for women veterans. Male-dominated veterans' organizations like the American Legion and the Veterans of Foreign Wars tacitly shut out women veterans or allowed them only as "auxiliaries." Female service members did, however, take advantage of the G.I. Bill to further their education. Also, many found the friendships forged in wartime service lasted throughout their lives.

Adjustment was difficult for returning POWs and civilian internees recovering from years of malnourishment and trauma. Having lived in extreme privation, most could never again waste food. Much had changed in their absence. Missionary and civilian internee Darlene Diebler, arriving after eight years in New Guinea and the Celebes, didn't know what to think when confronted with the new style dial telephone. "There was a circular metal affair with letters as well as numbers around it," she said. "I thought 'How do you work this thing?'" Many returnees were eager to forget and move on with their lives. Army nurse POW Ethel Thor rarely spoke about her war experiences. Instead she got married, had children, and launched into family life. "I never knew she was in the army," said her daughter, Carla Kingsbury. "I didn't know until after I was out of high school."

For Japanese Americans, war's end brought the release of the thousands still interned in U.S. "relocation" camps. Internees left the camps to rebuild their lives and livelihoods in a land where prejudice lingered. Jeanne Wakatsuki's parents returned to Long Beach from Manzanar to find their stored furniture "unaccountably robbed," their car repossessed, and no record of their fishing boats. In 1949, the government offered minimal compensation for their losses, awarding an average of $440 each to the 23,000 claimants who filed (a fraction of the estimated $400 million total in Japanese American losses). In 1982, a U.S. government commission verified that Japanese Americans had not committed a single act of espionage, sabotage or fifth column activity. Six years later, Congress voted to issue a formal apology to internees and to pay survivors

$20,000 each in reparations.

On the home front, women had to make adaptations. After years of separation and longing, their men were back. But things had changed. Wives who had learned self-reliance as sole managers of the household, finances, and child rearing—all while holding an outside job—found it difficult to go back to the prewar ideal of the demure, dependent wife. Barbara Gwynne, a WAC commanding officer, who married and had a baby after the war, noted, "we were used to making decisions for ourselves. . . . I suppose that it was a surprise for some of the men."

With victory, women's war jobs ended abruptly. Gladys Poese Ehlmann, a punch press operator at Emerson Electric Company in St. Louis, said, "The war was over on August 14th and we went in on the 15th. They lined us up and had our paychecks ready for us." In the first nine months after V-E Day, four million women left the U.S. work force. Posters and newsreels urged females to make way for the returning men and go back to homemaking. "I didn't mind leaving the job," said Ann McGhee, a worker at the Alameda Naval Air Station. "I was ready to find my soul mate and settle down and raise a family." Lola Weixel, a welder from Brooklyn, felt differently. "America wanted babies. And we wanted babies, but we gave up everything for that," she said. As factories retooled for peacetime production, women found high-skilled, higher paid positions closed to them. Still, some remained in the work force, and the public's view of suitable jobs for females expanded from teachers and nurses to now include clerical and office workers—positions previously dominated by men.

The war had brought hardship and loss to many; opportunity, self-confidence and independence to others. Looking back, women remembered World War II as a time of excitement, vitality, experience and intensity. "I didn't know what tired was," said shipyard worker Alice Caldwell. "Those were great years!"

The War is Over!

It was different for each person . . .

Helen Dunn celebrated amid the whistling and honking on Canal Street in New Orleans on V-J Day. "The sailors were grabbing people and kissing them. And I dodged them. I dodged about ten sailors. . . . And then I turned around, and this sailor came up behind me and grabbed me and gave me the *best* kiss . . . and then he disappeared."

Elizabeth Morrison, an aircraft template maker in Linden, Massachusetts, heard the news at work. "Oh my God, everybody stopped working and just celebrated. But we were sad to leave work too. . . . Within a week all production stopped."

Mabel Smith, a Rhode Island mother, cheered the war's end with her sister-in-law and their small children, who banged noise makers and marched about. "There was a remarkable feeling that it was finally over," she said.

Army nurse Clara Wynick was in the Philippines on V-J Day. "My patients were upset with me because I wasn't very jubilant. I was sad, thinking of the thousands who wouldn't be going home . . . the families who would never see their loved ones again."

Evelyn Whitfield, recovering from three-and-a-half years of imprisonment and near starvation under the Japanese in the Philippines, did not feel hatred for her captors. "I knew that war is the enemy," she said. "If we don't forgive and get over it, we can never go on."

Former first lady Eleanor Roosevelt wrote in her newspaper column, "The greatest opportunity the world has ever had lies before us. God grant that we have enough understanding . . . to live in the future as 'one world' and 'one people.'"

After the War

- **Major Charity Adams,** commander of the only African American WAC unit to serve overseas, fought a number of quiet battles against the U.S. Army's policy of overt segregation. Adams left the service in March 1946 and earned a master's degree in vocational psychology from Ohio State University. She married a physician and raised a son and daughter while establishing a distinguished career as a public administrator. After many honors, Adams died in 2002 at the age of 83.

- **The Andrews Sisters, Maxene, Patty and LaVerne,** were the most famous female vocal group in U.S. history at the end of World War II. Building on their wartime popularity, they headlined theater shows worldwide, hosted their own radio show, and did extensive commercial jingle work in the late 1940s and early 1950s. The group broke up in 1953, reunited in 1956, and continued with moderate success until the death of eldest sister, LaVerne, in 1967.

- **Josephine Baker,** the flamboyant, expatriate American dancer who smuggled papers and gathered intelligence for the French Resistance, spent her later years adopting a "Rainbow Tribe" of children from countries around the world. She also actively supported the American civil rights movement and spoke at the 1963 March on Washington beside Martin Luther King. She opened a retrospective revue in Paris on April 9, 1975 to critical acclaim, but lapsed into a coma the next day and died in Paris on April 12, 1975 of a cerebral hemorrhage at the age of 68. Twenty thousand people lined the streets of Paris to mourn her passing.

- **Margaret Bourke-White,** the daring photojournalist who witnessed the war in Russia and flew on a B-17 mission over North Africa, continued her legendary career after the war, covering the world for *Life* magazine. She interviewed Mohandas Gandhi just before his assassination in January 1948, and reported on the violent partition of India. She covered the Korean War before her career slowed down in the 1950s due to Parkinson's disease. In 1963, she published a best selling autobiography, *Portrait of Myself*. Margaret Bourke-White died in Connecticut in 1971 at the age of 67.

- **Iris Carpenter,** the British correspondent who covered the war in France and Germany, became a U.S. citizen and married Colonel Russell Akers of the U.S. First Army. Carpenter brought her two children to the U.S. while working for the *Boston Globe* and several English newspapers. She wrote a well received book, *No Woman's World,* detailing her war experiences, and later worked for the Voice of America.

- **Lee Carson,** the International News Service reporter who got an exclusive aerial view of the D-Day invasion, went home to the U.S. after V-E Day. She was married twice and worked for two decades as a magazine journalist before her death at a young age from cancer.

- **Dickey Chapelle,** the brash photojournalist who went ashore during the battles for Iwo Jima and Okinawa, continued to take risks to report on conflict zones after World War II. She covered the revolutions in Hungary, Algeria and Cuba, as well the fighting in the Vietnam War. In 1965, shrapnel from an exploding land mine struck and killed her near Da Nang, Vietnam. She was 46.

- **Ruth Cowan,** one of the first female correspondents to go ashore in North Africa, returned to Washington to report for the Associated Press. She served as president of the Women's National Press Club. In 1956, Cowan resigned from the AP to marry prominent government administrator, Bradley D. Nash. They retired to his Harper's Ferry farm. Cowan died in 1993 at the age of 91.

- **Muriel Daggett,** the SPAR who traveled to Seattle from Boston, got married and left the Coast Guard shortly before the end of the war. She settled in the Puget Sound area, raised her family there and became involved in veteran's activities. In 2001, she was one of 57 Spars present in Kodiak, Alaska for the commissioning of the Coast Guard cutter, *Spar,* commanded by a female and named in honor of the women who served in the Coast Guard Reserve in World War II.

- *Miriam Davenport,* who helped save prominent Jewish writers and artists through the Emergency Rescue Committee, left Marseille in October 1940 for Yugoslavia where her fiancé waited. With great difficulty, the two managed to get passage from Lisbon for the U.S., just days after the Pearl Harbor attack. Three times married, Miriam worked for numerous public causes, studied art and became a prize-winning painter and sculptor. She died in 1999.

- *Bette Davis,* film star and cofounder of the Hollywood Canteen, continued to star in motion pictures, but saw her popularity gradually decline. Four times married, she gave birth to a daughter, Barbara, and adopted two children. In 1950, she received an Academy Award nomination for the film, *All About Eve.* Her career revived in the early 1960s and in the next decade she moved into television work. Davis died in France in 1989 at the age of 81.

- *Darlene Diebler,* the young bride and missionary interned by the Japanese in the Celebes, returned to the United States in late 1945 and gradually recovered her strength. Three years later, she married missionary Gerald Rose, and they began a ministry in New Guinea that lasted until 1978. They next moved their ministry to the Northern Territories in the Australian Outback. The two returned to the U.S. late in life and settled in Tennessee. Darlene Diebler Rose died in 2004.

- *Marlene Dietrich,* the German-born film star, remained in Europe with the USO, performing for Allied soldiers until after V-J Day. During the next three decades, she toured internationally as a cabaret performer and appeared in a number of films, including *Judgement at Nuremberg* (1961). She died in Paris in 1992 at the age of 90.

- *Alice Dunn,* the Hungarian fashion designer who survived Nazi persecution at Auschwitz, made her way to Paris with the help of the Resistance, and from there to the United States. Shattered in body and mind, she arrived in New York in March 1946 and reunited with her mother and brother. Adjustment was difficult. In 1950, she married Jerry Adler. She dedicated her later years to visiting schools to tell her story.

- *Lisa Fittko,* who with her husband Hans, guided hundreds of anti-Nazi refugees across the Pyrenees to Spain, escaped by ship to Cuba in 1941, and from there went to the U.S. in 1948. Settling in Chicago, she wrote books and worked as a peace activist. Hans Fittko died in 1960. Lisa lived to the age of 95. She died in 2005.

- *Cornelia Fort,* the pilot and flight instructor who was in the air at Pearl Harbor when the Japanese attacked, and who later joined the Women's Auxiliary Ferry Squadron, died on March 21, 1943 from a midair collision with another army plane while ferrying a BT-13 to Dallas, Texas. Shortly after her close call at Pearl Harbor, she wrote in a foreshadowing letter to her mother, "I was happiest in the sky—at dawn when the quietness of the air was like a caress, when the noon sun beat down and at dusk when the sky was drenched with the fading light. Think of me there and remember me."

- *Martha Gellhorn,* the determined war correspondent who stowed away on a hospital ship to get one of the first eyewitness reports of the D-Day invasion, went on to cover many of the major conflicts of the 20th century. In 1945, she divorced her husband, novelist Ernest Hemingway. She adopted an Italian orphan boy in 1949, and began a nine year marriage in 1954 to T. S. Matthews, an editor at *Time* magazine. Gellhorn

After the War

wrote a total of six novels and continued working as a world reporter until her early eighties. She died in London in 1998 at the age of 90.

- *Mary Jayne Gold,* the Chicago heiress who aided the Emergency Rescue Committee's efforts to help artists, writers and anti-Nazis to escape Vichy France, left Marseille in 1941 for Lisbon and the United States. She returned to France after the war and lived on the Riviera. According to filmmaker Pierre Sauvage, Gold felt "that only one year in her life really mattered and it was the year she spent in Marseille." She never married. She died in 1997 at the age of 88.

- *Betty Grable,* the iconic "pin-up" actress, ruled the box office for eight years after war's end. In 1953, she moved to television and later starred in Las Vegas reviews. In 1965, she divorced her husband, band leader Harry James, with whom she had two daughters. Grable died of lung cancer in 1973 at the age of 56.

- *Ruth Gruber,* who accompanied 982 European refugees to the U.S., found her life after the voyage "inextricably locked with the Jews." As a correspondent for the *New York Herald Tribune* for 20 years and author of many books, she has worked throughout her life to "fight injustice with words and images."

- *Virginia Hall,* the OSS agent who escaped the Gestapo while working undercover in France, was awarded the Distinguished Service Cross in September 1945 for her work in occupied France. In 1950, she married fellow operative, Paul Goillot. Hall worked for the Central Intelligence Agency, the successor to the Office of Strategic Services, until 1966 when she retired to her farm in Maryland. She died in 1982.

- *Rita Hayworth,* the redheaded actress army flyers wanted most to be "cast adrift with," continued her movie career until 1948 when she left Hollywood to marry Prince Aly Khan. She returned to film after her divorce in 1951 and stayed in the movie business until 1972. She died in 1987 at the age of 68.

- *Marguerite Higgins,* the correspondent who made headlines for her coverage of the liberation of Dachau, ran the *New York Herald Tribune's* Berlin bureau after the war. She covered the Korean War and received a Pulitzer Prize for her frontline dispatches. Higgins married General William Hall and had three children. In 1963, she joined *Newsday* and while on assignment in Vietnam in 1965, contracted the parasitic disease, leishmaniasis, which led to her death in January 1966 at the age of 45.

- *Grace Hopper,* the navy computer scientist, was discharged from active duty in 1946, but remained in the Reserves. During the next 40 years she continued her innovative work with computers which included development of the first compiler, invention of the computer language, COBOL, and implementation of standards for early programming languages, including COBOL and FORTRAN. She retired from the U.S. Navy in 1986 at the age of 80 with the rank of rear admiral. She died in 1992.

- *Lena Horne,* singer and reluctant pin-up favorite of African American servicemen, made eleven films after the war, but found that major stardom eluded her due to pervasive prejudice in the movie industry and American society. She turned to a nightclub and recording career in the 1950s, as well as to work in the civil rights movement. Horne successfully recorded and performed well into her eighties.

- *Agnes Newton Keith,* mother and writer who survived the hardships of internment under the Japanese in Borneo, returned to North America after liberation. After six months of recuperation, the British Civil Service recalled her husband to Borneo to work in postwar reconstruction. Agnes and her son followed shortly after. In subsequent years they lived in Borneo and Libya. Agnes Newton Keith wrote about her experiences in the book (later made into a movie), *Three Came Home*. She died in 1982 at the age of 80.

• *Helen Kirkpatrick,* war correspondent for the *Chicago Daily News* who saw the liberation of Paris, served as a European reporter for the *New York Post* from 1946 to 1949 and covered the Nuremberg Trials. In the early 1950s she worked for the State Department, helping to implement the Marshall Plan for European reconstruction. Kirkpatrick joined Smith College, her alma mater, in 1954 as an administrator and married a trustee of Smith, Robbins Milbank, that same year. Kirkpatrick died in 1997 at the age of 88.

• *Veronica Lake,* the sultry actress who cut her hair to keep factory women who emulated her hairstyle from getting their hair caught in machinery, saw her career decline once she cut her "peek-a-boo" tresses. The film success Lake enjoyed before and during the war faded with the coming of peace. Other actors found her difficult, she developed a drinking problem, and Paramount cast her in a series of forgettable movies. By the late 1950s she suffered a series of financial and personal reverses that left her broke and in poor health. She died in Vermont in 1973 at the age of 50.

• *Frances Langford,* the USO performer who entertained GIs in North Africa and the South Pacific, made ten films after the war and continued her famous USO tours with the Bob Hope troupe. She had a radio variety show and worked in nightclubs. In 1955, she married industrialist, Ralph Evinrude, and moved to an estate in Florida. Langford died in 2005 at the age of 92.

• *Clara Lindholm,* missionary and mother of four, who with her children escaped from Japanese-occupied Negros Island in the Philippines by submarine, was reunited with her husband when he returned to the U.S. in July 1945. Acceding to the wishes of fellow missionaries, they returned to Silliman University on Negros for a year, and then transferred to a mission in Shanghai. They retired to California in 1979 after more than 35 years of missionary work. In 2005, Clara Lindholm celebrated her 102nd birthday.

• *Florene Miller,* the WASP who safely landed her crippled plane in Dallas, continued to ferry planes for the military until the Women Airforce Service Pilots was deactivated in December 1944. After leaving the WASP, Miller married her former flight student, Chris Watson, and had two daughters. She earned a master's degree in business and taught at the University of Houston for 30 years.

• *Lee Miller,* *Vogue* correspondent who photographed one of the first uses of napalm in St. Malo, France, divorced her first husband, Aziz Eloui Bey, after World War II and married the surrealist painter, Roland Penrose. They had a son, Anthony, in 1947. The family settled down on a Sussex farm and played host to many artists such as Picasso, Henry Moore, and Max Ernst. Miller largely gave up photography and took up gourmet cooking and music. She struggled with alcoholism, and died in 1977 at the age of 70.

• *Betty Willett Mowery,* who fell in love and married Oscar Rea Mowery in 1945, settled with her husband in San Diego and had four children. They traveled frequently throughout their lives and remained in contact Marine Corps friends.

• *Shelley Mydans,* war correspondent, who with her husband, Carl Mydans, was interned by the Japanese in Manila and then Shanghai, China, was repatriated to the U.S. on the diplomatic ship, *Gripsholm*. Beginning in January 1946, Mydans worked for Time, Inc., doing a syndicated radio network news program. She and Carl had a son and daughter, and moved to Tokyo where they held down the Time-Life Bureau. In addition, Shelley wrote three novels and co-authored a nonfiction work. She died in 2002 at the age of 86.

After the War

- *Betty Thorpe Pack,* the OSS spy known as "Cynthia" who infiltrated the Vichy Embassy in Washington D.C., married Charles Brousse, the press attaché turned OSS operative with whom she secured the Vichy cipher. Together they renovated a tenth-century chateau in Perpignan, France. "Cynthia" died of cancer in 1963.

- *Frances Perkins* served as U.S. Secretary of Labor from 1933 to 1945. After Franklin Roosevelt died in 1945, President Truman appointed Perkins to the United States Civil Service Commission, a post she held until the death of her husband in 1952. She wrote a well-received history about her time in the New Deal entitled, *The Roosevelt I Knew.* Perkins taught labor relations at Cornell University until her death in 1965 at the age of 83.

- *Claire Phillips,* the Resistance member who spied on Japanese officers at her night club, and supplied food and medicine to POWs, returned home to Portland, Oregon after liberation from the Women's Correctional Institution near Manila on February 10, 1945. In recognition of her work in the Resistance, the U.S. awarded her the Medal of Freedom in 1951. She died nine years later at the age of 52.

- *Jeannette Rankin,* congresswoman from Montana and the lone representative to vote against U.S. entry into World War II, remained active in the women's and peace movements after the war. She traveled widely, lecturing on progressive topics, and maintained a farm in Georgia. In 1968, she led the Jeannette Rankin Brigade, a group of 5,000 women, in a Washington D.C. protest against the Vietnam War. Rankin died in 1973 at the age of 93.

- *Eleanor Roosevelt,* First Lady of the United States, moved to New York after the death of her husband, President Franklin Roosevelt, on April 12, 1945. From 1946 to 1952, she served as a delegate to the United Nations, where as chair of the Human Rights Commission, she helped frame the Universal Declaration of Human Rights. Throughout her life she remained an influential political figure. She died in 1962 at the age of 77.

- *June and Ervin Schmidt,* who married in 1944, settled in Seattle and raised a family.

- *Sigrid Schultz,* the Berlin news bureau chief for the *Chicago Tribune* who left Germany in 1941, recovered from typhus contracted during the war, and continued to work as a reporter and as a contributor to *McCall's* magazine. She authored the widely read *Germany Will Try It Again,* and correctly predicted a number of features of the Cold War. Schultz died in 1980 at the age of 87.

- *Lois Sevareid,* wife of correspondent, Eric Sevareid, left Paris for the U.S. with her newborn twins just before the German occupation. After the war she suffered from manic depression. Her illness placed a great strain on her marriage. She and her husband divorced in 1962. Following the breakup, she moved to Flint Hill, Virginia and worked in the town's library. In 1972, she died of a stroke at the age of 59.

- *Margaret Sherk,* a wife and mother interned at Santo Tomás in the Philippines, fell in love with internee Jerry Sams, became pregnant, and gave birth to a baby daughter while imprisoned by the Japanese. Throughout her internment she struggled to nourish and protect her children, and to defend and take solace in a love born under extreme circumstances. Her husband, Bob Sherk, died on a POW transport ship in late 1944. After the war, Margaret and Jerry Sams were married. They settled in the Sierra Nevada foothills of California.

- *Etta Shiber,* the expatriate American widow in Paris who with her friend, identified in her memoirs as "Kitty Beaurepos," helped 150 downed Allied airmen to escape occupied France, returned to the U.S. in weakened health on the repatriation ship, *Drottningholm,* in an exchange for the German hairdresser spy, Johanna Hoffman. Her book, *Paris—Underground,* about her experiences in Nazi-occupied France became a major success in 1943. She died in 1948.

- *Tess Shirer,* wife of "Murrow Boys" correspondent, Bill Shirer, fled Europe for the U.S. in 1940 with her two-year-old daughter. In 1941, she and Bill had a second daughter. Tess and her husband divorced in 1970.

- *Dinah Shore,* singer and USO performer, starred in ten films after the war, but was most famous for her singing and television career. Shore had her own TV show from 1951 to 1962, producing over 500 broadcasts. From 1970 to 1980, she hosted two TV interview shows. She won nine Emmy awards. Dinah Shore died in California in 1994 at the age of 77.

- *Gwen Terasaki,* American wife of a Japanese diplomat who was "repatriated" to Japan with her husband and daughter, Mariko, in 1942, survived the war under American bombardment in that country. In 1949, she and her daughter left Japan so that Mariko could attend college in Tennessee. Her husband died two years later. Gwen wrote about her experiences in Japan in the best selling book, *Bridge to the Sun,* which was made into a motion picture. She died in 1990 at the age of 84.

- *Dorothy Thompson,* the prescient journalist expelled from Germany in 1934 for her criticism of Adolf Hitler, toured the U.S. speaking out against isolationism. After the war, Thompson worked for *Ladies Home Journal.* She became a commentator on issues in the Middle East and gradually evolved a pro-Arab position. She was married three times. Following her divorce from writer Sinclair Lewis in 1942, she married Austrian-Czech émigré artist, Maxim Kopf. Thompson died in Portugal in 1961 at the age of 67.

- *Ethel Thor,* the army surgical nurse who served in the jungles of Bataan and was a prisoner of war for three years in the Philippines, missed many of the receptions that greeted the rest of the liberated nurse POWs. Suffering from dengue fever and a carbuncle on her back that required a skin graft, she was hospitalized for six weeks before returning home to Tacoma, Washington in April 1945. Putting the war behind her, she married and had three daughters. She died in 2002 at the age of 91.

- *Sonia Tomara,* roving correspondent who covered the war in Poland, France and Italy, quit the *New York Herald Tribune* in 1945 upon her marriage to Colonel William Clark, a lawyer attached to General Eisenhower's staff. They moved back to Germany for six years, while her husband worked for the Allied High Commission in the reformation of the German court system. They then settled in Princeton, New Jersey. Tomara died in 1982 at the age of 85.

- *Ada Ulmer,* the navy wife and nurse who awoke to the Pearl Harbor attack, returned from Hawaii to the mainland with other military wives and children in May 1942. She and her husband, Jack, settled in Poulsbo, Washington after the war where they enjoyed a happy marriage for more than 55 years.

- *Margaret Utinsky,* who established the "Miss U" resistance network in the Philippines and smuggled food and medicine to hundreds of Allied prisoners of war, aided the Counter Intelligence Corps in uncovering collaborators at the end of the war. She returned to the U.S, eventually settling in Long Beach, California. In 1946, she received the U.S. Medal of Freedom in recognition of her service. She died in Lakewood, California in 1970 at the age of 70.

Chronology 1931–1941

Mussolini and Hitler

Japanese invade Shanghai

Neville Chamberlain

Winston Churchill

Paris falls to the Germans

- **September 1931:** Japan invades Manchuria as part of a plan to expand its empire in Asia and seize needed raw materials.

- **January 1933:** Adolf Hitler becomes chancellor of Germany and the National Socialist German Workers' (Nazi) party gains power. With army support, Hitler solidifies his authority and in August 1934 becomes *führer* (supreme leader).

- **October 1935:** Under Fascist dictator Benito Mussolini, Italy invades Ethiopia.

- **March 1936:** Repression and anti-Semitism grow virulent in Germany as Nazis sanction violence against Jews. Germany rearms and in March, sends troops into the demilitarized Rhineland in defiance of the 1919 Versailles Peace Treaty.

- **July 1937:** Japan provokes a clash with Chinese militia near Peking and the "incident" escalates to full-scale war with China. December: The Rape of Nanking. Japanese troops take Nanking, the Chinese Nationalist capital, in a brutal binge of looting, rape and murder that leaves over 40,000 Chinese dead.

- **March 1938:** Germany annexes Austria in violation of the Versailles Treaty. France and Britain take no action.

- **September 1938:** British Prime Minister Neville Chamberlain negotiates with Hitler to avert war. Sept. 29–30: Germany, Britain and France sign the Munich Pact, allowing Germany to annex the Sudetenland, a part of Czechoslovakia. Chamberlain declares this will satisfy Hitler and bring "peace in our time."

- **November 1938:** Nov. 9: *Kristallnacht* (the night of broken glass), Nazis loot, smash and burn Jewish houses and shops throughout Germany. Nazis kill 91 German Jews and force 26,000 into concentration camps.

- **March–May 1939:** Germany occupies the rest of Czechoslovakia in violation of the Munich Pact. Britain and France vow to defend Poland against German attack.

- **April 1939:** Italy occupies Albania. May: Italy and Germany become allies.

- **June–August 1939:** Britain, France and the Soviet Union fail to agree on an alliance. In August, the Soviet Union, under Josef Stalin, signs a nonaggression pact with Germany, including secret provisions for the partitioning of Poland.

- **September 1939:** Sept. 1: **World War II begins.** Germany invades Poland. Sept. 3: Great Britain and France declare war on Germany. Sept. 17: The Soviet Union attacks Poland from the east. Oct. 6: Fighting ceases in Poland with the Germans in control of western Poland and the Soviets in the east.

- **November 1939:** The U.S. modifies its Neutrality Act, enabling the sale of arms to Britain and France. Nov. 30: The Soviet Union invades Finland.

- **April 1940:** Germany invades neutral Denmark and Norway.

- **May 1940:** Neville Chamberlain resigns; Winston Churchill becomes British prime minister. May 10: Germany launches *Blitzkrieg* (lightning war) air attacks and occupies neutral Holland, Belgium and Luxembourg. The Germans push into northern France, encircling the British and French armies. Surrounded at

Dunkirk, 338,226 British and French troops evacuate across the Channel to England, May 27-June 4. Churchill declares: "We shall fight on the beaches. . . . We shall never surrender."

The Blitz—London bomb damage

- **June 1940:** June 10: Italy declares war on France and Britain. June 14: Paris falls to the Germans. Under an armistice, Germany holds northern and western France, while Marshal Philippe Pétain's collaborationist "Vichy" French government rules southern unoccupied France.

- **June 1940–June 1941**: Battle of the Atlantic. The German offensive at sea to blockade Britain sinks over 5 million tons of British shipping, with a loss of only 20 German U-boats (submarines).

- **July 1940–May 1941**: Battle of Britain. The German Luftwaffe launches air attacks on English ports, convoys, and airfields to open the way for invasion of England. Both sides suffer major losses. Sept. 7: The Luftwaffe starts daylight bombing of London. Royal Air Force (RAF) fighters beat back German attacks. Sept. 17: Hitler postpones the invasion. Germany begins "the Blitz," an intensive night bombing campaign over British cities.

Franklin Roosevelt

- **September 1940:** Sept. 27: Germany, Italy and Japan sign the Tripartite Pact. Hungary and Romania join them in the "Axis" alliance in November.

- **November 1940:** Franklin Roosevelt elected to a third term as U.S. president.

Hideki Tojo

- **December 1940–November 1941:** Britain launches offensives against Italians in Egypt, Ethiopia and Somalia. British advance to Libya. March: Germans and Italians drive British back. Nov: British mount a successful offensive in Libya.

- **March 1941:** U.S. Senate passes Lend-Lease, allowing the purchase of war materials to "lend" or "lease" to Allies.

- **April 1941:** Germany occupies Yugoslavia and Greece.

German troops in Russia, 1941

- **June 1941:** June 22: Germany breaks its nonaggression pact of 1939 and invades the Soviet Union, starting a protracted war. U.S. and Britain aid the Soviets. Nazi SS and police murder 500,000 Soviet Jews by December 1941.

- **July 1941:** Japan occupies French Indochina.

- **October 1941:** Hideki Tojo becomes prime minister of Japan.

- **December 1941:** Dec. 7: Japanese planes strike Pearl Harbor, Hawaii and cripple the U.S. Pacific Fleet—"a date that will live in infamy." The same day (across the dateline), Japan launches assaults on the Philippines and Guam, and begins a major offensive in Southeast Asia. Dec. 8: United States and Great Britain declare war on Japan. Dec. 11: Germany and Italy declare war on the U.S.

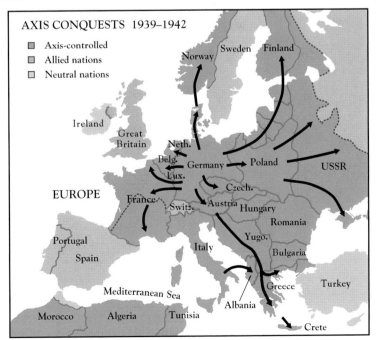

AXIS CONQUESTS 1939–1942
- ☐ Axis-controlled
- ☐ Allied nations
- ☐ Neutral nations

Norway Sweden Finland
Ireland
Great Britain
Neth.
Belg.
Lux.
Germany Poland USSR
Czech.
France
Switz. Austria Hungary
EUROPE
Romania
Portugal
Spain
Italy
Yugo.
Bulgaria
Mediterranean Sea
Turkey
Albania Greece
Morocco Algeria Tunisia
Crete

Chronology 1942–1944

Jews in the Warsaw Ghetto

U.S. Marines at Guadalcanal

German tanks in Tunisia

- **December 1941–May 1942:** Japanese troops invade the Philippines, Guam, Wake Island, Hong Kong, the Gilbert Islands, Caroline Islands, Sarawak, Borneo, Siam (Thailand), Burma, Malaya, Singapore, Sumatra, Celebes, Dutch East Indies, New Guinea, New Britain and the Solomon Islands.

- **January 1942:** Jan. 20: Wannsee Conference. German SS leaders make plans to deport and annihilate the Jews of Europe, a genocide that continues throughout the war. Between December 1941 and November 1942, the SS establishes death camps at Chelmno, Belzec, Auschwitz-Birkenau, Sobibor, Treblinka and Majdanek, Poland.

- **January–June 1942:** Germany sinks over 3 million tons of Allied shipping, with a loss of only 21 U-boats.

- **February 1942:** Feb. 19: Roosevelt signs Executive Order 9066, authorizing the internment of over 110,000 Japanese, German, and Italian Americans in the U.S.

- **April–May 1942:** Fall of the Philippines. April 9: Japanese assault on Bataan crushes U.S. and Filipino defenses in the Philippines. Japanese brutalize surrendered troops on the 65-mile "Death March" to prison camps. May 6: U.S. forces at Corregidor, the last holdout in the Philippines, surrender to the Japanese.

- **April–May 1942:** War in the Pacific. April 28–May 8: Battle of the Coral Sea. The first aircraft carrier battle in naval history. U.S. Navy repulses Japanese invasion forces headed for Port Moresby, Papua, New Guinea.

- **May–July 1942:** North Africa. May 26: Axis troops begin an offensive in Libya. June 21: Germans capture Tobruk. July 1–22: British stop the Axis advance into Egypt near El Alamein.

- **June 1942:** June 3–6: Battle of Midway. U.S. Navy drives back Japanese invasion forces—a turning point in the Pacific war.

- **June–August 1942:** June 28: Overextended Germans begin offensive into southern Russia and the Ukraine.

- **July 1942:** July 21: Japanese invade eastern New Guinea and begin advance toward Port Moresby.

- **July–December 1942:** German U-boats sink 3 million tons of Allied shipping in the Atlantic.

- **August 1942–February 1943:** August 7: U.S. Marines land on Guadalcanal in the first stage of an Allied counteroffensive in the Solomon Islands and New Guinea. Jan 22: Allies take southeastern tip of New Guinea. Feb. 8: After months of heavy fighting, Allies defeat Japanese at Guadalcanal.

- **August 1942–February 1943:** Battle of Stalingrad. August 22: Germans reach Stalingrad. The

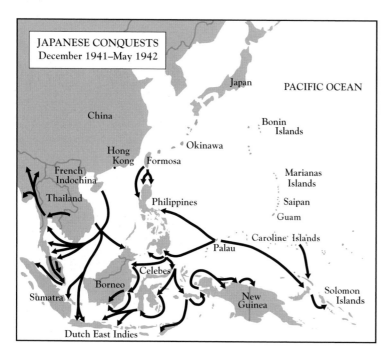

JAPANESE CONQUESTS
December 1941–May 1942

China

Japan

PACIFIC OCEAN

Bonin Islands

Okinawa

Hong Kong
Formosa

French Indochina

Thailand

Marianas Islands

Saipan

Philippines

Guam

Palau

Caroline Islands

Celebes

Sumatra

Borneo

New Guinea

Solomon Islands

Dutch East Indies

protracted battle for the city claims 750,000 Soviet and 850,000 Axis troops. Feb. 2: Soviet victory at Stalingrad is a turning point in the war against the Axis.

Siege of Stalingrad

- **October 1942–June 1943:** Allied offensive in North Africa stops German advance. Oct. 23: British win at El Alamein. Nov–Dec: Allies take Vichy French garrisons in Morocco and Algeria. Germans send reinforcements. British fight Germans in Tunisia while Axis forces continue to retreat through Libya. Jan. 23: Allies take Tripoli. Feb. 14: Germans launch counteroffensive and capture Kasserine Pass in Tunisia, but U.S. and British prevail on Feb. 22nd. May 13: Allied North Africa campaign ends with the surrender of 240,000 Axis troops.

- **April–June 1943:** April 19–May 15: Warsaw Ghetto Uprising. Jews revolt as German SS prepares to exterminate remaining ghetto inhabitants. 56,000 Jews die fighting or at Treblinka death camp. June 11: German SS commander Heinrich Himmler orders all Jewish ghettos in Poland liquidated.

General Patton in Sicily

- **July 1943–September 1943:** Invasion of Sicily. July 10: Allies land in Sicily off the Italian coast. Aug. 17: U.S. forces under Patton and British under Montgomery take Messina and claim victory in Sicily. German troops flee to Italy.

- **July 1943–July 1944:** Soviet Union. July 5: Germans launch offensive against Kursk, but withdraw on July 13th to shift troops after Allies invade Sicily. Aug. 3: Soviet forces begin major offensives, recapturing Kharkov (Aug. 23) and Kiev (Nov. 6). Soviets begin offensives in Ukraine (Dec. 24–26), Poland (Jan. 6), Belorussia (March 4), the Crimea (May), Finland (June 9), the German eastern front (June 22) and the Baltic states (July 3).

Soviet offensive in the Baltics

- **July 24–August 3, 1943:** Intensive day and night Allied bombing raids against Hamburg, Germany cause firestorms that kill 40,000 civilians.

- **September 1943–June 1944:** Invasion of Italy. Sept. 3: British troops land in southern Italy. Sept. 8: Italians surrender, but Germans occupy Italy and fight on for the Axis. Sept. 9: Allies land at Salerno and Taranto. Oct. 13: Italy declares war on Germany. Jan 4: Battle of Monte Cassino begins, a 5-month struggle that ends on May 18th with Allied victory. Jan 22: Allies land at Anzio and begin a bloody assault that ends with German retreat on May 23rd. June 5: Allies enter Rome.

Capture of Saipan

- **November 1943–June 1944:** Allied offensive in the Pacific. Nov. 23: U.S. forces take Tarawa and Makin atolls in the Gilbert Islands. Dec. 26: U.S. Marines land on New Britain. Feb. 4: U.S. forces capture Kwajalein in the Marshall Islands. Feb. 17 and 23: Americans land at Eniwetok atoll in the Marshalls. Feb. and April: U.S. carrier raids on Truk in the Caroline Islands. Feb. 29–March 18: U.S. troops take Admiralty Islands. April 22: Americans land at Hollandia in northern New Guinea. June 15: U.S. forces land on Saipan, securing an important air base for the bombing of Japan. June 19-20: Battle of the Philippine Sea. Japanese Combined Fleet attacks U.S. Fleet with a loss of 3 Japanese aircraft carriers and 330 planes to only 29 U.S. planes.

- **June 6, 1944:** D-Day. Invasion of Normandy. 155,000 Allied troops land on beaches in northern France in the largest amphibious assault in history, a pivotal event in the recapture of Europe from the Germans.

D-Day Invasion of Normandy

Chronology 1944–1945

Americans enter Paris

MacArthur returns to the Philippines

Belgium: Battle of the Bulge

- **June–August 1944:** Soviet Union. June 22: On the third anniversary of the German invasion of the USSR, the Red Army launches a massive attack against the Germans in Belorussia. Within two months, the Germans lose 670,000 men, thousands of tanks and guns, and retreat back into Poland.

- **June–October 1944:** Allied advance in France. In heavy fighting, the Allies gradually expand the Normandy beachhead. July 25: Allies launch Operation Cobra. Over the next two months Allies overcome German resistance, break out of Normandy and head eastwards toward the Seine River and Paris. Aug. 25: Allies liberate Paris after a 50-month German occupation. October: Allied armies battle toward the German border, constrained by inadequate supplies.

- **July 1944:** July 20: German army conspirators attempt to assassinate Hitler with a bomb at his headquarters. Hitler survives and crushes the resistance.

- **October 1944:** Oct. 20: U.S. forces invade the Philippines. Oct 23–26: The Japanese respond with a naval attack in Leyte Gulf, and in a three day battle lose most of their remaining large fleet units.

- **December 1944–January 1945:** Battle of the Bulge. Dec. 16: Germans launch an immense attack on U.S. troops in Belgium's Ardennes mountains, punching a "bulge" in the line. After large initial losses, the Americans manage to hold the Wehrmacht until reinforcements halt the Germans on December 24th. Dec. 25: Americans counterattack. Jan 15: Battle closes.

- **February 1945:** Feb. 4–11: U.S. President Franklin Roosevelt, British Prime Minister Winston Churchill, and Soviet leader Josef Stalin, meet at Yalta in the Crimea and make decisions on the occupation of Germany, Soviet participation in the war against Japan, and the organization of the United Nations.

- **February–March 1945:** Battle of Iwo Jima. Feb. 19: U.S. Marines land on tiny Iwo Jima island, 700 miles south of Tokyo. In a ferocious eight-day battle, 6,800 U.S. Marines are killed. Almost the entire garrison of 20,000 Japanese soldiers die.

- **March–April 1945:** Allied advance into Germany. March 7: American forces cross the Rhine into Germany. April 2: Allies capture the Ruhr and move across northern Germany toward the Elbe River. Soviets advance from the east.

- **March–June 1945:** Firebombing of Japan. March 9–10: Using incendiaries in a night raid, U.S. B-29 bombers create a firestorm in Tokyo, killing an estimated 100,000 Japanese civilians. Over the next four months, almost all of Japan's major cities are partially destroyed by fire bombing.

- **April–June 1945:** Battle of Okinawa. April 1: U.S. Marines invade Okinawa, a 1,200 square-

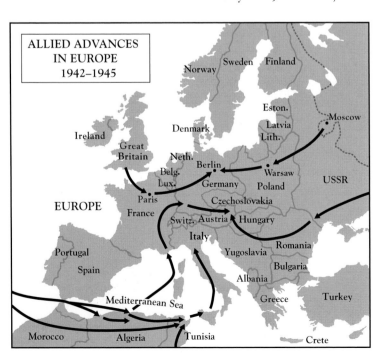

ALLIED ADVANCES
IN EUROPE
1942–1945

mile populated island, 350 miles from Tokyo. In a series of battles, Americans kill approximately 72,000 Japanese soldiers. U.S. forces lose 12,000 killed and 70,000 wounded. Another 150,000 Japanese civilians die during the fighting.

U.S. flag at Iwo Jima

- **April 12, 1945:** U.S. President Franklin Roosevelt, age 63, dies of a cerebral hemorrhage at Warm Springs, Georgia. Vice-President Harry S. Truman assumes the office.

- **April 1945:** Battle for Berlin. April 16: Soviets launch a huge offensive across the Oder River to take Berlin 45 miles away. April 25: U.S. and Soviet troops meet at the Elbe River in Germany. The Soviets assault the center of Berlin the next day. April 30: With Soviet troops only a quarter of a mile away from his bunker beneath central Berlin, Adolf Hitler commits suicide. His "thousand year Reich" lasted twelve years and two months.

- **May 8–9, 1945:** The Germans surrender unconditionally to the Allies ending the war in Europe. May 8th is declared V-E Day, Victory in Europe Day.

V-E Day in England

- **July 1945:** Allies increase aerial and naval bombardment of Japan.

- **July 16, 1945:** The United States successfully tests the first atomic bomb at the Alamogordo Test Range in New Mexico. It releases an explosive equivalent of 18,000 tons of TNT.

- **July–August 1945:** July 17–Aug 2: Truman, Stalin, and Churchill meet at Potsdam, Germany to arrange the political structure of the postwar world. The Soviets agree to enter the war against Japan in August unless the island nation obeys an ultimatum for unconditional surrender.

Atomic bomb at Nagasaki

- **August 6, 1945:** A U.S. B-29 bomber drops an atomic bomb on Hiroshima, Japan. The bomb detonates with a force of 13,000 tons of TNT and kills approximately 100,000 people.

- **August 8, 1945:** Soviets declare war on Japan.

- **August 9, 1945:** A U.S. B-29 bomber drops an atomic bomb on the city of Nagasaki, Japan. The bomb detonates with a force of 22,000 tons of TNT, initially killing 40,000 people. Forty thousand more die later from radiation burns and sickness.

- **August 14, 1945:** Led by Emperor Hirohito, the Japanese government accepts the Potsdam ultimatum and surrenders unconditionally. August 14 is declared V-J Day, Victory over Japan Day.

- **September 2, 1945:** The Japanese surrender formally on the deck of the U.S battleship *Missouri* anchored in Tokyo Bay. **World War II ends.**

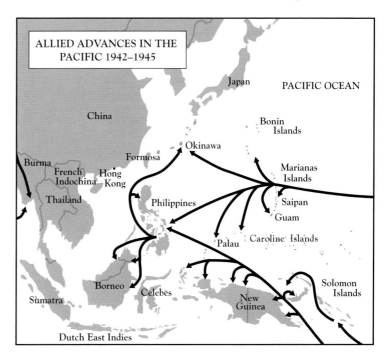

ALLIED ADVANCES IN THE PACIFIC 1942–1945

Bibliography

Adler, Alice Dunn. *Boriska's Prophecy: a True Story of Survival and Renewal.* Reston, VA: Acropolis Books, Ltd., 1991.

Allen, John. "Finding Safe Harbor." *On Wisconsin.* Spring 2002. http://waa.uwalumni.com/onwisconsin/spring02/harbor.html

American Red Cross Museum. "World War II Accomplishments of the American Red Cross." www.redcross.org/museum/history/ww2a.asp

Andrews, Maxene and Bill Gilbert. *Over Here, Over There: The Andrews Sisters and the USO Stars in World War II.* New York: Kensington Publishing Corp., 1993.

Bach, Steven. *Marlene Dietrich: Life and Legend.* New York: William Morrow and Company, Inc.,1992.

Bachrach, Deborah. *The Resistance.* San Diego: Lucent Books, Inc., 1998.

Bailey, Ronald H. *The Home Front: U.S.A.* Alexandra, VA: Time-Life Books, 1978.

Baker, Jean-Claude and Chris Chase. *Josephine: The Hungry Heart.* New York: Random House, 1993.

Beer, Edith Hahn with Susan Dworkin. *The Nazi Officer's Wife: How One Jewish Woman Survived the Holocaust.* New York: William Morrow and Company, Inc., 1999.

Bellafaire, Judith A. "Asian-Pacific-American Servicewomen in Defense of a Nation." www.womensmemorial.org/Education/APA.html

—ibid."The Women's Army Corps: A Commemoration of World War II Service." www.army.mil/cmh-pg/brochures/wac/wac.htm

Bernstein, Sara Tuvel with Louise Loots Thornton and Marlene Berstein Samuels. *The Seamstress: A Memoir of Survival.* New York: Berkley Books, 1999.

Billings, Charlene W. *Grace Hopper: Navy Admiral and Computer Pioneer.* Hillside, NJ: Enslow Publishers, Inc., 1989.

Binney, Marcus. *The Women Who Lived for Danger: The Agents of the Special Operations Executive.* New York: HarperCollins Publishers Inc., 2002.

Bourke-White, Margaret. *Portrait of Myself.* New York: Simon & Schuster, 1963.

Bradley, LaVerne. "Women at Work." *National Geographic.* August 1944, pp.193–220.

Bradley, Ruby G. "Prisoners of War in the Far East." http://history.amedd.army.mil/ANCWebsite/bradley.htm

Brion, Irene J. *Lady GI: A Woman's War in the South Pacific.* Novato, CA: Presidio Press, 1997.

Brysac, Shareen Blair. *Resisting Hitler.* New York: Oxford University Press, 2000.

Camp, LaVonne Telshaw. *Lingering Fever: A World War II Nurse's Memoir.* Jefferson, NC: McFarland & Company, Inc., 1997.

Campbell, D'Ann Mae. *Wives, Workers and Womanhood: America During World War II.* Ann Arbor, Michigan: University Microfilms International, 1979.

Cappon, Sally. "Pearl Harbor Memories Kept Alive by Letter." *Santa Barbara News-Press.* December 7, 1999, pp. A1, A10.

Chapelle, Dickey. *What's a Woman Doing Here? A Reporter's Report on Herself.* New York: William Morrow and Company, 1962.

Chapline, Neal. *Molly's Boots.* Detroit: Harlo Press, 1993.

Clandestine Women: Spies in American History. National Women's History Museum. www.nmwh.org/spies/14.htm

Cloud, Stanley and Lynne Olson. *The Murrow Boys: Pioneers on the Front Lines of Broadcast Journalism.* Boston: Houghton Mifflin Company, 1996.

Coffey, Frank. *Always Home: 50 Years of the USO.* McLean, VA: Brassey's (US), Inc., 1991.

Cogan, Frances B. *Captured: The Japanese Internment of American Civilians in the Philippines, 1941–1945.* Athens, GA: The University of Georgia Press, 2000.

Cohen, Rich. *The Avengers.* New York: Alfred A. Knopf, 2000.

Cohen, Stan. *V for Victory: America's Home Front During World War II.* Missoula, MT: Pictorial Histories Publishing Company, 1991.

Coleman, Penny. *Rosie the Riveter: Women Working on the Home Front in World War II.* New York: Crown Publishers, 1995.

—ibid. *Where the Action Was: Women War Correspondents in World War II.* New York: Crown Publishers, 2002.

Collins, Clella Reeves. *Army Woman's Handbook: Official Guide for the Association of Army Wives.* Macon, GA: Women's Defense League of Macon and The Infantry School Women's Club of Ft. Benning, Georgia, 1942.

Collins, Max Allan. *For the Boys: The Racy Pin-Ups of World War II.* Portland, OR: Collectors Press Inc., 2000.

Cooper, Page. *Navy Nurse.* New York: McGraw-Hill Book Company, Inc., 1946.

Daniels, Roger. *Prisoners Without Trial: Japanese Americans in World War II.* New York: Hill and Wang, 1993.

Danner, Dorothy Still. *What a Way to Spend a War: Navy Nurse POWs in the Philippines.* Annapolis: Naval Institute Press, 1995.

"Death in Line of Duty Comes to LIFE Correspondent Jacoby." *Life.* May 11, 1942.

Davis, Bette with Michael Herskowitz. *This 'n That.* New York: G.P. Putnam's Sons, 1987.

Earley, Charity Adams. *One Woman's Army: A Black Officer Remembers the WAC.* College Station: Texas A & M University Press, 1989.

Ebbert, Jean and Marie-Beth Hall. *Crossed Currents: Navy Women from WWI to Tailhook.* New York: Brassey's (US), 1993.

Ebel, Miriam Davenport. "An Unsentimental Education." Miriam Davenport Ebel, 1999. Chambon Foundation. Varian Fry Project. www.chambon.org

Edwards, Julia. *Women of the World: The Great Foreign Correspondents.* New York: Ivy Books, 1988.

Eisner, Peter. *The Freedom Line: The Brave Men and Women Who Rescued Allied Airmen from the Nazis During World War II.* New York: Harper Collins Publishers Inc., 2004.

Elliott, Andrea. "V-J Day is Replayed, but the Lip-Lock's Tamer This Time." *New York Times,* August 12, 2005.

Elfendahl, Gerald. "Island Waves." *The Bainbridge Voice.* November/December 1997, pp. 30–32.

Eman, Diet with James Schaap. *Things We Couldn't Say.* Grand Rapids, MI: William B. Eerdmans Publishing Co., 1994.

Fessler, Diane Burke. *No Time For Fear: Voices of American Military Nurses in World War II.* East Lansing: Michigan State University Press, 1996.

Fisher, M. F. K. *How to Cook a Wolf.* San Francisco: Northpoint Press, 1954.

Fittko, Lisa. *Escape Through the Pyrenees.* Translated by David Koblick. Evanston, IL: Northwestern University Press, 1991.

Frank, Miriam, Marilyn Ziebarth and Connie Field. *The Life and Times of Rosie the Riveter: The Story of Three Million Working Women During World War II.* Emeryville, CA: Clarity Educational Productions, 1982.

Freedman, Russell. *Eleanor Roosevelt: A Life of Discovery.* New York: Scholastic, Inc., 1994.

Fry, Varian. *Surrender on Demand.* Boulder, CO: Johnson Books published in conjunction with the United States Holocaust Memorial Museum, 1997.

Gellhorn, Martha. *The Face of War.* New York: Simon and Schuster, 1959.

Gluck, Sherna Berger. *Rosie the Riveter Revisited: Women, the War, and Social Change.* Boston: Twayne Publishers, 1987.

Gold, Mary Jayne. *Crossroads Marseilles, 1940.* Garden City, NY: Doubleday & Company, Inc., 1980.

Goldberg, Zosia as told to Hilton Obenzinger. *Running Through Fire: How I Survived the Holocaust.* San Francisco: Mercury House, 2004.

Goodwin, Doris Kearns. *No Ordinary Time: Franklin and Eleanor Roosevelt: The Home Front in World War II.* New York: Simon & Schuster, Inc., 1994.

Gott, Kay. *Women in Pursuit: Flying Fighters for the Air Transport Command Ferrying Division During World War II. A Collection & Recollection.* McKinleyville, CA: Kay Gott, 1993.

Green, Anne Bosanko. *One Woman's War: Letters Home from the Women's Army Corps 1944–1946.* St. Paul: Minnesota Historical Society Press, 1989.

Gruber, Ruth. *Haven: The Unknown Story of 1000 World War II Refugees.* New York: Coward-McCann, Inc., 1983.

—ibid. *Inside of Time: My Journey from Alaska to Israel.* New York: Carroll & Graf Publishers, 2003.

Gruhzit-Hoyt, Olga. *They Also Served: American Women in World War II.* New York: Birch Lane Press, 1995.

Harris, Mark Jonathan, Franklin D. Mitchell and Stephen J. Schechter. *The Homefront: America During World War II.* New York: G.P. Putnam's Sons, 1984.

Hartmann, Susan M. *The Home Front and Beyond: American Women in the 1940s.* Boston: Twayne Publishers, 1982.

Hayes, Joanne Lamb. *Grandma's Wartime Kitchen: World War II and the Way We Cooked.* New York: St. Martin's Press, 2000.

Heide, Robert and John Gilman. *Home Front America: Popular Culture of the World War II Era.* San Francisco: Chronicle Books, 1995.

Holm, Jeanne M. *In Defense of a Nation: Servicewomen in World War II.* Washington, D.C.: Military Women's Press, 1998.

Honey, Maureen, ed. *Bitter Fruit: African American Women in World War II.* Columbia, MO: University of Missouri Press, 1999.

Hoopes, Roy. *When the Stars Went to War: Hollywood and World War II.* New York: Random House, 1994.

Hosley, David H. *As Good as Any: Foreign Correspondence on American Radio 1930–1940.* Westport, CT: Greenwood Press, 1984.

Houston, Jeanne Wakatsuki and James D. Houston. *Farewell to Manzanar.* New York: Bantam Books, 1974.

Hughes, Kaylene. "Women at War. Redstone's WWII Female Production Soldiers." www.redstone.army.mil/history/women

Hunt, Heather C. *Women in the 1950's Workplace. What Happened to Rosie?* http://honors.umd.edu/HONR269J/projects/hchunt/main.htm.

Hynes, Samuel, Anne Matthews, Nancy Caldwell Sorel et al. (advisory board) *Reporting World War II. Part One: American Journalism 1938–1944.* The Library of America, 1995.

—ibid. *Reporting World War II. Part Two: American Journalism 1944–1946.* The Library of America, 1995.

Inada, Lawson Fusao, ed. *Only What We Could Carry: The Japanese American Internment Experience.* Berkeley, CA: Heyday Books, 2000.

Jackson, Kathi. *They Called Them Angels: American Military Nurses of World War II.* Westport, CT: Praeger Publishers, 2000.

Jacoby, Mr. and Mrs. Melville. "Bataan Wounded Lived with Pain." *Life.* April 20, 1942, pp. 32–35.

Johnson, Forrest Bryant. *Hour of Redemption: The Heroic Saga of America's Most Daring POW Rescue.* New York: Warner Books, Inc., 2002.

Jordan, Killian, ed. *Our Finest Hour: The Triumphant Spirit of the World War II Generation.* Time, Inc., 2000.

Kaminski, Theresa. *Prisoners in Paradise: American Women in the Wartime Pacific.* Lawrence, KS: University Press of Kansas, 2000.

Keil, Sally Van Wagenen. *Those Wonderful Women in Their Flying Machines: The Unknown Heroines of World War II.* New York: Rawson, Wade Publishers, Inc., 1979.

Keith, Agnes Newton. *Three Came Home.* New York: Time Inc., 1965.

Kimmett, Larry and Margaret Regis. *The Attack on Pearl Harbor: An Illustrated History.* Seattle: NavPublishing, LLC, 1999.

Klein, Gerda Weissmann. *All But My Life.* New York: Hill and Wang, 1995.

Kohlhoff, Dean. *When the Wind was a River: Aleut Evacuation in World War II.* Seattle: University of Washington Press, 1995.

Korson, George. *At His Side: The Story of the American Red Cross Overseas in World War II.* New York: Coward-McCann, Inc., 1945.

Larson, C. Kay. *'Til I Come Marching Home: A Brief History of American Women in World War II.* Pasadena, MD: The Minerva Center, 1995.

Lawson, Don. *An Album of World War II Home Fronts.* New York: Franklin Watts, 1980.

Leuthner, Stuart and Oliver Jensen. *High Honor: Recollections of Men and Women of World War II Aviation.* Washington, D.C.: Smithsonian Institution Press, 1989.

Lewis, Vickie. *Side-by-Side: A Photographic History of American Women in War.* New York: Stewart, Tabori & Chang, 1999.

Lindholm, Paul R. *Shadows From the Rising Sun: An American Family's Saga During the Japanese Occupation of the Philippines.* Quezon City, Philippines: New Day Publishers, 1978.

Litoff, Judy Barrett and David C. Smith, eds. *American Women in a World at War: Contemporary Accounts from World War II.* Wilmington, DE: Scholarly Resources, Inc., 1997.

—ibid. *Since You Went Away: World War II Letters from American Women on the Home Front.* New York: Oxford University Press, 1991.

Littleton, Cynthia. "Why We Fought: The Entertainment Industry Rallied to Help Win WWII." *The Hollywood Reporter.* July 1, 2005.

Livingston, Jane. *Lee Miller Photographer.* New York: Thames and Hudson, 1989.

Lovell, Mary S. *Cast No Shadow: The Life of the American Spy Who Changed the Course of World War II.* New York: Pantheon Books, 1992.

Lyne, Mary C. and Kay Arthur. *Three Years Behind the Mast: The Story of the United States Coast Guard SPARs.* [Washington, D.C.]: n.p., [1946].

Mangerich, Agnes Jensen as told to Evelyn M. Monahan and Rosemary L. Neidel. *Albanian Escape: The True Story of U.S. Army Nurses Behind Enemy Lines.* Lexington: The University Press of Kentucky, 1999.

Marino, Andy. *A Quiet American: The Secret War of Varian Fry.* New York: St. Martin's Press, 1999.

May, Antoinette. *Witness to War: A Biography of Marguerite Higgins.* New York: Beaufort Books, Inc., 1983.

Maynard, Mary McKay. *My Faraway Home: An American Family's WWII Tale of Adventure and Survival in the Jungles of the Philippines.* Guilford, CT: The Lyons Press, 2001.

McClendon, Sarah. *Mr. President, Mr. President! My Fifty Years of Covering the White House.* Santa Monica, CA: General Publishing Group, Inc., 1996.

McIntosh, Elizabeth P. *Sisterhood of Spies: The Women of the OSS.* Annapolis: Naval Institute Press, 1998.

McLaughlin, Kathleen. "Allies Open Trial of 20 Top Germans for Crimes of War." *New York Times.* November 20, 1945.

Miller, Frieda S. "What's Become of Rosie the Riveter?" *New York Times.* May 5, 1946.

Miller, Grace Porter. *Call of Duty: A Montana Girl in World War II.* Baton Rouge: Louisiana State University Press, 1999.

Miller, Russell. *The Resistance.* Chicago: Time-Life Books, 1979.

Mills, Kay. *From Pocahontas to Power Suits: Everything You Need to Know About Women's History in America.* New York: Penguin Books, 1995.

Monahan, Evelyn M. and Rosemary Neidel-Greenlee. *All This Hell: U.S. Nurses Imprisoned by the Japanese.* Lexington: The University Press of Kentucky, 2000.

—ibid. *And If I Perish: Frontline U.S. Army Nurses in World War II.* New York: Anchor Books, 2003.

Moore, Brenda L. *To Serve My Country, To Serve My Race: The Story of the Only African American WACs Stationed Overseas During World War II.* New York: New York University Press, 1996.

Mullener, Elizabeth. *War Stories: Remembering World War II.* Baton Rouge: Louisiana State University Press, 2002.

Mulvey, Deb, ed. *We Pulled Together and Won! Personal Memories of the World War II Years.* Greendale, WI: Reiman Publications, 1993.

Norman, Elizabeth M. *We Band of Angels: The Untold Story of American Nurses Trapped on Bataan by the Japanese.* New York: Random House, 1999.

Norwalk, Rosemary. *Dearest Ones: A True World War II Love Story.* New York: John Wiley & Sons, Inc., 1999.

O'Brien, Mary Barmeyer. *Jeannette Rankin: 1880–1973. Bright Star in the Big Sky.* Helena, MT: Falcon Press Publishing Company, 1995.

Okubo, Miné. *Citizen 13660.* Seattle: University of Washington Press, 1983.

Opdyke, Irene Gut. *In My Hands: Memories of a Holocaust Rescuer.* New York: Alfred A. Knopf, 1999.

Ostroff, Roberta. *Fire in the Wind: The Life of Dickey Chapelle.* New York: Ballantine Books, 1992.

Paldiel, Mordecai. *Saving the Jews: Amazing Stories of Men and Women Who Defied the "Final Solution."* Rockville, MD: Schreiber Publishing, 2000.

Pearson, Judith L. *The Wolves at the Door: The True Story of America's Greatest Female Spy.* Guilford, CT: The Lyons Press, 2005.

Penrose, Antony. *The Lives of Lee Miller.* New York: Holt, Rinehart and Winston, 1985.

Phillips, Claire and Myron B. Goldsmith. *Manila Espionage.* Portland, OR: Binfords & Mort, 1947.

Ramsey, Mary Ann. "Only Yesteryear." *Pearl Harbor Gram.* November 1993, pp. 1–2.

Redmond, Juanita. *I Served on Bataan.* Philadelphia and New York: J.B. Lippincott Company, 1943.

Resnick, Abraham. *The Holocaust.* San Diego: Lucent Books, 1991.

Riding, Alan. "Mary Jayne Gold, 88; Helped Refugees Flee Nazis." *New York Times.* October 7, 1997.

Rivas-Rodriguez, Juliana A. Torres, Melissa DiPiero-D'Sa, et al. *A Legacy Greater Than Words: Stories of U.S. Latinos and Latinas of the World War II Generation.* Austin: University of Texas Press, 2006.

Rogansky, Barbara. *Smoke and Ashes: The Story of the Holocaust.* New York: Holiday House, 1988.

Rollyson, Carl. *Nothing Ever Happens to the Brave: The Story of Martha Gellhorn.* New York: St. Martin's Press, 1990.

Roosevelt, Eleanor. *This I Remember.* New York: Harper & Brothers, 1949.

Roosevelt, Eleanor. David Emblidge, ed. *My Day: The Best of Eleanor Roosevelt's Acclaimed Newspaper Columns, 1936–1962.* Da Capo Press, 2001.

Roscoe, Theodore. *United States Submarine Operations in World War II.* Annapolis, MD: United States Naval Institute, 1949.

Rose, Darlene Deibler. *Evidence Not Seen: A Woman's Miraculous Faith in a Japanese Prison Camp During WWII.* San Francisco: Harper & Row, 1988.

Sams, Margaret. *Forbidden Family: A Wartime Memoir of the Philippines, 1941–1945.* Madison: University of Wisconsin Press, 1989.

Savary, Gladys. *Outside the Walls.* New York: Vantage Press, Inc., 1954.

Schenone, Laura. *A Thousand Years Over a Hot Stove: A History of American Women Told Through Food, Recipes and Remembrances.* New York: W.W. Norton & Company, 2003.

Schomp, Virginia. *World War II: Letters from the Homefront.* New York: Benchmark Books, 2002.

Schroeder, Alan. *Josephine Baker.* New York: Chelsea House Publishers, 1991.

Severo Richard. "Frances Langford, Trouper on Bob Hope Tours, Dies at 92." *New York Times.* July 12, 2005. p. A21.

Sforza, John. *Swing It! The Andrews Sisters Story.* Lexington: The University Press of Kentucky, 2000.

Shiber, Etta with Anne and Paul Dupre. *Paris—Underground.* New York: Charles Scribner's Sons, 1943.

Shirer, William L. *20th Century Journey. Vol. 2: The Nightmare Years, 1930–1940.* Boston: Little, Brown and Company, 1984.

Shukert, Elfrieda Berthiaume and Barbara Smith Scibetta. *War Brides of World War II.* New York: Penguin Books, 1989.

Sides, Hampton. *Ghost Soldiers: The Forgotten Epic Story of World War II's Most Dramatic Mission.* New York: Doubleday, 2001.

Simbeck, Rob. *Daughter of the Air: The Brief Soaring Life of Cornelia Fort.* New York: Atlantic Monthly Press, 1999.

Smith, Steven Trent. *The Rescue: A True Story of Courage and Survival in World War II.* New York: John Wiley & Sons, Inc., 2001.

Soderbergh, Peter. *Women Marines: The World War II Era.* Westport, CT: Praeger Publishers, 1992.

Sorel, Nancy Caldwell. *The Women Who Wrote the War.* New York: Arcade Publishing, 1999.

South Kingstown High School students. *What Did You Do in the War Grandma? An Oral History of Rhode Island Women during World War II.* www.stg.brown.edu/projects/WWII_Women/

Stenbuck, Jack, ed. *Typewriter Battalion: Dramatic Front-Line Dispatches from World War II.* New York: William Morrow and Co, Inc., 1995.

Sterner, Doris M. *In and Out of Harm's Way: A History of the Navy Nurse Corps.* Seattle: Peanut Butter Publishing, 1997.

Stodolsky, Catherine. "Lisa and Hans Fittko and Varian Fry." 2007. www.lrz-muenchen.de/~catherine.stodolsky/lisa/ff.html

Stremlow, Mary V. *Free a Marine to Fight: Women Marines in World War II.* Marines in World War II Commemorative Series. Washington, D.C.: Marine Corps Historical Center, 1994.

Suberman, Stella. *When it Was Our War: A Soldier's Wife in World War II.* Waterville, Maine: Thorndike Press, 2003.

Sutin, Jack and Rochelle Sutin. Lawrence Sutin, ed. *Jack and Rochelle: A Holocaust Story of Love and Resistance.* St. Paul: Graywolf Press, 1995.

Terkel, Studs. *"The Good War:" An Oral History of World War Two.* New York: Ballantine Books, 1985.

Thomas, Helen. *Front Row at the White House: My Life and Times.* New York: Scribner, 1999.

Thomson, Robin J. "SPARS: The Coast Guard & the Women's Reserve in World War II." http://www.uscg.mil/history/h_wmnres.html

Tomblin, Barbara Brooks. *G.I. Nightingales: The Army Nurse Corps in World War II.* Lexington: The University Press of Kentucky, 1996.

Uchida, Yoshiko. *Desert Exile: The Uprooting of a Japanese-American Family.* Seattle: University of Washington Press, 1982.

Utinsky, Margaret. *"Miss U."* San Antonio, TX: The Naylor Company, 1948.

USO. "USO Camp Shows." www.uso.org/whatwedo/entertainment/historicalusocampshows/

Vail, Margaret. *Yours is the Earth.* New York: J.B. Lippincott Company, 1944.

Van Sickle, Emily. *The Iron Gates of Santo Tomás: The Firsthand Account of an American Couple Interned by the Japanese in Manila, 1942–45.* Chicago: Academy Chicago Publishers, 1992.

Vaughan, Elizabeth. Carol M. Petillo, ed. *The Ordeal of Elizabeth Vaughan: A Wartime Diary of the Philippines.* Athens, GA: The University of Georgia Press, 1985.

Verges, Marianne. *On Silver Wings: The Women Airforce Service Pilots of World War II, 1942–1944.* New York: Ballantine Books, 1991.

von Miklos, Josephine. *I Took a War Job.* New York: Simon & Schuster, 1943.

Wagner, Lilya. *Women War Correspondents of World War II.* Westport, CT: Greenwood Press, 1989.

Warren, James R. *The War Years: A Chronicle of Washington State in World War II.* Seattle: History Ink, 2000.

Waterford, Van. *Prisoners of the Japanese in World War II.* Jefferson, NC: McFarland & Company, Inc. Publishers, 1994.

Weatherford, Doris. *American Women and World War II.* New York: Facts on File, 1990.

Weitz, Margaret Collins. *Sisters in the Resistance. How Women Fought to Free France 1940–1945.* New York: John Wiley & Sons, Inc., 1995.

Whitfield, Evelyn. *Three Year Picnic: An American Woman's Life Inside Japanese Prison Camps in the Philippines During WWII.* Corvallis, Oregon: Premiere Editions International, Inc., 1999.

Wilding, Jennifer. "Warriors in Greasepaint." *Articles On War.* www.onwar.com/articles/0201.htm

Williams, Vera S. *WASPs: Women Airforce Service Pilots of World War II.* Osceola, WI: Motorbooks International, 1994.

Winfield, Pamela with Brenda Wilson Hasty. *Sentimental Journey: The Story of G.I. Brides.* London: Constable and Company Ltd., 1984.

Wingo, Josette Dermody. *Mother Was a Gunner's Mate: World War II in the Waves.* Annapolis, MD: Naval Institute Press, 1994.

Winn, Viola S. *The Escape.* Wheaton, IL: Tyndale House Publishers, Inc., 1975.

Wise, Nancy Baker and Christy Wise. *A Mouthful of Rivets: Women at Work in World War II.* San Francisco: Jossey-Bass Publishers, 1994.

Women of Courage: The Story of the Women Pilots of World War II. Lakewood, CO: KM Productions, 1993. Videotape.

Yellin, Emily. *Our Mother's War: American Women at Home and at the Front During World War II.* New York: Simon & Schuster, Inc., 2004.

Picture Credits

Index

Women's Army Corps PFC
Dorothy Bretty (right) in England.

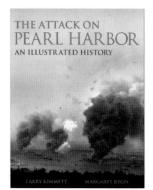
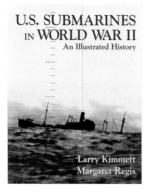